D0938418

Make Music with Your iPad®

Ben Harvell

John Wiley & Sons, Inc.

In memory of Steven Paul Jobs,
without whose genius and vision,
this book, the iPad, and a whole new way of making music
wouldn't exist.

Make Music with Your iPad®

Make Music with Your iPad®

Published by
John Wiley & Sons, Inc.
10475 Crosspoint Boulevard
Indianapolis, IN 46256
www.wiley.com

Published simultaneously in Canada

ISBN: 978-1-118-14558-6

Manufactured in the United States of America

10 9 8 7 6 5 4 3 2 1

For general information on our other products and services or to obtain technical support, please contact our Customer Care Department within the U.S. at (877) 762-2974, outside the U.S. at (317) 572-3993 or fax (317) 572-4002.

Wiley also publishes its books in a variety of electronic formats and by print-on-demand. Some content that appears in standard print versions of this book may not be available in other formats. For more information about Wiley products, visit us at www.wiley.com.

Library of Congress Control Number: 2011940544

Colophon: This book was produced using the ITC Giovanni typeface for the body text, Calcite Pro for the titles, ITC Stone Sans for the sidebar text, and Rotis Semi Serif for the caption text.

Acknowledgments

Throughout my career as a writer and an editor, I've often been told that creating digital music, especially on mobile devices, is too niche a topic for the mainstream. Fortunately, there are some people who, like me, dispute that fact. Aaron Black at Wiley is one such person who loved the idea of this book from the start and helped me get it to print. I hope that, as an audiophile himself, he enjoys it as much as a consumer as he does from an acquisitions editor's standpoint.

I'd also like to thank Galen Gruman and Carol Person for above-and-beyond levels of support and unwavering patience throughout the production of this book. Through conflicting time zones and my relentless queries they've turned a good book into a great one.

On the artist front, Evan Taubenfeld and Jordan Rudess deserve special mention for taking time from being bona fide rock stars to answer my questions and provide support when I needed it. Their advice and approachable nature have truly enhanced this book.

Thanks also to the many music and tech PR pros who provided me with swift responses, images, and links to the right people, especially Leslie Buttonow at Korg, Elizabeth Sachs at MWPR, and Paul and Tia at IK Multimedia.

Finally, special thanks go to Hayley and select friends who, perhaps overestimating my talents, always believed I could make a go of this writing thing even when I questioned it.

Credits

Acquisitions Editor
Aaron Black

Editorial Director
Robyn Siesky

Business Manager
Amy Knies

Senior Marketing Manager
Sandy Smith

Vice President and
Executive Group Publisher
Richard Swadley

Vice President and
Executive Publisher
Barry Pruett

Editor
Carol Person, The Zango Group

Technical Editor
Joe Marquez

Design and Layout
Galen Gruman, The Zango Group

Cover Designer
Michael E. Trent

Copy Editing, Proofreading,
and Indexing
The Zango Group

About the Author

Ben Harvell is a freelance writer based in Bournemouth, U.K., writing for almost all magazines with the word "Mac" in the title, including *Macworld, MacFormat, MacLife,* and *MacUser*.

Formerly the editor of *iCreate Magazine*, the creative magazine for Mac, iPad, and iPhone users, as well as a staff writer at *Digital Music Maker* magazine, Ben has been writing about Apple and digital creativity for more than ten years.

He has also been recording his own music since computers were capable of it. As iOS devices began to take off, Ben specialized his writing in the field, writing several books on iPhone and iPad creativity.

He blogs at `www.benharvell.com` when he has time but can be found more regularly on Twitter (`@benharvell`).

Contents

Contents

Introduction

So you bought an iPad and you are wondering if those Apple ads promoting its music-creation prowess are true. My aim with this book is to provide an answer to a question I've heard countless times: "Can I really use the iPad to make music?" My answer has always been yes.

Although I do cover using the iPad as a supplementary tool for your existing music setup, most of *Make Music with Your iPad* is dedicated to making music with the iPad as the hub. It is genuinely exciting that with an iPad, a few apps, and the right cables, you have a full-fledged mobile music studio in your hands.

And you don't have to take my word for it either. There is huge acceptance of the iPad in musical circles — and not just for passing time on the tour bus, either. From producers to chart-topping musicians, the iPad is finding its own niche in a world that has seen some huge technological improvements over the past decade. Whether all these advancements are a good thing for music (Auto-Tune, I'm talking to you) is a matter of opinion. Throughout this book you will find sidebars labeled "Artist Lesson" that convey the thoughts of major musicians and industry figures who use the iPad as part of their day-to-day work. These snippets show that the iPad isn't just a plaything anymore and is in fact becoming a must-have tool for music production, practice, and even publishing.

More than 'Just a Big iPhone'

It still makes me laugh when I think back to the day I received my first iPad in the mail. Assembled friends and family were interested but, within spending five minutes looking at it, they came to the conclusion that it was "just a big iPhone." They weren't alone, either. The blogosphere and some corners of the media jumped on the same bandwagon, writing off the iPad as nothing more than a novelty gadget for wealthy businessmen to use in bars as a symbol of status.

Fast-forward a couple of years and you can't walk past a coffee shop, library, or bar (those businessmen are still at it) without seeing the gleaming product of Apple's design and manufacturing teams. But the fact that iPads are now ubiquitous doesn't alone mean they are any better than a large-format iPhone or iPod Touch.

What makes the key difference in the iPad's overall usefulness is the selection of apps available. As the porn industry decides which video format will succeed, the slightly less seedy community of software developers are the ones with the power to give a Roman-style thumbs-up or thumbs-down to a new platform like the iPad. Fortunately for Apple, many developers already knew the ins and outs of iPad app development given its similarity to the iPhone and its almost identical operating system. And so, as more and more iPad apps began flooding the App Store, the iPad's uses and features were increased. Without the App Store, the iPad is effectively an expensive, yet pretty web browser, media player, and e-book reader.

You Have to Spend Money to Make Music

That little segment of iPad history, sponsored by my nigh on ten years experience writing for the consumer Mac press, helps emphasize an important point regarding your enjoyment of this book. Take the age-old adage "If you want to make an omelet, you gotta break some eggs" and substitute the omelet for making music on the iPad and the eggs for your bank balance.

I hope the thought of a creamy snack has softened the idea of spending a little money doesn't have quite the sting it might have. I'm sure 90 percent of readers are currently thinking "Well, duh!" but I simply want to explain the same fact that Apple hides in the small print of its ads: You can do very little with the iPad when it comes to actually making something unless you take a few trips to the App Store.

How This Book Is Organized

That said, I'm not talking about breaking the bank, either. I have structured this book in a way that you can quickly find the precise tools and techniques that you need to make the music you want.

That is why Part I is dedicated to specific music types and the apps and the artists related to them. As I leafed through one of Jamie Oliver's cookbooks recently, he recommended a selection of key utensils to help the reader get the most from his recipes. The total amount ran into the hundreds of dollars. But even if you bought every app I mention in this book, you would be hard-pressed to reach even half that amount.

The second part of the book deals solely with GarageBand for iPad because it is currently the ultimate music tool for the iPad — bar none. Even if you don't invest in the apps and kit I recommend in Part I, you can still do a lot of music-making with GarageBand alone. And Part II shows you how.

The third part of the book takes the GarageBand techniques explained in Part II and walks you through the creation of an example song. It's a great way to put that theory in Part II to actual use.

Throughout the book you'll find several special elements:

- **Sample audio clips:** So you can hear actual examples of some of the techniques I describe in the book, I've made audio clips that you can play on your iPad or other device, if you have an Internet connection for pulling them from the Internet. These audio clips are featured in sidebars throughout the book that have the ♪ icon at the beginning of their titles. Use the QR code in a sidebar to download and listen to its audio clip.
- **Artist lessons:** Several professional musicians have shared their insights and experiences of using the iPad in their own work, and you'll find the "Artist Lesson" sidebars throughout the book that profile these working musicians' iPad expertise.
- **Tips:** Although most of the book offers hands-on advice, you'll see periodically paragraphs labeled "tip" that provide a little extra help.

Okay, it is time to get down to business as long as you have a few things straight. One, as I just mentioned, you are willing to pay less than a round of drinks for quality music apps. Two, you install GarageBand on your iPad; you will be sorry if you don't. Three, you are ready to turn your expensive toy into a music production powerhouse. If you are happy with those conditions, let's get going.

Conventions Used in This Book

Computing, like music, has its own special language. That's especially true for the iPad, which introduces a whole new way of interacting: via gestures. If you're new to the language of computing or of the iPad in particular, read on to get the essentials used in this book.

All about gestures

Throughout this book, I cover how to use the iPad. The iPad is a lot different from your computer. There is no keyboard or mouse. Instead, the iPad just requires your fingers. There are several common gestures used throughout the iPad's iOS operating system and its apps, which I describe here.

Tap: A tap is the most common iPad gesture. It is commonly used to select an item or press a virtual button. To perform a tap, hold your finger over the iPad screen and then quickly touch the screen and lift your finger back up. In other words, tap it.

Tap and hold: The tap-and-hold gesture requires you to press your finger against the screen and hold it there without lifting. Many apps use the tap-and-hold gesture to select an object so you can move it elsewhere on the screen.

Drag: iPad apps often require the drag gesture to move and resize items on the screen. Drags on the iPad are almost always preceded by a tap and hold. To drag an item, slide your finger across the iPad screen. Lift your finger when you are done dragging an item.

Pinch: Many apps use the pinch gesture to zoom in. To perform a pinch, place your thumb and index finger on the screen at the same time and then pinch them together.

Expand: The opposite gesture of pinch is expand, which is used to zoom out. Put both your index finger and thumb on the screen close to each other, then move them away from each other.

Rotate: Use the rotate gesture to rotate objects on the screen. To do so, place your thumb and index finger on the screen as if starting the pinch gesture but, instead of pinching, rotate your fingers on the screen clockwise or counterclockwise.

Scroll: Scrolling is the most common gesture to move up and down through the contents in a window or pane. To scroll on the iPad, place your finger against the screen and, while keeping your finger against the screen, slide it up and down or right and left as the context requires. Note that some apps require you use two fingers to scroll content in a pane, to differentiate scrolling in the surrounding window.

All about iOS controls, computer menus, and codes

iOS has a simple user interface, with just a few elements to note:

Windows and panes: As on a computer, apps run in windows. But in iOS, they take up nearly the full screen (except for the iOS status bar), so people often use the term *screen* instead of *window*. As on a computer, windows can be divided into sections called *panes*.

Buttons: These can be made of text and/or icons. Tap them to activate a control, such as initiating an action or opening a menu.

Menus: As on a computer, a menu contains a list of options to choose from; it may contain submenus with additional options (indicated by the > symbol).

Popovers: iOS's equivalent of a computer's dialog box or panel, it contains multiple controls, such as switches, sliders, buttons, menus, and steppers (small controls that increment you through settings values). Popovers can also contain sub-popovers (indicated by the > symbol).

Contextual menus: Like their computer counterparts, these appear for text or objects. Unlike on a computer (where you Control+click or right-click to get them), you tap and hold on an iPad's screen. Also unlike on computers, iOS's contextual menus can be a regular (vertical) menu or a horizontal row of buttons.

This book also uses a special symbols within sequences of computer menu actions: ➪. So, File ➪ Save means to choose the File menu, then choose the Save option, and File ➪ Library ➪ Import Playlist means to choose the File menu, then choose Library from the menu and then choose Import Playlist from the submenu.

Finally, I use the `code font` to indicate URLs and other text you type in literally, such as in text fields.

All about QR codes

Throughout this book you will see images in the margin that look sort of like digital mazes. These are called QR (quick response) codes and act as visual links to the Internet and the App Store.

I also use them to provide you audio clips so you can hear examples of what I'm describing in those sidebars throughout the book that have the ♪ icon at the beginning of their titles. When you scan the QR code for an audio clip from your iPad or other device, that clip will play on your device.

To take advantage of QR codes, point your iPhone's or iPad's camera at the QR code while running a QR-scanning app to have your device open the appropriate web page, App Store description, or audio file. This saves you the trouble of typing website URLs that look like cryptic gibberish. (You'll also see the icons for iOS apps themselves in the margins, so you can quickly tell you're looking at the intended app in the App Store.)

Okay, we can now start to make music!

PART I

iPad Music-Making Basics

In this part of the book, I look at the many ways your iPad can help you make music. From adding the iPad to your existing studio setup to jamming and practicing with a plethora of music apps, Part I shows you how to make the most of your iPad from a musical perspective.

I recommend reading through each chapter to get your complete fill of mobile music. Those readers interested in specific aspects of iPad music — such as guitarists and pianists — can flick straight through to the chapter that relates to you. In each chapter, you'll find a selection of apps, guides, and advice on how to make the best use of your iPad with your chosen instrument or style of music.

To make things even better, as well as to prove I'm not making most of this up, I've enlisted the help of some friends. You'll no doubt have heard songs by most, if not, all the professional musicians featured in the Artist Lessons sections throughout this part. Their advice is not only encouraging to those excited by this new music-making platform but also helpful as they share their own tips on how to get the best results from your music apps.

As well as advice for specific instruments and genres, I've also included advice on general topics like practicing your instrument, connecting your iPad to external equipment, and sharing your finished songs.

The iPad is a truly amazing tool for the modern music maker with almost limitless possibilities, so I've done my utmost to make sure the burning questions are covered. "How do I hook up my guitar?" "What's the best microphone to use?" "Can I mix songs together?" "How do I export my tracks?" All these questions and many more are answered in this part, to get you ready for pulling the whole lot together in Part II where I get into creating projects in GarageBand.

1

Get Yourself Connected

First, let's deal with some equipment issues. There are a few bits and bobs, in addition to the iPad's out-of-the-box accessories that although not essential will make your iPad music experience far superior. Ultimately, the kit you buy should be determined by importance. The following add-ons will be more or less important depending on your style of music and choice of instruments.

You don't need to run out and buy everything mentioned right away, either. As and when the situation arises, extra devices and cables might come in handy but there's no requirement to use any of them. You can still follow the advice in this book and then improve things with new toys when you have the time or money. For example, until you reach a stage where recording clarity is essential, you can record vocals and even instruments through the iPad's headphone mic to get a feel for the way things work. If you then decide you want to enhance your production, go ahead and grab a new microphone.

The beauty of the iPad is that, in most cases at least, you shouldn't need anything more than the device itself and your chosen apps to start making music. Everything is possible at a default level. You just need to choose what aspects you would like to improve with suitable third-party products. For when that time comes, the following are my recommendations.

Apple's iPad Camera Connection Kit

One thing the iPad doesn't offer is a USB port. Many people thought this decision was the height of stupidity on Apple's part but,

FIGURE 1-1

The iPad Camera Connection Kit

as ever, the company had a trick up its sleeve, a trick you might not be aware of that could seriously improve the way you make music. For quick transfer of photos from your camera to your iPad, Apple introduced its iPad Camera Connection Kit, shown in Figure 1-1, that is comprised of an SD card reader and USB adapter.

People, including many music geeks like me, soon discovered that a camera wasn't the only device that could be attached to the iPad via this method. As long as they don't draw too much power, a wide range of music peripherals — headphones, microphones, MIDI keyboards, controllers, and more — can be connected to the iPad and used with your music apps, including GarageBand. For its minimal cost, this small kit is a worthwhile purchase for iPad musicians, especially if you already own any USB peripherals that you could use to connect to it.

Unfortunately, there's no official list of hardware that works with the Camera Connection Kit, so you are left to trial and error. I've found most of my old kit works perfectly. A device that works with the connection kit won't provide any kind of feedback that the connection has been successful, but you might receive a message telling you that the USB device you are connecting draws too much power. Sadly, my workhorse MIDI keyboard, a three-octave M-Audio model, fell into this category, so I've had to downgrade to a more portable and lower-power device for iPad work. You might find the same, but if you're lucky you will be using your USB devices with your iPad in a matter of minutes with this handy kit. You can pick up the Camera Connection Kit at Apple stores or online for $29.

Line-In Connections: Guitar, Bass, and More

So what about instruments and devices that use a standard lead? In most cases, it's not as simple as finding an adapter to fit the iPad's headphone/audio-in port. For one thing, you remove the option to monitor your work with headphones because the iPad offers only one jack for input and output. Second, a simple adapter might not work at all.

To avoid both problems, IK Multimedia, Apogee, and Peavey provide solutions with their respective iRig, Apogee Jam (see Figure 1-2), and AmpKit Link products. These small boxes, no bigger than a smartphone, offer a line-in jack and, in the case of the IK Multimedia and Peavey devices, headphone output. Apogee's Jam is the only device of the three that attaches via the dock connector, freeing you to use the

FIGURE 1-2

Apogee's Jam guitar connector

iPad's headphone jack to monitor your recording or send the output to speakers. The other two devices connect to your iPad's headphone jack with a standard minijack lead and provide an additional jack for headphones.

Certified to work with the iPad, these devices offer the quickest and most reliable way to record electric string instruments and are a must-have if you want to record at the highest quality with any Core Audio-compatible application.

Here's how to connect USB devices with the iPad Camera Connection Kit:

1. Start by connecting your device — be it a keyboard, microphone, or speakers — to the USB jack on the Camera Connection Kit using the cable that came with your device. Make sure you do this first; otherwise, the iPad may not accept the connection.
2. If your device uses external power, make sure it is plugged in and connected to a power source.
3. Plug the dock connector end of the Camera Connection Kit into your iPad and launch the relevant app. GarageBand is a good choice for most instruments, and speakers should work automatically. If your device uses too much power, an alert box appears indicating that fact (see Figure 1-3).

FIGURE 1-3

The USB power warning alert

4. Play a song on your iPad to test the speakers or launch an instrument in GarageBand to make sure your device is working correctly. Try the GarageBand Keyboard instrument for USB keyboards and the Audio Recorder instrument for microphones.

Microphones

Let's face it: The built-in iPad microphone isn't going to cut it when it comes to recording quality, and neither is the microphone on the iPad's headphones (unless you're after a specific kind of lo-fi effect). Fortunately, there are several solutions available for iPad users.

The first I've touched on already: Apple's iPad Camera Connection Kit allows you to use some USB microphones as an input option. If you happen to already have a microphone, there may be a route from it to your iPad but it will take an extra kit to make it work. A dynamic microphone (one that doesn't require power) might work through a device for guitar input like the iRig or others mentioned in the previous "Line-In Connections" section.

FIGURE 1-4

IK Multimedia's iRig Mic

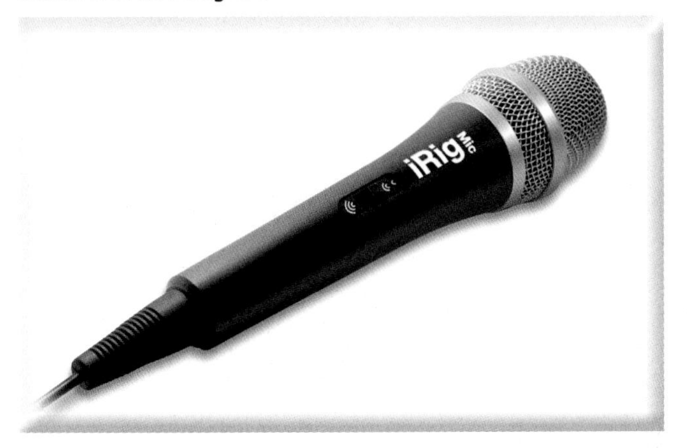

Condenser microphones require phantom power if they're not connected by USB and thus will need to run through a separate interface. If you use a condenser microphone with your computer, the chances are you already have a device to mix and power it and, if so, you can run it through an iRig or similar device. If not, you'll need a compact audio interface that provides phantom power. There are many available from companies like M-Audio and Edirol that should do the job.

For a more dedicated option, IK Multimedia's iRig Mic (shown in Figure 1-4) is a cost-effective choice. A simple handheld mic with three gain settings, the iRig Mic provides the same headphone out option as its sibling for guitars, the iRig. Using this method, you can quickly record live instruments, vocals, and even samples wherever you happen to be and without an additional power supply. Apogee also offers an iPad-friendly microphone in the form of its unoriginally titled Mic, featuring PureDigital technology for vocals and acoustic instruments.

MIDI Keyboards and Other Devices

IK Multimedia seems set to rule the iPad connectivity roost when it comes to music with its third adapter for iPad, this one for connecting MIDI devices. The iRig MIDI, shown in Figure 1-5, is a compact device that uses Core MIDI technology to connect any MIDI device to your iPad. This includes controllers and drum machines that can be used to control a wide range of MIDI-compatible iPad apps, including Apple's GarageBand.

FIGURE 1-5

The iRig MIDI

The device comes with IK Multimedia's own SampleTank app that includes a library of more than 500 sounds that can be played back live through any controller you connect via iRig MIDI. Alternatively, and if you're very lucky, you might be able to connect a USB-based MIDI device to your iPad using the Camera Connection Kit if it draws only a small amount of power. You'll find more information starting with Chapter 6, but I have to warn you that the USB route is hit-and-miss, but certainly worth a try before trying other options.

Headphones and Speakers

I don't recommend using Apple's iPad headphones to monitor your music. There, I said it. Don't get me wrong, I love the Apple kit but the headphones are for people to enjoy compressed MP3 music, not to accurately monitor music production. The default headphones also aren't noise-canceling, so you will be able to hear any background noise that might be present. First, they don't help you accurately gauge how your music sounds, and second they make it harder to focus if you're playing or recording an instrument and listening to it via headphones.

Ultimately, I suggest you get the best headphones you can find. The major manufacturers — Sennheiser, Sony, and Shure — all offer a wide range of headphones for monitoring and fit most budgets. I've been quite excited by the Monster Beats by Dr. Dre series, too.

When it comes to music production, there are few professionals who could offer a better sonic subscription than the doctor himself. The Beats range comes in all shapes and sizes with the excellent but fairly expensive Studio model (see Figure 1-6) as well as the more portable yet production-friendly Tour ear buds that also offer noise cancellation while being suitably lightweight.

If you already own a tried and tested set of headphones, I suggest you stick with it. Even if it uses a different connection than the iPad's standard. After all, you can pick up an adapter for headphones that use the ¼-inch stereo headphone adapter to make them fit the iPad's 3.5mm headphone jack for less than a dollar, a serious saving by comparison to buying a brand new set of cans.

Speakers are a less tricky prospect for the iPad, with many options available. It's best to stick to a direct connection through the dock

FIGURE 1-6

The Monster Beats by Dre Studio headphones

connector or headphone jack rather than use Bluetooth as there is often a slight delay when working with audio wirelessly.

The major manufacturers — JBL, Phillips, Bose, and Altec Lansing — all offer iPad-specific devices, some of which include a docking station so you can support and power your iPad while audio plays through the speakers. If you are planning to get one of these devices, check that the iPad can be positioned in both portrait and landscape orientation when docked, or else you may have difficulty using some apps that require the iPad to be positioned in a certain way.

Altec Lansing's Octiv Stage MP450 provides multiple positions while docked through its rotating arm. For standalone speakers that connect via the headphone jack, a more expensive but high-quality option is Bose's Computer MusicMonitor speakers that provide a very small footprint but excellent quality nonetheless and are suitable for monitoring projects when away from your main speaker system.

Connecting to 3G Networks

It's not essential, but having your iPad connected to the web can be a huge advantage for accessing new tracks when you're on the move, sharing your creations with others, or sending them to your computer. If you have an iPad with a built-in 3G connection, connecting to the web is simple.

If you have a Wi-Fi-only model, you could be left stranded if you can't find a suitable hot spot. If you fall into the latter category, you can ensure an almost constant connection by investing in your own mobile broadband device. Commonly known as MiFi (a brand name for one model), these small wireless devices are equivalent to a 3G dongle for laptops that connects to a carrier's data network and transmits it as a Wi-Fi signal to your iPad. Of course, you need to sign up for a data plan with a cellular provider that will charge a monthly fee but for the convenience it provides it's certainly worth it. If you already have a plan for your cell phone, you might even be offered a promotion or discount rate for purchasing an additional plan for your iPad.

Connecting to Wi-Fi Networks

Whether you want to connect to a public Wi-Fi hot spot, a personal MiFi device, or your home network, you need to tell your iPad which network to use. (Perhaps you have a Wi-Fi-only iPad, but even if you have a 3G-capable model, you might want to use Wi-Fi for its faster connections or to not use up your 3G bandwidth allocation.) Here's how:

1. If you want to connect to a personal Wi-Fi access point, router, or MiFi, make sure it is turned on and set up per the manufacturer's instructions.
2. Head to the iPad's Settings app and tap the Wi-Fi option in the Sidebar.
3. In the Wi-Fi Networks pane, make sure that Wi-Fi is switched on. Under the Choose a Network section, look for the Wi-Fi network you want to connect to. If you see a lock icon next to a network name in the list, as in Figure 1-7, the network is password-protected, so you will need to enter a password before you can connect and access the network.
4. Tap the network you want to join and enter its password if requested. In a public hot spot, you may need to log in or acknowledge the terms of service. Some public hot spots automatically open the Safari browser so you can do that;

FIGURE 1-7

Connecting to a Wi-Fi network

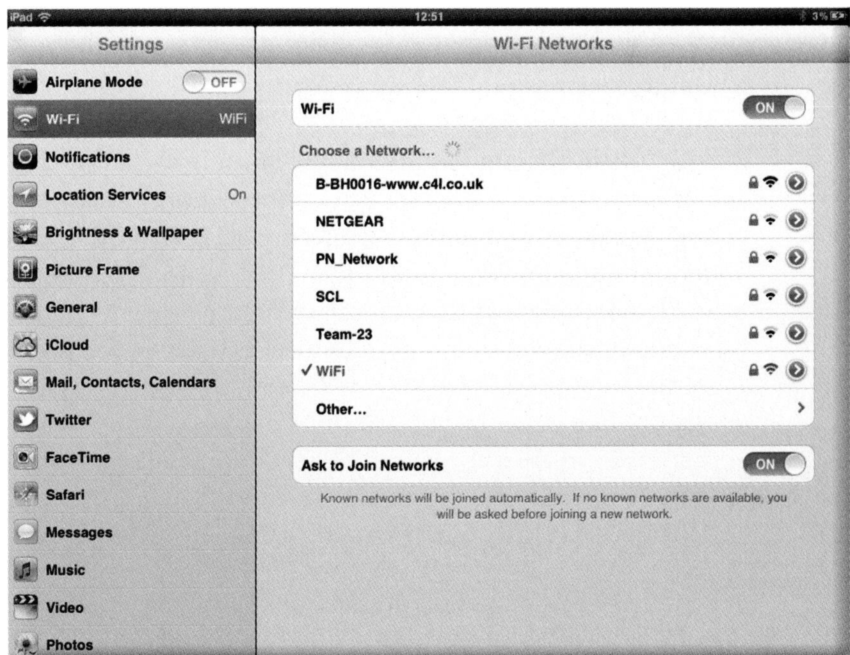

others will appear to not respond after you connect, in which case you need to go to Safari yourself and try to open any web page to get that public hot spot's login page to appear.

Charging Your iPad and Preserving Power

One of the worst things that can happen when you're using your iPad on the move is to run out of battery power. The iPad holds a decent charge and can easily last all day if used sparingly but, unfortunately, most music apps demand a lot of the tablet's processors and graphics and, as a result, its battery capacity.

To avoid running out of power, you can take several steps to limit battery usage before it's too late:

1. Turn off Wi-Fi and Bluetooth if you're not using them, in the Settings app. Alternatively, you could switch your iPad into airplane mode from the Settings app to prevent 3G, Wi-Fi, and Bluetooth from connecting or looking for a connection, which uses valuable juice.
2. If you can manage it, reduce the brightness of the iPad's screen. Keeping the large display lit and bright is another power-sapping task, so use the iPad at the lowest brightness level before you can't see the screen at all can be handy.
3. If you haven't opted to use airplane mode, you should also turn off location services in the Settings app; location detection also uses power while trying to determine your GPS location.
4. If you are still using a Wi-Fi or 3G Internet connection, limit how often the iPad checks for new e-mails by going the Mail, Contacts, Calendars pane in the Settings app and changing the Fetch New Data setting to a specific interval or Manually. By turning off the Push setting, you have your iPad stop constantly checking for new messages and using battery as it does it. You can set the iPad to check every 15, 30, or 60 minutes. If you set it to Manual, the iPad checks for e-mail only when you launch the Mail app or tell it to check for new mail.
5. If you are using your iPad near a computer or power outlet, plug it in when convenient to avoid draining the battery as you work. (This sounds obvious but it's easy to forget, even when you are sitting in front of multiple USB or wall sockets just waiting to provide power to your iPad!)

To keep a closer eye on your battery usage and the charge you have remaining, make sure you turn on the Battery Percentage option in the Settings app so the percentage of charge remaining displays at the top of the iPad's screen, allowing you to better gauge how much power you have left.

There are also several apps available on the App Store, such as Battery Plus for iPad, Battery Doctor, and Battery HD+ (shown in Figure 1-8) that monitor how long your iPad will last when using specific applications.

Of course, there are times when even the most careful battery preservation won't stop the inevitable shut down as your iPad runs out of charge. In this instance, the only route is a power outlet or a suitable charger. Although most people are content to connect their iPad to a computer via USB or to a wall jack to charge it, if you're on the move or working outdoors, this can become a tricky proposition. If you think you might run in to this problem, I recommend checking out one of the many iPad chargers on the market.

A particularly useful device is the New Trent iCruiser, shown in Figure 1-9, that packs an impressive 11,000mAh capacity, which means

FIGURE 1-8

Battery HD+

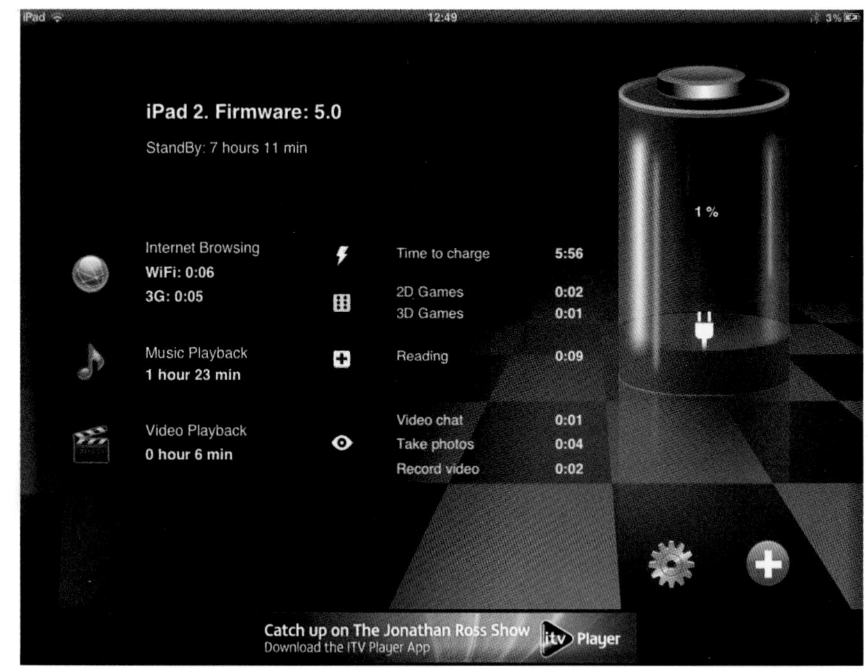

FIGURE 1-9

The New Trent iCruiser

that it can charge the iPad 2 fully and an iPhone more than five times without requiring main power. The lightweight device connects to several other devices, too, so it could help keep any additional music kit you are using topped up as well. Having the iCruiser in your kit bag means that, should you need it, you can double your battery life when you're away from a suitable power source.

If you spend a lot of time making music outdoors, another favorite charging accessory of mine is the Powermonkey Extreme. Not only is the device rugged and, incredibly, waterproof, it can provide power to your iPad and recharge itself using solar rays. With a 9000mAh lithium-polymer battery, the device can give you a power boost when your iPad really needs it and continue to provide you with charge while the sun shines.

2

I Write the Songs

There are many ways the iPad can help you make music without making a sound. For those quiet times, the classically trained and the eager amateur can use the large touchscreen to plot notes, write lyrics, and do more without disturbing the world around them. The iPad's portability means that you can use your iPad almost anywhere, be it commuting to work or relaxing on the couch. Not only can you write music on the iPad but you can also display it. In fact, the iPad could be the most stylish music stand ever made.

If your band, class, or even orchestra needs to work from the same sheet of music, printing should be the last resort where the iPad is involved. Sharing via e-mail and Wi-Fi are the new cool. This chapter takes a look at how you can create, edit, and view sheet music and chords on your iPad to keep your music with you wherever you go and provide the freedom to create on the move.

Viewing Sheet Music on the iPad

Think about it: You get a printed piece of paper or music book and you slap it on a music stand to read as you play. The paper is susceptible to being blown away (especially if you're playing a brass instrument), you have to turn its pages manually, and it can tear or bend. Surely there is an easier way of reading music? With an iPad, there is.

Not only can you download sheet music in formats such as PDF or Word or view them on the web, but there are dedicated apps to help you read sheet music far more easily than on the printed page. The iPad offers a clear view of the music, and allows you to store hundreds if not thousands of songs that you can take with you wherever you go. And, when it comes to the dreaded page turn while you're playing, a sweep of your finger is far more accurate and reliable than turning a physical page.

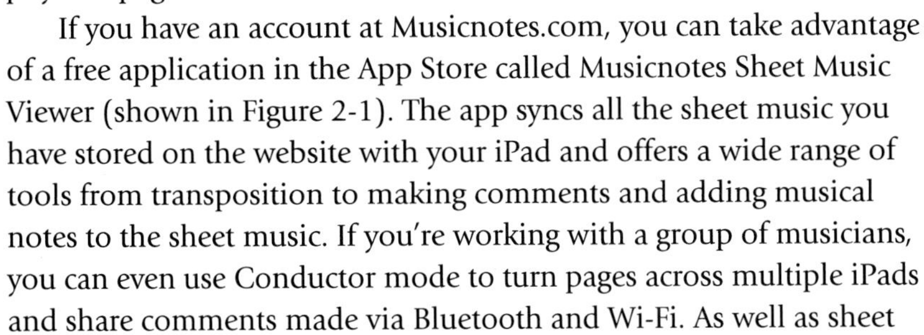

If you have an account at Musicnotes.com, you can take advantage of a free application in the App Store called Musicnotes Sheet Music Viewer (shown in Figure 2-1). The app syncs all the sheet music you have stored on the website with your iPad and offers a wide range of tools from transposition to making comments and adding musical notes to the sheet music. If you're working with a group of musicians, you can even use Conductor mode to turn pages across multiple iPads and share comments made via Bluetooth and Wi-Fi. As well as sheet

FIGURE 2-1

Musicnotes.com's sheet music viewer

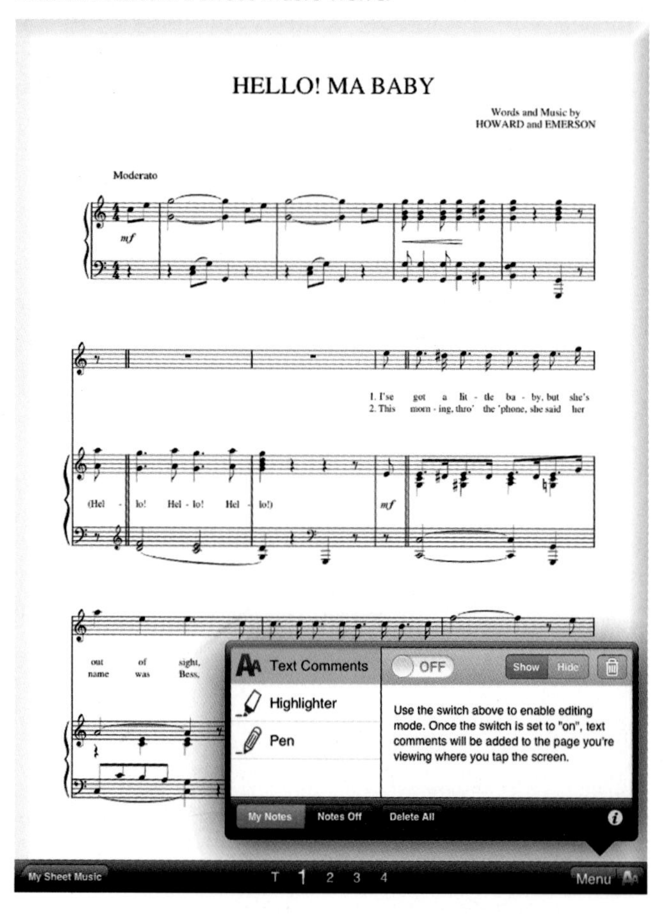

music, Musicnotes also works with guitar tablature so it isn't just a tool for those working classically.

Another excellent app for viewing sheet music is ForScore, a highly praised viewer and organizer that not only works well but looks beautiful. Offering a visual metronome, automatic page turning, and portrait and landscape orientation options, ForScore keeps the focus on your music with all menus hidden by default. Searching your sheet music is also easy in ForScore, with tagging and keyword options as well as the ability to create set lists.

If you need to focus on playing without worrying about that crucial upcoming page turn, the iPad's Bluetooth capabilities offer an additional accessory to make your life easier. AirTurn's BT-105 is a page-turner pedal that connects wirelessly to your iPad and turns pages with a single press. Connecting via Bluetooth, the BT-105 is compatible with several sheet music apps for iPad, including Musicnotes Sheet Music Viewer, ForScore, MusicReader, and OnSong. If you use your iPad to view sheet music on a regular basis, whether you are practicing or performing live, the BT-105 device could be a worthy investment to help avoid embarrassing pauses.

Annotating sheet music

Here's how to mark up sheet music with Musicnotes:

1. Start by launching Musicnotes and selecting the sheet music you want to edit from the My Sheet Music pane. Either tap a

FIGURE 2-2

Highlighting sheet music with Musicnotes

song title or swipe across the sheet music images to locate the file you want.

2. With the sheet music loaded, tap the Menu button at the bottom right of the pane and choose Highlighter from the popover. Pick a color for your highlights from the selection on the right.
3. Tap the sheet music you have loaded to hide the popover and swipe a finger across the sections you want to highlight (see Figure 2-2). These could be notes you are having trouble with or a section you want to practice.

You can also add notes to sheet music by following the same process but selecting the Pen tool from the Menu popover. This allows you to draw on the sheet music or write reminders to yourself. Use both the Highlighter and Pen tool to make detailed notes.

Importing printed sheet music for iPad use

It's likely that you have a collection of printed sheet music or guitar tab books already. If so, you should think about adding them to your iPad. Not only will digitizing your music mean you don't have to carry as much around with you, but you can also share music with others far more easily.

By using a scanner, your iPhone, or even the iPad's camera, you can quickly turn a printed page into a digital file that you can keep with you wherever you take your iPad. Of course, scanning is the best route, as you will achieve the highest quality replication. But using the iPad or iPhone camera does provide greater convenience even if the clarity of the image isn't the best. Here are your options:

- If you have access to a scanner, this is your best option. Import all the sheet music you need as PDF files and store them on your computer, ready to be synced with your iPad. Once you have transferred these PDFs via e-mail or syncing, you can open them in the iPad's default Quick Look viewer or download Apple's free iBooks app to view them.
- If you don't have a scanner, in a well-lit room, place the sheet music you want to import on a flat surface and launch the Camera app on your iPad. (If you have an iPhone, use its camera as the results will be better.) Position the camera above your sheet music and tap where the notes are shown on the Camera app's preview to focus on the detail and set

the exposure. When the music is framed and in focus, tap the Camera button or, in iOS 5, use the Volume Up physical button on your iPhone or iPad to take a picture of the sheet music (see Figure 2-3). The image is stored in your iPad's Photos app, where you can view it in full-screen mode to play from it. If you want to send the image to an app like iBooks or GoodReader, such as to organize and annotate the sheet music, there are several PDF converters such as Pictures 2 PDF in the App Store for converting images in your photo library into PDFs.

- If you don't have an iPad with a camera or an iPhone, use a digital camera to photograph the sheet music and then sync the photos to your iPad through iTunes or use the iPad Camera Connection Kit to transfer them from your camera to iPad.

FIGURE 2-3

Shooting sheet music with the iPad's camera

Writing Sheet Music

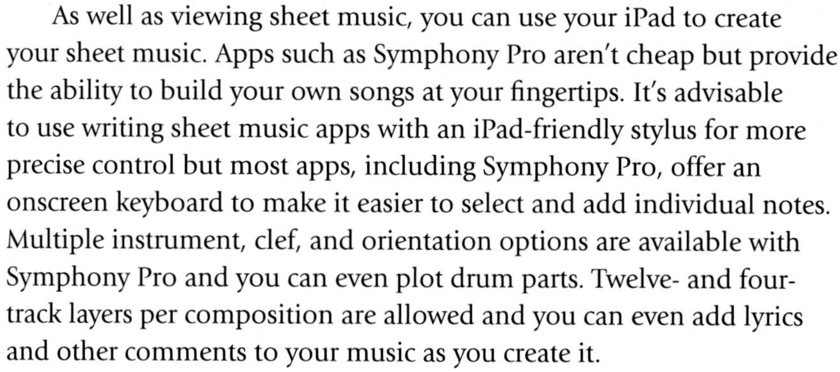

As well as viewing sheet music, you can use your iPad to create your sheet music. Apps such as Symphony Pro aren't cheap but provide the ability to build your own songs at your fingertips. It's advisable to use writing sheet music apps with an iPad-friendly stylus for more precise control but most apps, including Symphony Pro, offer an onscreen keyboard to make it easier to select and add individual notes. Multiple instrument, clef, and orientation options are available with Symphony Pro and you can even plot drum parts. Twelve- and four-track layers per composition are allowed and you can even add lyrics and other comments to your music as you create it.

For guitarists who want to write music there's GuitarScript, a tab editor that allows you to quickly write tablature that includes hammer-ons and pull-offs in an intuitive interface that makes the writing process easy. Designed to work with the iPad's touchscreen, GuitarScript allows you to import documents from a number of sources, including iTunes and the Mail app. You can even print from the iPad.

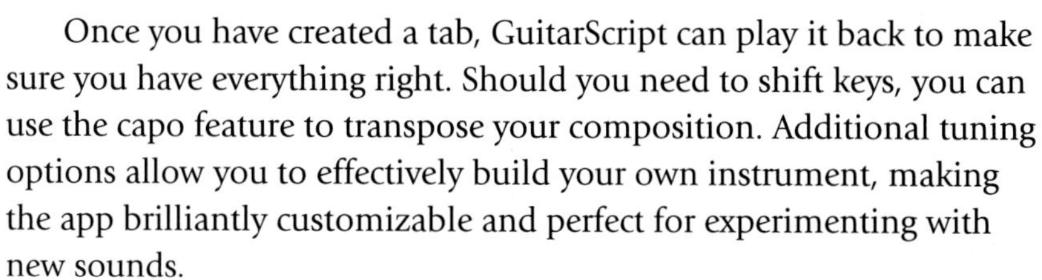

Once you have created a tab, GuitarScript can play it back to make sure you have everything right. Should you need to shift keys, you can use the capo feature to transpose your composition. Additional tuning options allow you to effectively build your own instrument, making the app brilliantly customizable and perfect for experimenting with new sounds.

Writing Lyrics

The iPad makes writing lyrics the simplest part of the songwriting process. The built-in Notes app (see Figure 2-4) is probably the easiest way to jot down quick ideas, however there are more advanced options available such as Apple's Pages and iA's Writer. Both allow file export via e-mail, and Pages offers printing (if you have a compatible printer) straight from the iPad to quickly commit your songs to paper.

Using the iPad's onscreen keyboard is the quickest way to write using these apps. But if your writing becomes more extensive, you might want to look into a wireless Bluetooth keyboard option. Apple offers its own keyboard that connects wirelessly as well as a keyboard dock that connects via the iPad's dock connector.

FIGURE 2-4

The iPad Notes app

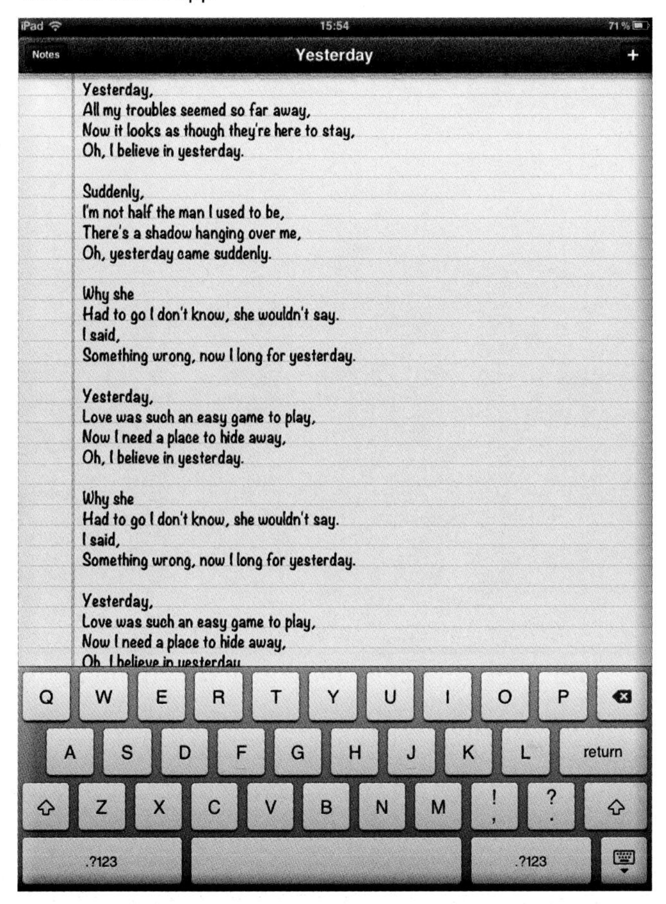

Alternate lyric-writing options

There is another method that may help your ideas flow when writing the words for your song: Using transcription software to record your voice and turn it into text, you can simply speak the lyrics rather than be foiled by that blank canvas in front of you and, in many cases, find inspiration in the most unlikely of places.

I recommend the free Dragon Dictation app, shown in Figure 2-5. Not only is it cheap, but it comes from the people responsible for the voice-recognition technology used by Siri, the virtual personal assistant on the iPhone 4S. The app is available for the iPhone and iPad, so you can transcribe lyrics whenever the mood strikes — and enjoy surprising accuracy from it. Whether you record via the iPad's built-in

FIGURE 2-5

Dragon Dictation

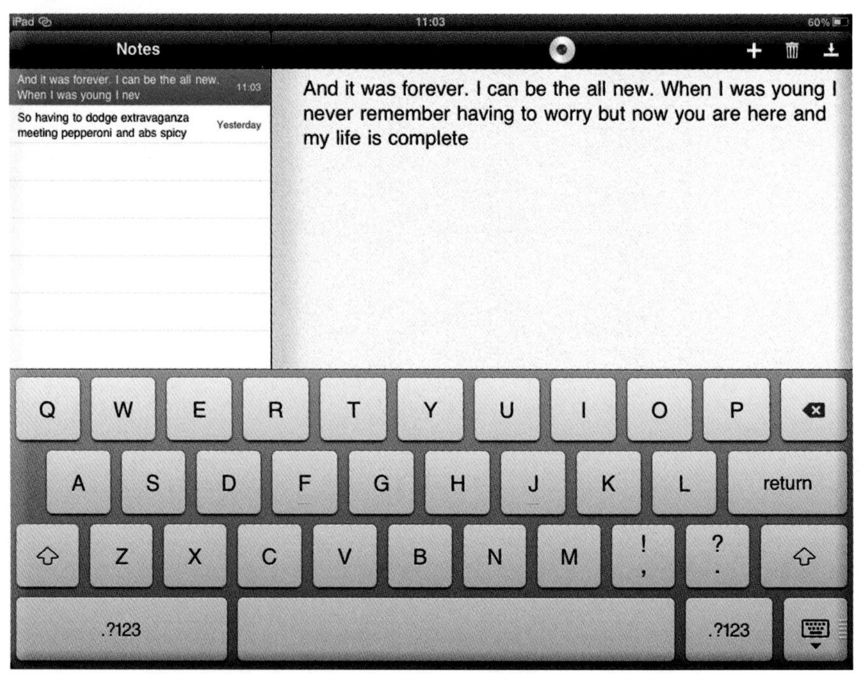

microphone, the headphone mic, or any other mic, Dragon does a good job of understanding what you say and making tweaks to the text should be a rarity.

You will also achieve some success — believe me, I've tried it — by singing to the app as you formulate lyric and harmony ideas. Some words will inevitably get lost in the process of recording and converting, but for a quick way to write lyrics, Dragon Dictation is a worthy addition to your iPad's app list.

Advanced songwriting methods

When playing an instrument isn't an option but you are still in creative mood when using your iPad, you can use apps to help you write music that don't require external devices or traditional touchscreen playback techniques.

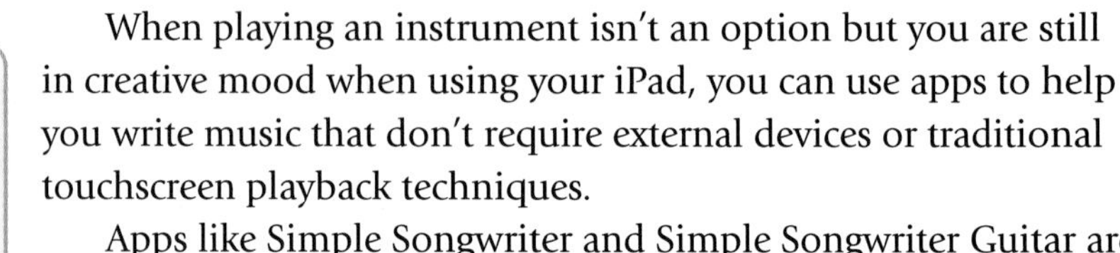

Apps like Simple Songwriter and Simple Songwriter Guitar are perfect for those times when you want to get a song idea down but don't have an instrument handy. Whether it's a chord progression you particularly like or an entire song you want to plot out, these apps offer

FIGURE 2-6

Simple Songwriter

a simple way to do just that. British band Scouting for Girls even used Simple Songwriter to come up with the melody for its song "Love How It Hurts."

Both apps are made for the iPhone but work perfectly well on the iPad using the 2X zoom feature to expand the window of an iPhone app on the iPad, and both are an easy route to building a song in just a few taps. Once you've found chords that work nicely together (from a selection of hundreds with multiple variations), you can record the progression and, when the time comes to record for real, the app can play back your song and show the chords as they play.

If you need to fit your song to a particular key, these apps can transpose recorded songs up or down, too.

Simple Songwriter also offers a useful way to learn the chords of other songs. Listening to an existing song and matching the chords with those in Simple Songwriter lets you accurately define the chords used and store them for future reference.

Here's how to plan song chords with Simple Songwriter:

1. Launch Simple Songwriter and tap the New Song button to begin a new project (see Figure 2-6).

2. Tap the chord buttons you want to play to figure out the chords you want to use and hold the inversion and 7th modifier buttons to the right of the window to create variations on those chords.
3. When you have a progression you want to remember, tap the Record button at the bottom left of the window and choose from a variety of settings that appear, such as turning the metronome on or off.
4. When you are ready, tap the large Start button and play your chords in time with the metronome and hit the Stop button when you're done.
5. To listen to your progression, tap the Play button and then tap the From Beginning button that appears to play back your song with each chord name displayed on the screen as it plays.

3

Practice Makes Perfect

Getting your instrument in tune is one of the little chores that musicians have to put up with. There are many physical tuners, from pitch pipes to small digital devices, that listen to your notes and give you feedback (on your tuning, not the good, rocking kind). These tools are all well and good and if you are happy with your current tuning method, by all means stick with them.

But if your device happens to run out of battery power or you are in a loud room where it cannot pick up individual notes, you need another method. This is where inline tuners are handy: those that are built into the pickup of an acoustic guitar or connected to your amp or lead to pick up the exact sound coming from your instrument.

Even these tuners can fall victim to battery requirements, though, and they are less flexible than software equivalents, which leads me to iPad-based tuners. Yep, as the phrase goes, "there's an app for that"; in fact there are hundreds of apps for that.

The first port of call is Apple's own GarageBand for iPad, which has a tuner built in to the Guitar Amp instrument. This tuner offers a simple visual interface that shows when a note is flat, sharp, or in tune. Major providers such as IK Multimedia's AmpliTube and Peavey's AmpKit include tuners you can use when your instrument is connected to your iPad via the iRig or AmpKit Link.

A third-party option, Bitcount's Cleartune Chromatic Tuner for iPad (see Figure 3-1), offers professional-level control and supreme tuning accuracy. Used by artists like The Black Keys and Gorillaz, Cleartune supports transposing and can run through notes manually or automatically. The app also tunes a wide range of instruments, including electric guitar, bass, bowed string instruments, woodwinds, brass, and piano.

Slow Down Music for Learning and Practice

If there is a particular solo or riff you want to learn but it's just too quick to follow at normal speed, there are ways to slow them down without altering the pitch. Normally, slowing down a piece of music brings about a severe pitch decrease, making it impossible to identify the correct notes. However, with some app trickery, you can avoid that happening and hear each note, even if it is as quick as the lead break from "Sultans of Swing."

AmpliTube offers just such a tool with its SpeedTrainer feature (see Figure 3-2) that is, incredibly, bundled for free with the basic app. The

FIGURE 3-1

Cleartune for iPad

process of slowing down a part is simple: Tap the Song button at the bottom of the display, load a song from your music library, and start it playing back. When you reach the beginning of the part you want to learn, tap the Loop and A buttons one after the other and then the B button at the end of the part. The music then loops the section you selected. Using the SpeedTrainer slider at the bottom of the window, you can adjust the playback speed to a tempo that suits you and even opt to turn off the vocals by tapping the No Voice button, although this isn't particularly effective for all songs.

Although you will notice some anomalies in the sound, the original pitch is perfectly preserved, so you can practice to your heart's content and gradually increase the speed as you become more accomplished.

FIGURE 3-2

Importing songs to slow down in AmpliTube

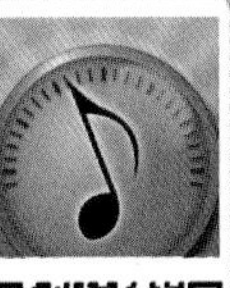

The fact that the SpeedTrainer is built into AmpliTube is a major bonus too, as you'll be able to set your guitar sound to match the part you're playing using the amp and effect controls. You can even record your practice using the built-in AmpliTube recorder so you can pick up on any mistakes.

App Store alternatives include the popular and free Anytune that works with both iPhone and iPad and there is also the high-priced yet highly praised Capo that offers a desktop version with advanced features for slowing down songs and pitch shifting.

Here's how to slow down songs for practice with AmpliTube's SpeedTrainer, shown in Figure 3-3:

1. Start by launching AmpliTube and tapping the Song button at the bottom of the window, denoted by the icon of an iPod Classic. Tap the Add Song button and select an import method. The easiest import route is iPod Library, which allows you to select a song from your iPad's music library
2. From the list of available songs, select one or tap the Add All Songs button to import all the songs in your library. Be warned, however: This may take a little time. When the song

FIGURE 3-3

AmpliTube SpeedTrainer

or songs you selected appears in the Songs list, you can simply tap a song title to select it. Once you've selected a song, you can play it back by tapping the Play button (the ▶ icon).

3. During playback, you can skip through the track using the first slider below the Play button. You can also adjust the volume of the song using the Volume slider. When you have found the beginning of the section in the song you want to practice, tap the A button at the top right of the Songs popover.
4. Play the song until you reach the end of the part you want to practice, then tap the B button to set the end of the region. Now tap the Loop button to the left of the A button.
5. Pressing Play loops the playback of the song between the A and B points you set. You can access SpeedTrainer as it plays by dragging the third slider to the left to slow the song down or to the right to speed it up.

Find Chords, Tabs, and Music for Popular Songs

It's no good bashing your head against a wall trying to learn a song if you are not sure of the notes or chords involved in the first place. Although some people are lucky to have the gift to simply pick up music by ear, the rest of us need a little push in the right direction. This is where some particularly useful apps come in to help you hit the right notes.

Songsterr Plus is a brilliant tool with more than 300,000 tabs that can be displayed and even played back in the app at regular or half speed to aid your learning. Based on the Songsterr.com database, tabs are tweaked and amended regularly to root out errors and provide a more accurate service. Users can search the app by genre tags too so you will never be short of a song to learn when you need one.

FIGURE 3-4

Ultimate Guitar HD

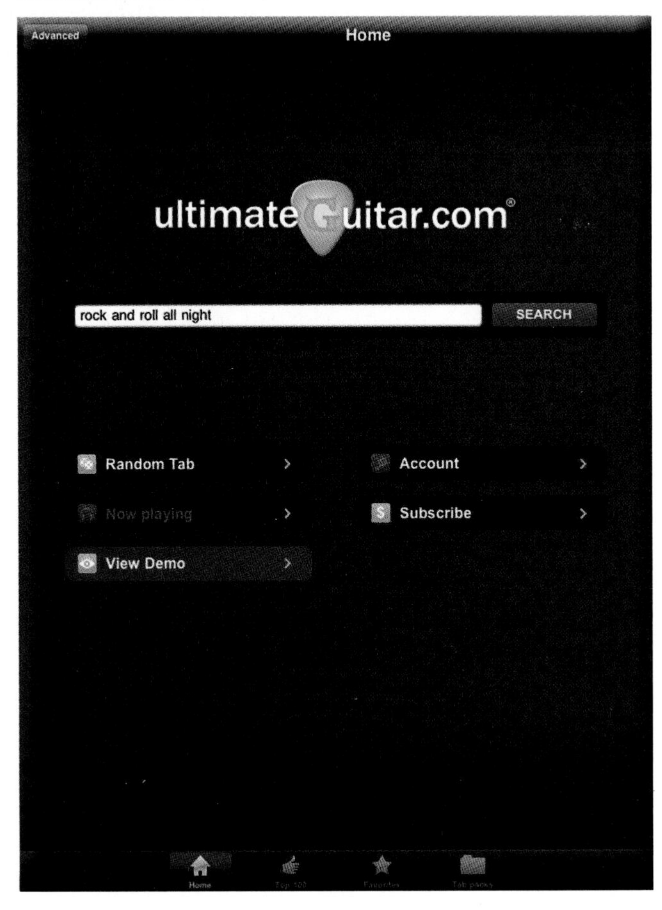

The popular website Ultimate Guitar also offers an iPad app, Ultimate Guitar Tabs HD (see Figure 3-4), for hunting down elusive chords for guitar and bass but does require a subscription. If you're not keen on spending the money, however, you can use the website from your iPad and view all the chords you want for free.

Musicnotes.com is also a great online source for downloading sheet music and includes sheet music for a range of instruments. Used with the Musicnotes.com iPad app, you can store your sheet music and view it whenever you need it, as Chapter 2 explains.

Although there are apps that help you access guitar and bass tabs as well as other music documents, many charge a subscription fee for the privilege. To avoid paying for tabs that are readily available for free online while keeping them accessible, you have a couple of options.

FIGURE 3-5

Reading tab from the Photos app

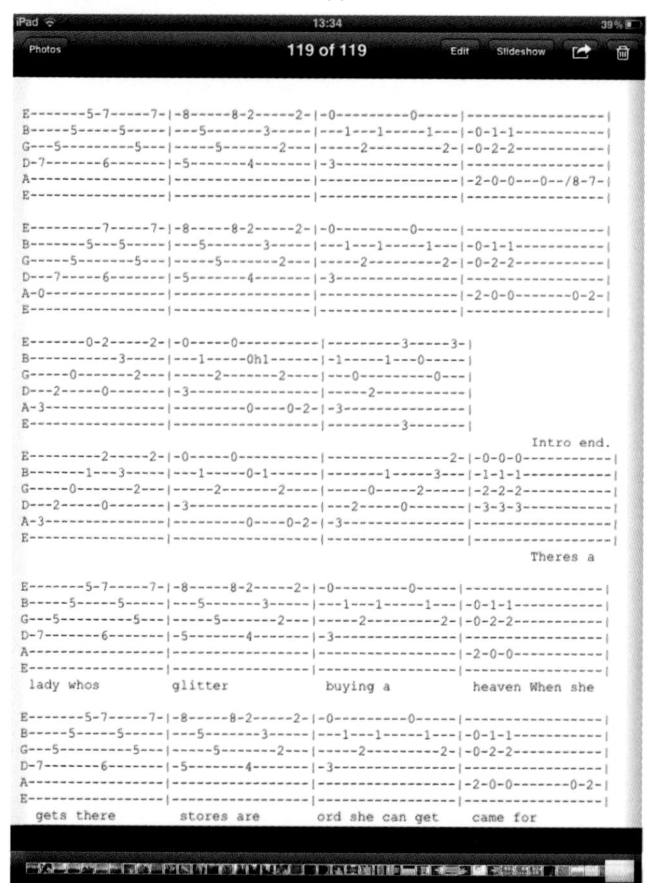

First, you can use the bookmarking features of your iPad's browser. For Safari, this means using the standard bookmarks list or using the Reading List feature introduced in iOS 5.0. By storing tabs you want to access again as bookmarks, you can create a collection of tabs that you can access whenever you have an Internet connection. If you use a service like Read It Later or Instapaper, you also can store tabs and may even be able to view them offline.

Second, you can take screen grabs of tabs from a website and store them in your iPad's Photos app. To do so, center as much of the tab on the Safari window as you can and press the iPad's Home button and Sleep/Wake button simultaneously. The screen flashes white and you hear a camera shutter sound, indicating the screen image has been captured. Head to the iPad's Photo app to find your new image. From here you can edit it, crop it, or share it via e-mail (see Figure 3-5). If you took multiple screenshots of tabs, your photos will be next to one another so you can quickly swipe among them while playing.

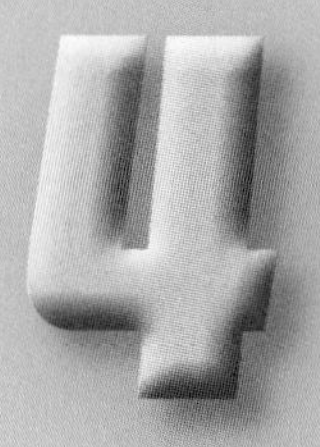

You Send Me

With your recording or mix finished, the time comes when your music is ready to share with the world. Even before this point, you might want to start firing out demos to your audience or sections of songs to other band members for them to work on. This chapter is all about getting your musical creations out of your iPad and onto the web. Of course, simply uploading a track isn't the end of the story.

If you want to maximize the number of people who actually listen to your songs, you need to know the right places to put them. You also need a little marketing knowledge to break through the sea of artists trying to do the same thing. Fortunately, there are plenty of services that can help you share and promote your music.

You also need to get involved in competitions. Even if you don't sweep the board with awards for every entry, your name and music will be listened to more than if it were just languishing on your iPad, and you will begin to build a reputation online. Unlike the days when gigging was the only way to promote your craft, the web provides a unique route to a much larger audience. Although I certainly wouldn't suggest ditching live performance entirely, harnessing the power of the Internet can be an effective tool for gaining fans.

Of course, there comes a time when creating just for the love of music isn't enough and, as you improve, it would be a waste not to make some money from your talent. If you believe your music is good enough to sell, there are many ways you can do so, including setting up your own web store and using the Holy Grail of music delivery, the iTunes Store. Even if you don't top the charts, the more promotion you do for your music, the more money you stand to earn, which you can then plow back into your music by adding new apps and hardware to your setup.

Uploading Your Music to the Web

How you get your music online from your iPad largely depends on the app you use. If your only choice is to export your music, then it's likely you will have to send the files to a computer to upload them to the Internet. However, if your chosen app offers an upload feature, you can quickly send finished songs or parts of a song to the web straight from your iPad.

Some apps like GarageBand offer an e-mail export feature, which provides workarounds for uploading to the web. One such method is to use the Send To Dropbox service that allows you to e-mail files to a unique address where the attachments are then copied to your Dropbox online storage account. By making the shared folder "public," you let other users access and listen to your music when provided with a special link. Using the public folder with the Dropbox app for iPad is a quick way to export and share your tracks without a computer.

Dropbox is a little flaky when it comes to actually opening audio files, however. More often than not it will allow you to play a file and that's it. If you simply want people to listen to your music, Dropbox is an easy solution for sharing, but sticking to the standard e-mail export features allows more options that are covered in the next section.

More and more apps are adding export options to one of the most popular music sharing sites, SoundCloud, which offers a YouTube-like sharing experience for audio with both desktop and mobile apps available (shown in Figure 4-1). I suggest signing up for a free subscription as this is fast becoming the go-to service for musicians who want to share their music with the world.

There are hundreds of iPad apps that allow you to upload to SoundCloud, including Peavey's AmpKit, MultiTrack DAW, iRig Recorder, and Nanostudio. Alternatively, using SoundCloud, you can record live and upload directly. Unfortunately, there is no way to

FIGURE 4-1

SoundCloud

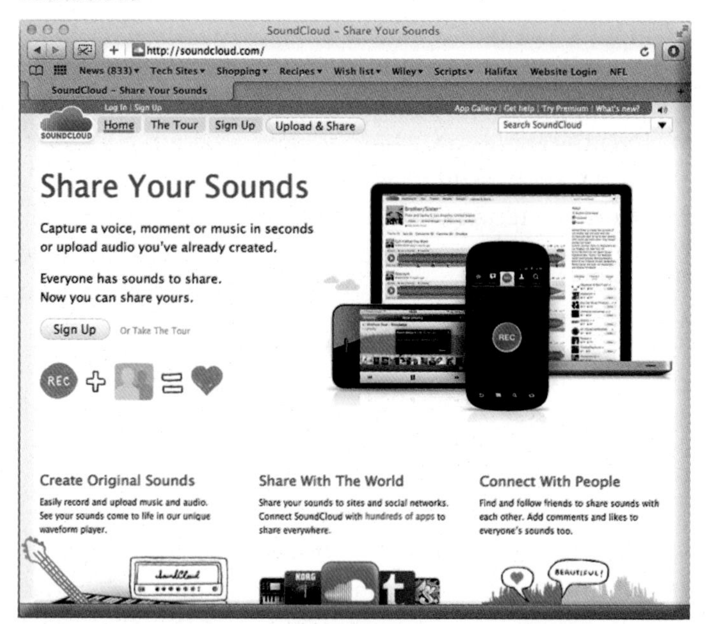

upload an individual file from your iPad to SoundCloud, so you need an app with a specific SoundCloud upload feature. This, of course, rules out GarageBand. Although you may be lucky and already use an app that offers SoundCloud support, you will likely need to access the audio files on your computer to upload them, or you could try these two supergeeky techniques to upload music directly from your iPad:

Geeky upload technique 1

If you have an app that either accepts pasted audio or can load audio files and uploads to SoundCloud, you can export a GarageBand project as an audio file via the e-mail export option and send the e-mail to yourself.

A great application choice, Harmonicdog's MultiTrack DAW, allows you to import audio files and export to SoundCloud. When the e-mail arrives on your iPad, download the attachment and tap and hold its icon until the Open In menu appears. Load the file in any compatible app that offers SoundCloud uploads and share your songs. If your app isn't listed, open the e-mail attachment in an audio editor like Hokusai Audio Editor and copy and paste it to your SoundCloud-compatible app.

Yes, it is a fiddly process but nonetheless is a convenient way to upload songs without having to sync files back to your computer.

Here's how to upload a GarageBand song to SoundCloud via MultiTrack DAW:

1. First you need to download MultiTrack DAW from the App Store.
2. Next, from GarageBand's My Songs window, pick the project you want to send to SoundCloud and tap the Share button (the icon of a rectangle with an arrow) and choose Email Song from the menu. The song is exported as an audio file, attached to a new e-mail message. In the To field, enter an e-mail address and send the e-mail.
3. When the e-mail arrives in your inbox, tap and hold on the attachment until a contextual menu appears. If MultiTrack doesn't appear on the list, tap the Open In option and select it from the list that appears. MultiTrack DAW opens with your song listed in its Shared menu. Tap the name of your song and then tap the Import Copy button. Tap the Menu button at the bottom of the window and close any songs that may be open.

FIGURE 4-2

A SoundCloud upload from MultiTrack DAW

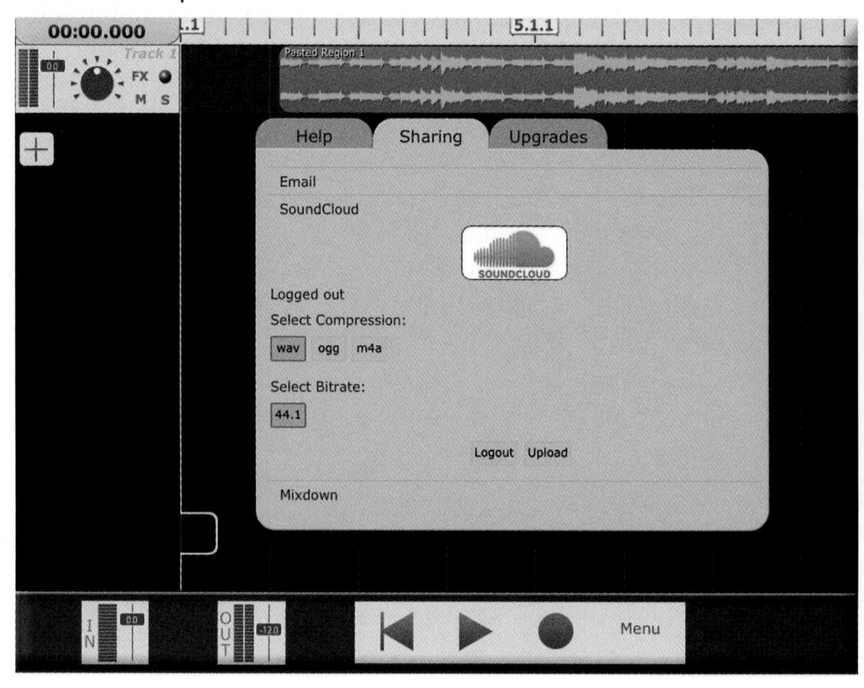

4. Tap the New Song button (the + icon) at the bottom of the window and enter a name for your song. Select the icon for your new song at the top left of the window. By default, one track is loaded in the project. Tap and hold on the time line until the contextual menu appears and drag your finger to the Paste button to import your song, then tap the Menu button again.
5. Choose Help/Sharing/Upgrades from the list that appears when you tap the Menu button and move to the Sharing pane. Tap SoundCloud and enter your login details when prompted (see Figure 4-2). When you're done, tap Upload to send the song to your SoundCloud page.

Geeky upload technique 2

If you have an iPhone and an iPad as well as a line-in product such as an iRig or AmpKit Link, you can use SoundCloud's own app to upload audio. You will need one additional adapter.

Start by launching the SoundCloud app on your iPhone and readying the project you want to share on your iPad. Next, connect the iRig to your iPhone and, instead of connecting the other end of the adapter to an instrument, plug it into your iPad using a 1/4-inch-to-1/8-inch (6.3mm to 3.5mm) adapter.

Begin recording with SoundCloud on your iPhone and begin playback of the track you want to share on your iPad. It might not be the best quality, but your song will be recorded to your iPhone. Unfortunately, the audio file becomes mono using this method.

Once you are done recording, you can upload the track to your SoundCloud account via a 3G or Wi-Fi connection from your iPhone.

Collaborating and Sharing Audio Files and Projects

With the e-mail export feature in GarageBand, it is easy to quickly share mix-downs of your projects from your iPad. Sharing project files requires iTunes and your computer, and it is currently the only route other users can use to load them in GarageBand on their iPad. This means that collaboration can be a bit tricky when sharing a complete song that can then be edited as opposed to just listened to. Of course, you can always drop a mixed-down version of a GarageBand project into a new GarageBand project, but mixing and removing elements from the original project is not possible.

I have tried long and hard to find a solution to GarageBand's sharing limitations, which annoy me and I'm sure will annoy you. At the moment, as far as my research is concerned, it's not possible. The problem is the app developers' lack of access to the iPad's file. As Apple works on more wireless features for the iPad, such as AirPlay and wireless syncing, I hope that ways to transfer files like GarageBand projects between iPads become available.

Another problem with a GarageBand project file is that it appears to most systems (other than in the GarageBand app and on Mac OS X) as a folder rather than a file (essentially, it is just a folder with the `.band` filename extension). Although this extension causes all sorts of issues when syncing with Dropbox (see Figure 4-3) and other services, it also means you can dig inside the folder and pick out the individual audio files that make up your project and share them one by one. I know this is not hugely helpful, but it may help you find your own way to collaborate on iPad-based GarageBand projects. If this method

FIGURE 4-3

Opening a GarageBand track in the Dropbox

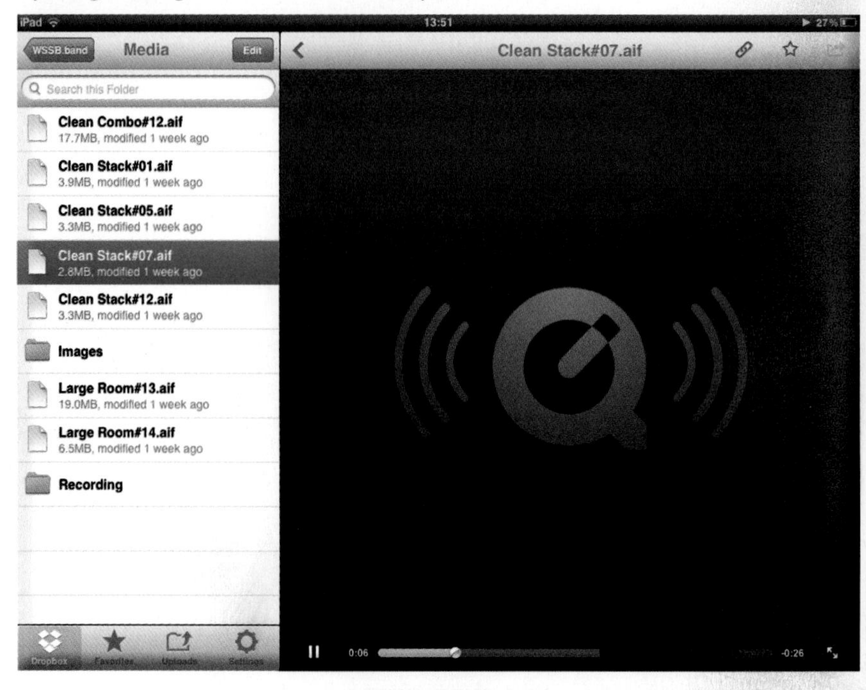

doesn't work for you, for the foreseeable future, you will have to sync back to your computer every time you want to share a GarageBand project file.

So what can you do instead? It is often best to share individual tracks bounced (exported) from your GarageBand projects so that they can be imported to a fresh project one at a time. Say your friend wants to add vocals to your track; simply send him the drum, bass, and guitar parts so he can create a new project from these tracks. You could simply mute all but one track in your project and then export it via e-mail. Only the unmuted track is shared so, essentially, you are just sharing one instrument part with any effects applied to it. The only real drawback of this process is that you will have to perform this time-consuming task for each track you want to share. (Chapter 18 covers this technique in more detail.)

Alternatively, some apps, such as AmpliTube, allow audio files to be opened as backing tracks, making them a perfect option for guitarists and vocalists who want to record parts over your existing GarageBand music. You could simply export your entire project and let your friend load the audio file in his chosen app as backing. Once he is done recording, he can export the product and send it back to you so you can add it to your project or create a new one.

But how do you add audio files to a GarageBand project? Unfortunately, like exporting, it is not as simple a technique as it should be. The first route is to use a computer and iTunes to sync the files as loops to your iPad and then import them in GarageBand.

I prefer a solely iPad route, which is where things tend to get tricky. Depending on the apps you have, it may also cost a bit of money, as adding audio to your tracks requires an extension to the normal cut and paste route in GarageBand. Chapter 18 explains the whole process, but the basic method requires loading the audio file you want to add to GarageBand from the Mail app in any app that appears in the Open In menu.

It sounds strange, but some apps aren't listed as available options when you try to open a file from Mail. Any app that 1) loads files from Mail and 2) supports copy and paste will be fine; otherwise I recommend you use Hokusai Audio Editor (and a small in-app purchase to enable copy and paste) or MultiTrack DAW. With a suitable app installed, you can then load the file you receive via e-mail, and copy and paste it to a vacant audio track in GarageBand. Sounds tricky, doesn't it? But it's not once you get the hang of it. Still, I wouldn't be surprised if you stick to using your computer to share files between iPads.

Promoting Your Songs

It can seem like a daunting task to promote your music online, but you should feel comforted (or more worried, depending on the way you look at it) that there are many people doing it.

Build your own website using a free service like Blogger or a paid subscription like Squarespace (see Figure 4-4) and start uploading your songs and telling people where to find them. Alternatively, create your own channel on a site like SoundCloud or even YouTube and promote that site. If you do create a site for your music, you also have the option to embed your SoundCloud and YouTube uploads on your page with a simple link. This link saves you from fiddling with complex file uploads in your website software.

You know what's coming next, right? Yep, the wonderful world of social networking. If you want the hits or, in this case, listeners, I advise starting accounts on at least Facebook and Twitter. By building up a

FIGURE 4-4

Squarespace

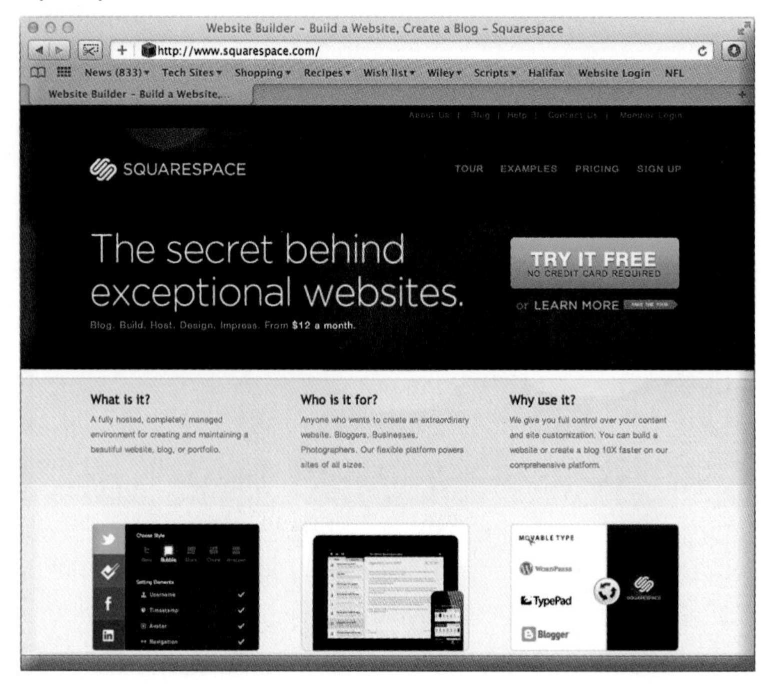

following for your music, sharing your thoughts on the production, and letting people know where you will be performing live, you can engage your audience in ways that weren't previously possible.

Social networking is also a handy route for people to learn more about you and your style. If they hear one track they like and then can't find any more, that's where the story ends. If, however, you have an online presence, they can find you and, if you're lucky, even buy your music or book you to play live if that's what you are after.

Social networks, especially Twitter, are brilliant ways to mix in the right circles online, too. By following artists similar to yourself as well as reviewers and industry professionals, you are likely to find people who will be interested in you.

Twitter is especially useful for categorizing your updates using its hashtag feature. By adding a hash (#) symbol before a specific section of text in a tweet (`#newmusic` for example; see Figure 4-5), people searching for specific items on Twitter can find your tweets among all others with the same hashtag. If your tweets and hashtag prove really popular, you could even become a trending topic!

FIGURE 4-5

Searching hashtags on Twitter

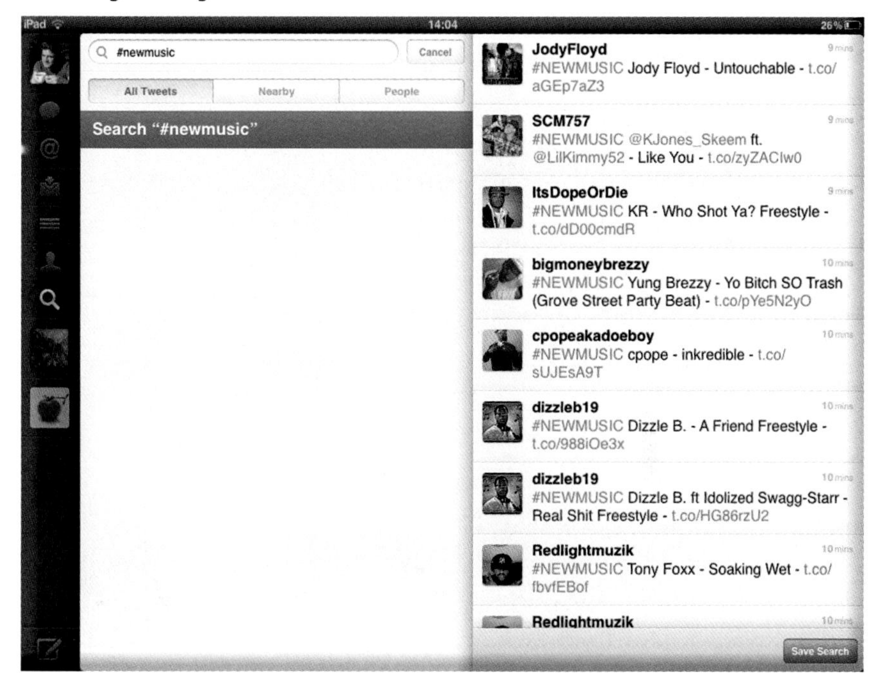

Of course, all these social networking site are accessible from your iPad, and several music apps make it possible to upload music directly to the sites.

Another great way to increase awareness is to enter your music into as many online competitions as you can. Most competitions allow you to include a short bio you can link to your site or social network pages so that those who enjoy your entry can find out more. Of course, winning a few competitions won't hurt your brand, either, but the fact that your music regularly crops up should be enough for you to pick up fans.

It is also worth regularly checking the websites of music app developers as well as manufacturers of music hardware, as they are always keen to promote their products and the work of their customers through competitions. As well as the recognition, there are normally amazing prizes to be won as well.

Selling Your Music on iTunes and Other Stores

Before you eagerly scan this section looking for the magic route to getting your music on iTunes, let me first explain: It's not that easy. Although there are plenty of places to sell your music online, even if you end up doing it yourself, iTunes is a little more tricky and, like most things Apple, far more curated than the rest. That said, it's not impossible to do and should be worth trying even if you don't end up making it on to Apple's store.

Bear in mind that although it might sound nice to say you have an album on iTunes, you are in the company of thousands of other artists, many of whom have huge record labels and marketing budgets behind them (see Figure 4-6). So, even if you do get your tracks on iTunes, they may be hard to find and won't receive the top billing afforded established stars. Apple also takes a 30-percent cut of the sale of every song. It's tough, but, hey, that's the music business.

Before you begin blindly submitting your music, there are some things you need to do. First, make sure your music is completely original to you. Unauthorized use of samples from copyrighted works, reused lyrics, or any other derivative works like covers will not fly when it comes to selling your music — and you could land yourself in some

FIGURE 4-6

The iTunes Store

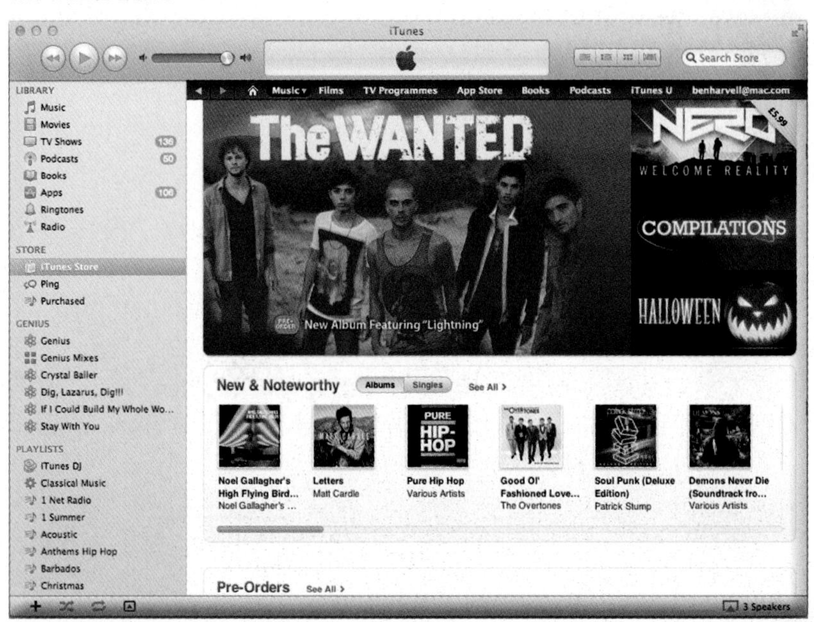

GETTING YOUR MUSIC ON SPOTIFY

Spotify's Sally Whatley explains how unsigned artists can add their music to Spotify and pick up new fans along the way.

What's the best route for an unsigned artist to get their music on Spotify

Artists don't need to be signed or have a record deal to get their music on Spotify. Unsigned artists should upload their music to one of the artist aggregators we work with: `http://www.spotify.com/work-with-us/labels-and-artists/artist-aggregators`. They help artists to license their music to online music services such as Spotify.

What are the benefits you believe Spotify offers artists?

Spotify is generating serious revenues for rights holders, labels, publishers, and the artists they represent. We have paid tens of millions of euros to rights holders since our launch. We do not have direct, contractual relationships with artists; we compensate collecting societies, who pay publishers and songwriters, and the record companies/aggregators who in turn compensate the artist for use of a track.

How can Spotify benefit up-and-coming bands?

Spotify also offers a powerful promotional platform for artists and exposure to more than 10 million users across Europe. Here's a quote from John Davis, manager of The Sounds, who explains how Spotify can benefit up-and-coming bands with an example: "The Sounds sold 3,000 tickets at €35 in Madrid, without ever having released an album there, never gone to radio, etc. The month before the show though, they had 110,000 streams of one song alone — in one month — on Spotify! They then went back and headlined a festival there for 20,000 people."

Each time a track is streamed, it earns more money for an artist, whereas if someone buys a download they have paid once to own the music, which they can listen to over and over again without paying any more back to the artist.

serious legal trouble if you ignore the warnings. Second, make sure your music is mixed and produced to the highest possible degree. Not only will decent production stand your recordings in better stead in comparison to major label recordings, stores will be far more interested in selling a professional-quality product over an unbalanced, muddy-sounding collection of tracks.

Before uploading or even submitting your music, listen to it on a wide range of devices, from headphones and computer speakers through to more expensive systems, to make sure your mix sounds as good as it possibly can across all media.

If mixing isn't your strong point, there are plenty of tutorials available online as well as books to help you hone your craft. There is even a section on mixing your projects in GarageBand in Chapter 16. If your music still doesn't sound right after fine-tuning and finessing, look for a local or web-based music producer to do the job for you. You don't have to spend a fortune, but if you can provide the individual tracks or project files to someone who knows what he or she is doing, you might be surprised at just how much better your music can sound.

Finally, if you are trying to sell an album or EP, make sure it looks the part with finished titles, liner notes if required, and album artwork that represents the music. It doesn't have to be a work of art but it does need to look polished enough for the casual listener to take a chance on your music.

When it comes to selling, start things off gently and explore the more niche music sellers online. If your music fits into a certain genre, explore whether there are any targeted online music stores that fit your style that might be able to find you a decent audience. Then move on to the bigger services commonly referred to as "aggregators." Services such as CDBaby charge a small fee per album and allow you to upload masters of your music as well as album artwork or send a physical CD or even vinyl record to the company that will digitize it for you. The music is then posted on CDBaby.com and distributed to all CDBaby's partners, which include iTunes, Spotify, and Amazon.com. Whenever a song or album is sold, money is added to your balance on the site. You then choose when and how you are paid.

There are other services to look at, too. TuneCore claims to allow users to keep 100 percent of their royalties and will also create an iTunes artist Ping page for you, while The Orchard offers more marketing opportunities as well as distribution. It sounds easy and, often for less than $50, these services will do as they promise. They just can't guarantee you the sales; that part is up to you.

If you choose to share music via SoundCloud, it also offers a commercial service called VibeDeck that makes it easy to sell songs right from your SoundCloud page. In terms of effort, this method is a no-brainer and allows you to simply add a Buy button to your page as well as offer your music for sale on Facebook, YouTube, and your own website. Rather than dealing with expensive shopping carts on your website or paying to have your music listed, this offering is among the most painless and certainly worth considering if you believe there are people willing to part with their cash for your songs.

As a footnote, I think it is important to realize that selling your music right away might not be the best idea. Remember, you need to build your audience and gain its trust before you start asking people to part with hard-earned cash to listen to your songs.

Don't look at each free download as money wasted but instead see it as a marketing opportunity. Everybody loves getting things for free and, if your music is up to scratch, most will see genuine value in it even if you don't immediately see the benefit. Think about how many times you've shared songs with your friends or a friend has sent you an MP3 of a band you ended up loving.

Word of mouth is one of the ultimate marketing tools and, without copyright restrictions and costs getting in the way, your sound is free to make its way from person to person, gaining you fans in the process. If you do make your songs available for free, make sure you tag the MP3 with the right metadata so that the song and artist names show up on iPods and music players like iTunes. You can also include lyrics and a link to your website if you like. You can easily adjust this information using iTunes on the Get Info dialog box for a particular song or group of songs and filling in the relevant data. The last thing you want is for people to hear and enjoy your music but not know what it's called, who it's by, or where they can get more.

5

Are Friends Electric?

Before I delve into the many, many ways you can make music with your iPad, I want to first explain how it can fit into your existing music setup. No matter whether you're making music in a professional studio, in your bedroom, or a shed at the end of the garden, the chances are you mix and edit music on a computer-based system. Apple's iPad is a great tool for making music on the move, but when you're back at your computer it offers many unique possibilities as well.

In this chapter, I describe how the iPad can become an integral part of your desktop music-making experience through applications that can enhance the way you record and produce. I also take a look at ways you can export your projects and recordings from your iPad back to your computer so you can work on them using your chosen software or system. Yes, I know this book is called *Make Music with Your iPad* but, at the end of the day, these tips will help you to do that, just not in the way you might expect. Fear not, however, as I'll be into the meat of mobile music making by the next chapter, so if you don't use any music software other than apps on your iPad, you can skip this chapter. Of course, reading it might just open your eyes to what you're missing.

Extend Your Desktop with Air Display

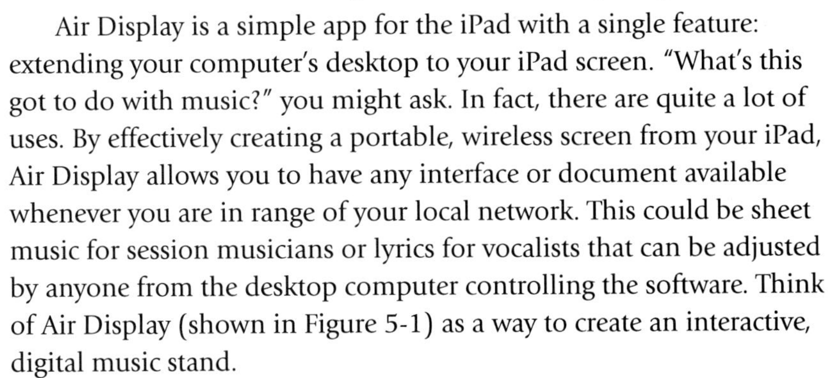

Air Display is a simple app for the iPad with a single feature: extending your computer's desktop to your iPad screen. "What's this got to do with music?" you might ask. In fact, there are quite a lot of uses. By effectively creating a portable, wireless screen from your iPad, Air Display allows you to have any interface or document available whenever you are in range of your local network. This could be sheet music for session musicians or lyrics for vocalists that can be adjusted by anyone from the desktop computer controlling the software. Think of Air Display (shown in Figure 5-1) as a way to create an interactive, digital music stand.

Air Display requires a Wi-Fi connection to work with your iPad, and you'll also need to download additional software for your computer from Avatron Software's website to pair the two devices. Once that's done, your iPad performs like any external display with the added benefit of being wireless. But wait, there's more… Air Display also provides control of the screen you are displaying on it via the iPad's touchscreen. Yes, you can actually move the cursor with your finger and click, drag, and select items on the iPad's screen. This

FIGURE 5-1

Air Display for iPad

means (you guessed it) you can even control music software on your computer from your iPad, allowing you far more flexibility to move about your recording space and avoid running back to the computer to make changes.

Now, I have to point out that there is a little lag time in the signal on your computer reaching your iPad, so don't expect to be able to actually edit projects as if you were using the computer itself, but triggering recordings and adjusting levels remotely is perfectly possible. Whether you have a small bedroom recording setup or a full-fledged studio, using your iPad can make things a great deal easier and allow you more flexibility to get on with the actual process of making music without technology getting in the way.

Here's how to use Air Display:

1. Start by installing the required software for your computer by heading to `http://avatron.com/d`. Download the software and follow the prompts to install it.
2. Make sure your computer and iPad are connected to the same Wi-Fi network and then launch the Air Display app on your iPad.

ARTIST LESSON

Who? Evan Taubenfeld

Experience: Evan is a singer/songwriter and former music director and lead guitarist for Avril Lavigne. Throughout his solo career, he has been signed to Warner Brothers Records, Sire Records, and EMI Music. Evan is also a certified AppleCare technician.

Favorite apps: GarageBand and Korg iElectribe.

Uses iPad for: "I use GarageBand for making quick eight-bar ideas of chord progressions and melodies, I sing into the built-in mic and send myself the idea that I then build later in Pro Tools or Logic. In the studio, I use it as a DAW controller via AC-7 Control and also via LogMeIn remote desktop. It's the perfect way to trigger things on my main recording computer remotely while singing in the vocal booth or sitting on the couch writing. On the road I'll use it for lyrics, melody ideas and fun sampling in GarageBand.

"The iPad can't replace any of my DAWs at present but it's a wonderful, portable, lightweight extension of certain parts of the DAW, so I don't need to be tied to a traditional computer or studio. I love starting songs and ideas on it and then moving onto a full-scale DAW to build them up."

Top tip: "The GarageBand sampler is an incredible, quick, and easy way to grab a sound or sample and manipulate it for your usage in ways you never thought possible. It's pretty incredible to have it with me and grab a quick sample of a street sound or someone talking that I couldn't capture in the studio. It also makes a superslick lyric stand. I'll throw it up in the vocal booth for singers."

3. On a Mac, click the Air Display icon in the menu bar left of the Spotlight icon and choose your iPad from the menu that appears. On a PC, click the Air Display icon in the Windows system tray and choose your iPad from the menu that appears.
4. An extension of your desktop should now display on your iPad's screen. To adjust the display layout, choose ➪ System Preferences ➪ Displays ➪ Arrangement on a Mac or go to the control panel and choose Air Display ➪ Display Arrangement on a PC.

Transfer Projects and Loops to Your Computer

If you're using your iPad on the move and want to send projects, sounds, and ideas back to your computer for editing, you can. Various apps rely on different methods to transfer projects and files, so you will need to figure out how your chosen app works. More often than not, iTunes is the choice for file transfer, but there are other methods you should be aware of.

File transfer via iTunes

When you have your iPad plugged into your computer or synced over Wi-Fi, open iTunes and select your iPad from the iTunes Sidebar's Devices section (see Figure 5-2).

Here's how to transfer files from your iPad to your computer via iTunes:

1. Connect your iPad to your computer using the standard USB Dock Connector cable and wait for your iPad to appear in the Devices section of the iTunes Sidebar.
2. Select your iPad in the Sidebar and then go to the Apps pane. Scroll down to the File Sharing section and select the app with the files you want to import.

FIGURE 5-2

Document transfer using iTunes file sharing

3. With your chosen app selected, browse the files available to import. If you don't see the file you want, you may need to launch the app on your iPad and designate it for transfer to iTunes. GarageBand, for example, provides a Sent to iTunes option.
4. When you have located the file you want to import, select it in iTunes and then click the Save To button to choose a location on your computer to store the file.

File transfer via e-mail

Other applications give you the option to export audio files to the iPad's Mail app and e-mail them to yourself or others using the Share menu (see Figure 5-3). (For the e-mail option, you need to make sure that you have a 3G or Wi-Fi connection available.) Here's how to send the files:

1. Open your chosen app, launch the project you want to share and head to its export menu or use its export button and share it using the app's export feature. GarageBand, for example, provides the Email Song option (see Figure 5-4).

FIGURE 5-3

Exporting a GarageBand project via the Share menu

FIGURE 5-4

E-mailing a project through the iPad's Mail app

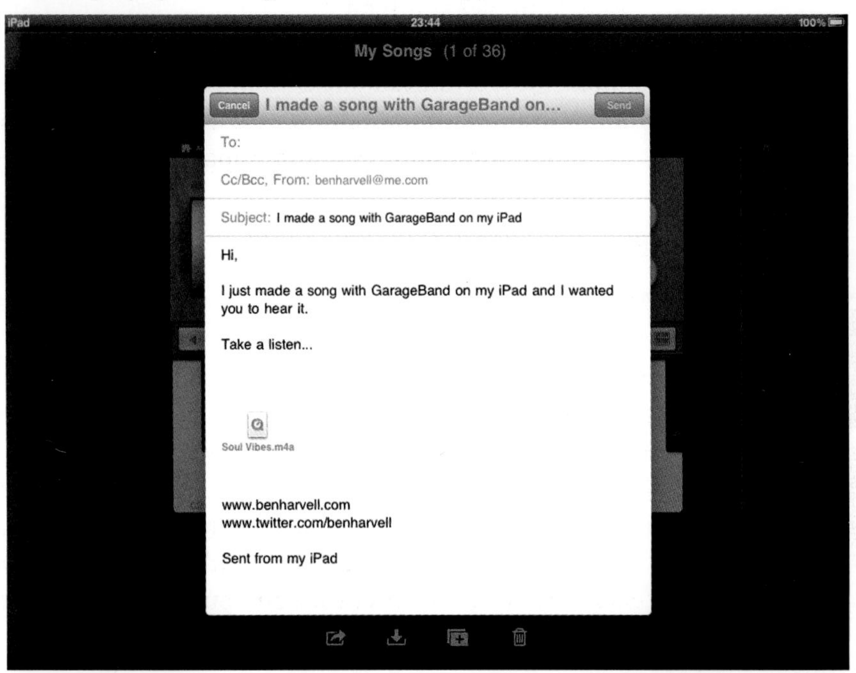

FIGURE 5-5

Shared files between a computer and iPad via Dropbox

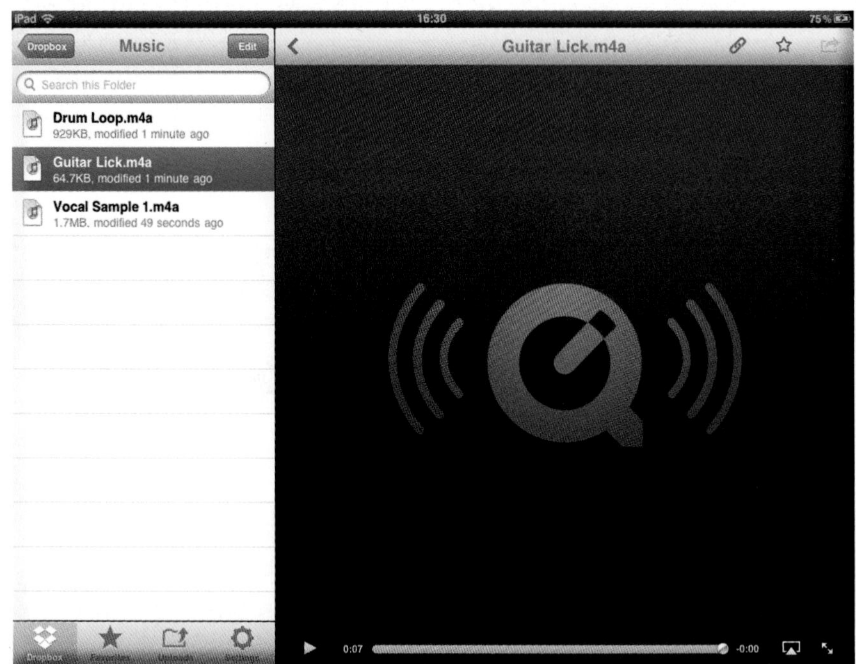

2. The app exports your project and adds it to a new e-mail message. Address the e-mail to an account you can access on your computer and send it.
3. Open your computer's e-mail client and check for new mail. The file you sent should appear with the attachment.
4. Download the attachment and store it on your computer. You can now open it in a compatible application on your computer.

Dropbox and beyond

Finally, some applications may provide the option to transfer your projects and files to cloud (online) services like Dropbox and Box.net. This method requires that a Dropbox or equivalent account be set up — which is, fortunately, pretty easy and free. I personally prefer Dropbox for its ease of use and decent support across a range of applications; it also offers a great iPad app to boot (see Figure 5-5). Services like Dropbox can become invaluable to the mobile musician as they afford you the ability to access recordings, projects, and other documents on all your devices be it a computer, iPad, or iPhone.

FIGURE 5-6

AC-7 Core for iPad controlling Logic for Mac

Once files are edited, added, or removed on one device, the changes are then pushed to the others to ensure you're kept in sync wherever you are. It's also a useful backup technique. The other benefit of cloud-based storage is that it works wirelessly rather than requiring a connection to iTunes each time but of course, this does have its drawbacks in terms of speed.

Control Desktop Software with AC-7 Core for iPad

There are iPad apps that allow dedicated control of your music software from the iPad's screen.

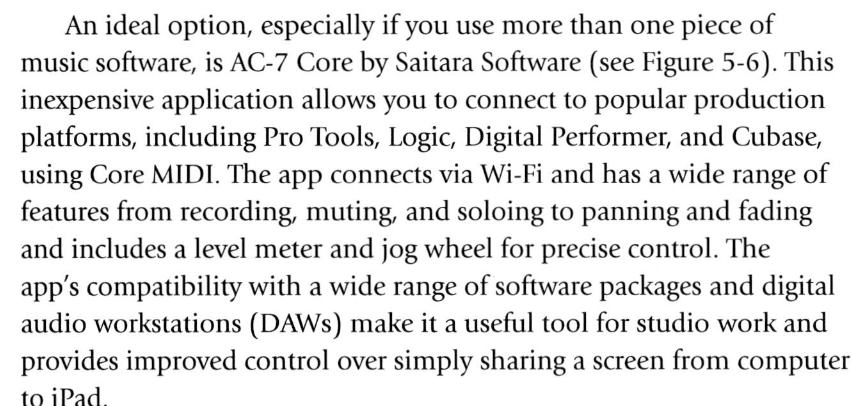

An ideal option, especially if you use more than one piece of music software, is AC-7 Core by Saitara Software (see Figure 5-6). This inexpensive application allows you to connect to popular production platforms, including Pro Tools, Logic, Digital Performer, and Cubase, using Core MIDI. The app connects via Wi-Fi and has a wide range of features from recording, muting, and soloing to panning and fading and includes a level meter and jog wheel for precise control. The app's compatibility with a wide range of software packages and digital audio workstations (DAWs) make it a useful tool for studio work and provides improved control over simply sharing a screen from computer to iPad.

6

All Mixed Up

Some call it music, some call it inane bleeping, but what you can't get away from is that digitally created music is very popular. Before computers as we know them today were common, sampling and electronic beat creation were already being used. And even earlier, vinyl turntables were even harnessed as rudimentary samplers.

The rise of the DJ certainly wasn't brought about by computers, but digital has done a lot for the craft. Genres such as house, trance, and electronica have all seen significant creativity and productivity boosts as software has developed and has empowered many aspiring turntable enthusiasts to begin practicing digital music on their computers at home. Other genres, including hip hop and dubstep also benefit from the digital strides made over the years where analog systems once ruled the roost.

Whether you are a four-to-the-floor dance master or a wannabe Dr. Dre, the iPad has something to offer you. Unlike those who believe in the analog-only route for music production, the modern DJ, remixer, and producer has a wealth of convenient digital options on the iPad. The age-old process of digging through a record collection to find beats and rhythms, for example, has given way to the billions of MP3s available on the web. Even the most obscure tracks from past decades can be found online if you look hard enough. Then there is the input of samples themselves. Rather than finding pre-recorded material, it's easier than ever before to record your own samples wherever you are and add them to your projects in seconds.

In this chapter, I look primarily at sampling, mixing, and beat creation using the iPad through a number of apps available in the App Store as well as useful ways to connect existing devices to your tablet for additional control.

Sampling with the iPad

How you use the iPad as a sampler is determined by the sampling you want to achieve. If you simply want to grab an audio snippet from a song or movie or even your own voice and drop it into your project, you don't need any tools more advanced than a simple sound recorder and editing application.

By default, the iPad doesn't offer a built-in recording solution like the iPhone's Voice Memos, but there are plenty of apps that can help you do the same job. Using such an app, you can record a sound using

♪ SYNTH SAMPLES

This audio recording is a guitar chord being played through the Synth app. The chord was recorded using the app's built-in recording tool and then played on the keys provided by the app. The pitch bend wheel is also used during this clip.

the iPad's built-in microphone, an attached microphone, or a line-in and then trim it down to create your sample. This recording can then be loaded into your project via iTunes, copy and paste, or from your iPad's music library. You could even forgo an iPad-based recorder and editor for software on your computer, but that limits the options available for remote recording.

There is also the option to import recordings from your iPhone to your iPad via iTunes or even e-mail if you want to retain your recording flexibility but don't want to shell out for another recording app for your iPad. Free apps like Pocket WavePad are a good solution, especially considering this specific tool allows you to set the sample rate, format, and recording level.

Also bear in mind that Apple's GarageBand app for iPad includes an audio recorder that I describe in detail in the GarageBand section. If you intend to use GarageBand as your main music-making tool on the iPad, you're all set to record. GarageBand for iPad also offers a traditional sampler, which leads nicely to the second type of sampling you might want to use.

That "other" sampling method for digital music makers allows sounds you've recorded to be played like an instrument. Harking back to the days of Casio samplers, this method has been used for decades as part of dance music tracks. The process effectively assigns a single audio file to each note on a keyboard and plays the sound back at the corresponding pitch when a key is pressed. GarageBand's Sampler instrument is the easiest route to achieving this style but applications such as the inexpensive Synth by Retronyms (shown in Figure 6-1) are also worth looking at. Synth was, in fact, a key instrument used on the Gorillaz album *The Fall,* if you were wondering about its pedigree.

The difficulty you will encounter with applications outside GarageBand, however, is that you need to get your sampler recordings back into your project once you have created them. With an app like

FIGURE 6-1

Synth for iPad by Retronyms

Synth, you need to record your sampler work to an external source to store it as an audio file or play it back into your project via the audio recorder and line-in, which makes things a little more difficult. Other applications do allow you to export your recordings, so make sure you choose wisely if you opt for an additional synth app.

Here's how to record and play samples with Synth:

1. Launch the Synth app and attach a microphone if you intend to use one.
2. When you're ready to record, tap the Sample Rec button at the top right of the window. Recording starts as soon as you tap the button, so make sure the sound you are recording begins quickly to avoid any dead air at the beginning of the sample.
3. When you want to finish recording, tap the Sample Rec button again. Your sample is applied to the keyboard and plays at the corresponding pitch when you tap a key on the onscreen keyboard.
4. You can adjust the sound of your sample using the virtual control knobs across the center of the window, as well as delay

and/or add distortion to your sound. Tap and hold on a knob and drag your finger up or down to adjust the setting.

5. To play more notes with your sample, tap the Oct buttons to the left and right above the onscreen keyboard to move up or down an octave. You can also adjust the modulation and pitch of your sample by moving the control wheels at the top left of the window as you play.

Mixing and DJing with the iPad

Many people were outraged when the laptop became a tool for the DJ, with software and hardware combinations like Serato Scratch replacing the traditional ones and twos. Now the iPad wants to join the party and will likely raise a few eyebrows in the process, too. As yet, the software doesn't exist on the iPad to allow it to do away with a turntable altogether, but the development of more and more advanced digital mixing tools is testing that statement.

If you're a hardened turntable enthusiast, it's unlikely you will find an app for the iPad that will do everything your existing setup can. But the iPad does offer extreme portability by comparison to two decks, a mixer, and a huge case of vinyl. If you become comfortable with an app-based DJing tool, the iPad can provide the most convenient way of performing live: All you need to do is plug your iPad into some speakers and you're ready to perform.

That dream scenario isn't possible in all apps, however, as you lose the ability to mix behind the scenes while you continue to play music to your audience. This is due to the iPad's single headphone socket and, therefore, single audio output, unlike a traditional multiple-I/O mixer. Of course, if you are confident enough, you can simply mix tracks live without previewing them, but that's quite a gamble, especially in front of a large crowd.

Before you throw down your iPad in disgust, there is a solution through software and hardware magic. Algoriddims' Djay app (shown in Figure 6-2), which I highly recommend, offers a function called Split Output. This feature, used with the DJ Cable from Griffin Technology, allows you to listen to your performance and cue tracks through headphones just like using a real turntable and mixer setup. Griffin goes to great lengths to explain that this $20 device isn't just a splitter cable either (although a standard Y splitter should work), and that it is specifically designed for use with Djay and its Split Output mode.

Using the DJ Cable and Djay, the output from the app is split into two mono signals so that the main signal you want your audience to hear is sent to one channel while your cueing is sent to another. Through headphones, you hear both channels, allowing you to DJ as you would on a normal set of decks.

The Turntable Alternative

Where you once had to spend hundreds of dollars to acquire the requisite kit to DJ with, an iPad and an app like Djay are now pretty much all you need, but the hard-core DJs may not be quite as positive toward this suggestion. Although spinning virtual records on the iPad's touchscreen is certainly possible and a great deal of fun, it lacks the tactile feedback of real turntables and a certain level of control. That's why Numark — yes, the company that makes turntables and mixers for the pros — has come up with the iDJ Live system. As you can see in Figure 6-3, it is effectively an iPad dock with two turntables and a mixer attached and, for an inexpensive system, brings back a little more realism for the traditionalists. The iDJ Live system is designed to work

FIGURE 6-2

Djay for iPad

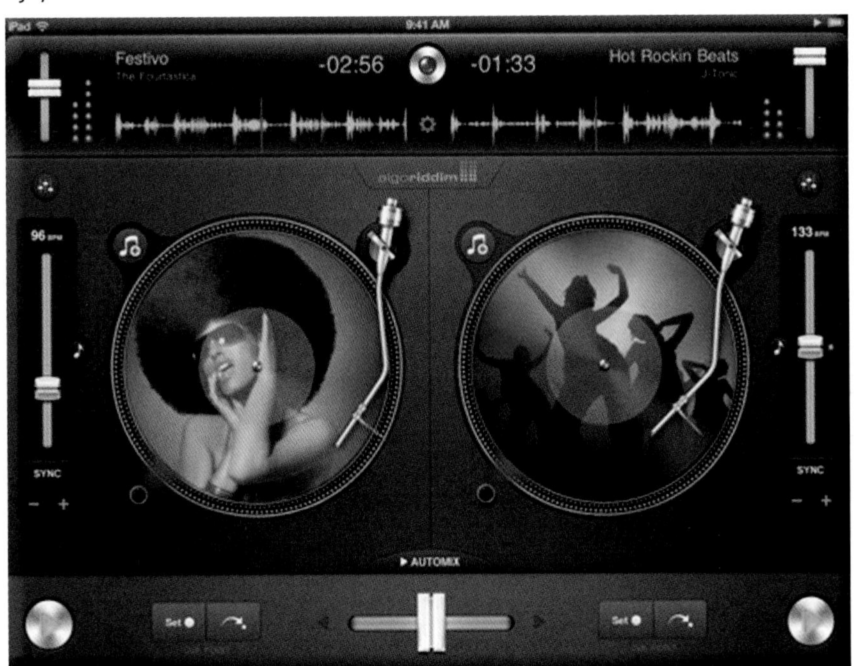

FIGURE 6-3

iDJ Live (Courtesy of Numark)

with the Djay app or any Core MIDI-enabled software, and it replicates the traditional two decks and a mixer setup, providing greater accuracy with two physical turntables controlling the virtual decks. This accuracy even extends to scratching, which is a little more difficult to perform with fingers on a screen.

The Djay software allows you to load tracks from your iPad's music library as if they were records and quickly switch between them as you mix. This goes a long way toward removing the need to lug a heavy bag of vinyl with you wherever you plan to perform, and it also means that you can mix and scratch tracks that you don't even own on vinyl. On top of this and, again unlike vinyl, an iPad connected to a Wi-Fi or 3G network allows you to download and add tracks to your library while you perform — perfect for those obscure requests.

Here's how to mix songs with Djay:

1. Launch Djay; two empty turntables appear.
2. In the first turntable. tap the button of a glowing note with a + symbol to bring up songs in your iPad's music library. Select the song you want to load by tapping it.

3. Do the same with the second turntable and load the song you want to mix with the original you loaded on the first turntable.
4. Songs begin playing once loaded, but you can stop them by tapping the Play button for each turntable; the button is located at the bottom left and right of the window.

ARTIST LESSON

Who? Jason LaRocca

Experience: Jason LaRocca has seen success in many facets of the music industry over the course of his career. He has shared the stage with such acts as Bad Religion and Rage Against the Machine. He has engineered and mixed scores for composer Mark Isham on films like *Crash* and *Moonlight Mile*. And on the small screen, he has worked on the music for such television shows as CBS's *CSI: Miami* and NBC's *Chuck*. Jason's most recent work can be heard in Gavin O'Conner's drama *Warrior* as well as the new fantasy series from *Lost* producers *Once upon a Time* on ABC. Jason is also a founding member of acclaimed L.A. punk band The Briggs, signed to SideOneDummy Records.

Favorite apps: V-Control for Pro Tools. "I use it most when I am mixing. It gives me eight channels of touch-sensitive faders and transports. It's awesome!"

Uses iPad for: "The iPad is great because it is one of those chameleon devices. When I am in the studio recording, I use it as a tuner, a synth, and even drum machine. For mixing, it can act as a control surface. On the road, it's a great idea-maker for songs, a control surface for a console, and even a great SPL meter. It has become a necessary extension of the modern studio. It has made certain things a lot easier for me to accomplish. I think the ability to do things that really require your hands or fingers is a lot better with a device like this. The soft synths are amazing in here. You can quickly grab a filter envelope and make a sweep of it with your fingers. No more mouse clicks on things that need your fingers on them!"

Top tip: "The Stylo synth can make some pretty amazing and original synth sounds based on audio it records from the built in mic. You can simply say one word into it and it ends up making it sound like a Dr. Dre bass line. It's very cool."

5. Adjust the tempo of each turntable using the sliders on either side of the window or, to match the tempo of one turntable to the other, tap the Sync button below the tempo sliders.
6. Use your finger to move the turntables as you would a real set of decks. A waveform above each turntable displays the position with a red marker showing the point where the needle is touching the virtual vinyl. To mark a point on the vinyl, tap the Set button (below the turntable) to set a cue point. Tapping the button next to the Set button automatically moves the vinyl to that point at any time.
7. When both turntables are playing, use the mixer slider at the bottom center of the window to switch between the audio from one turntable or the other. Or move the slider to the center to play the audio from both turntables. You can also record your mixes by tapping the Record button in the center of the window, between the turntables.

Creating Beats and Rhythms

As a platform for idea creation, the iPad is second to none. Several artists I've spoken with use apps like Korg's iElectribe (shown in Figure 6-4) to build beats, and it is probably the perfect marriage of old-school electronic music creation and the iPad. iElectribe is a modern day reworking of the Electribe R synthesizer and sequencer launched in 1999, rebuilt in software form for the iPad. Considering that buying an original Electribe R will set you back hundreds of dollars, the comparatively tiny asking price for iElectribe is almost too good to be true.

Here's how to create a beat with iElectribe:

♪ IELECTRIBE RHYTHMS

This clip was created using iElectribe and was built from scratch using one of the empty presets. The beat uses automation to adjust pitch for some of the instruments and effects have been applied to some of the drum sounds to give a crunchy, lo-fi feel to the loop.

FIGURE 6-4

Korg's iElectribe

1. Start by tapping the main synthesizer LED indicator at the top left of the window. In the popover that appears, scroll down to Section D. Tap one of the empty Init templates to load it. A basic beat begins playing. Tap anywhere on the screen to close the popover.
2. Tap the Synth 1 button near the bottom of the window. The steps that trigger this synth are highlighted across the bottom, as shown in Figure 6-4. Tap a red step (the numbered keys below the Synth buttons) to deselect it; tap a white step to select it. Experiment with different selections to create a kick drum pattern. As your pattern plays back, a green highlight shows the step the beat is on.
3. Tap the Synth 2 button; this is normally a snare sound. None of the steps should be selected at the bottom of the window, so highlight some to build up your beat. Do the same for any of the other sounds until you are happy with the beat you have created.
4. Adjusting how some synths sound can help make your beat more distinctive. When you have selected a sound, use the

Oscillator and Amp settings to adjust the sound and use the Effect control in the center of the window to apply effects to all sounds.

5. When you are happy with your beat, export it by tapping the main LED again and then tapping the Export button at the top of the window. From here, you can record your beat or bounce the pattern for export to a computer via iTunes.

The iPad app even offers features not found in the original hardware Electribe, including the exporting of patterns from the iPad to your computer. iElectribe also offers preset templates to help you get going and, with several effects and modifiers built in to the app, you can quickly create your own unique sounds and beats to form the basis of a new project. The app is regularly updated with new features, many requested by the community of iElectribe users. If you are using the iPad Camera Connection Kit or an iRig MIDI, you can even connect MIDI devices to your iPad and use them with iElectribe.

Although iElectribe is the go-to choice for most iPad users, there are plenty of alternatives available in the App Store for creating beats and loops. Rhythm Studio by Pulse Code is certainly worth a look with its multiple devices, including drum machine, synths, mixers, and controllers.

FIGURE 6-5

ReBirth for iPad

Another favorite beat-creation tool is also a reworking of a classic piece of music hardware: ReBirth for iPad, shown in Figure 6-5. A faithful emulation of the Roland TB-303 and TR-808, ReBirth is a bass synth and drum machine in one that is capable of creating classic sounds on the fly. Arguably easier to use than the original devices, ReBirth is an exciting option for all kinds of beat creation from hip hop to techno, and it offers export options so you can quickly add your composition to a full production.

7

Different Strings

Now for one of the most popular sections of the book, I'm sure. The chapter for the aspiring Satrianis and wannabe Fleas that explains how to connect your guitar, bass, or any other electric string instrument to your iPad. It's not always just a case of plug and play when it comes to making music with your instrument and the iPad, so in this chapter I fill in the blanks about connections.

Beyond connections, it's all about rocking out and finding new techniques to make your jamming, recording, and practicing more enjoyable than ever before. I also describe how the switch from hardware to software for effects, tuners, and pedals can save you a pretty penny. Now, finally, that expensive iPad will begin to pay for itself as you discover that, in many cases, it is all you need to create and record incredible sounds with your stringed instrument.

The art of playing guitar and bass has its fair share of purists, much like the DJ fraternity, but many are realizing that digital is not only a money and space saver, but also a creativity enhancer. With so many unique apps and accessories tailored for iPad guitarists, the iPad can actually broaden your creative options. So, unless you're a die-hard analog user (in which case, why the iPad, huh?) or a member of The White Stripes, this chapter reveals the potential the iPad offers guitarists. I hope it also provides a little understanding why so many guitar and bass pros are using the iPad, be it on tour or in the studio.

Jamming and Practicing

Once your instrument is in tune, the next step is the one you've been waiting for: actually playing your instrument with your iPad. Let's not forget how cool this is. No practice amp, no power cables, just your guitar and your iPad. Of course, monitoring on headphones is a must, if not for you then those in the surrounding area. If you want to show off a bit, connecting speakers at this stage is also possible. Just imagine busking with your electric guitar, iPad, and a set of battery-powered speakers. The possibilities are endless. New York-based rockers Atomic Tom performed a gig on the subway in front of bemused commuters using only their iPhones. Imagine what they could have done with both their instruments and an iPad!

With all your kit wired up, you need to pick the app you want to use to play your instrument through. The first port of call is likely going to be GarageBand, which is covered in detail later in the book. But there are plenty of other apps you should look at, most

♪ AMPLITUBE ROCK

This recording was created by playing an electric guitar through the AmpliTube app for iPad. The guitar was connected using IK Multimedia's iRig and recorded in the application. The default amplifier was used when recording and a number of effects including chorus and overdrive were turned on and off throughout the performance.

of which are free, that can turn a standard experience into an epic one. Whether you want to practice a new lick, master the playing of a popular tune, build up multiple instrument parts, or just rock out, your iPad has the answer. Before you get cracking, make sure you've read how to connect your guitar to your iPad as described in Chapter 1.

Start by picking a convenient position to work. Once you're wired up to your iPad, you have as much flexibility to move as your instrument lead and headphone or speaker cable allow. Ideally, you should place your iPad on a flat surface in front of you, tilting it with the Smart Cover or other stand if you have one, and sit or stand in easy reach of the screen. If things get a little cramped while you work, you can always buy longer cables or extensions to make more room. If you are using an iRig or similar device (see Chapter 1), you can buy a longer minijack-to-minijack cable to run from the device to your speakers or a male-to-female minijack extension lead that adds more length to your connection.

Get Rocking with Legendary (Virtual) Amps

Once you have a guitar or bass connected to your iPad, you need an app to play through. A great choice for instant gratification is IK Multimedia's AmpliTube, a ridiculously generous free application that simulates a bunch of amps and pedals as well as provides other features. The first window you see is a representation of an amp with virtual pedals attached and, if you give your instrument a quick strum, it sounds like it's playing through those devices. Once you finish playing a few licks (believe me, you'll waste a lot of time having fun), you can start adjusting your sound by simply tapping and dragging any of the control knobs on the amp or pedals. You can also load

FIGURE 7-1

Recording with the Peavey AmpKit app

new amplifiers and effects to further adjust the sound, and there are plenty more to be had via in-app purchase, including classic Fender kit. Elsewhere, you can record your performance and load tracks from your iPad's music library to play along with.

Another music hardware heavyweight, Peavey, features yet another free app with amplifiers, AmpKit (see Figure 7-1). It offers the Peavey ValveKing amp, plus two cabinets, two pedals, and two mics by default; you can add more via in-app purchases.

The beauty of both AmpliTube and AmpKit is that, once you've recorded a part, you can go back and edit the amp or effects applied to it and completely change the sound without re-recording the part. Both apps allow you to save your recordings to iTunes, e-mail them, or share them online.

Here's how to record a guitar part with AmpliTube:

1. Start by connecting your guitar to your iPad using an iRig or similar device, and connect the iRig to speakers or headphones depending on your preference. Play a few chords or notes to check that you can hear your guitar's input. If not, check the

iPad's volume setting as well as the connection between your guitar and iPad.

2. Tap the Tools button (the guitar icon at the bottom of Figure 7-2) and tap the On button below the tuner. Play through all the strings on your guitar one at a time to check that they are in tune. Adjust them if needed.
3. In the Tools popover, tap the On button below the metronome settings and slide a finger across the Metronome bar to select the tempo. If you don't know what tempo you want to use, tap the Tap button next to the metronomes On button at a speed you roughly think is right for your recording. The tempo is set according to the speed of your taps.
4. Tap anywhere on the AmpliTube window to hide the Tools popover and tap the Rec button (the icon of a reel-to-reel tape recorder) next to the Tools button at the bottom of the window. Tap the Record button and begin playing your guitar part. Make sure to keep an eye on the VU meter.
5. When you want to stop recording, tap the Record button again to end the recording and then tap the Play button. An orange

FIGURE 7-2

Recording in AmpliTube

ARTIST LESSON

Who? Stefan Lessard

Experience: Stefan is the bassist and founding member of the Grammy Award-winning Dave Matthews Band. With seven studio albums as well as several live albums, as of 2010, Dave Matthews Band has sold about 40 million copies worldwide.

Favorite apps: "AmpliTube for sure!"

Uses iPad for: "I like to sketch out ideas on the iPad using a variety of musical apps. AmpliTube allows my ideas to come to life while on the road.

"I have always liked new technology and how it relates to music and music production. The benefits depend on how you use it. I use mine for preproduction and also for sheet music. There are a lot of great sheet music apps out there also!"

Top tip: "I'm still developing my tricks! Get AmpliTube, all the Korg apps, and the Bassline apps to start developing your own."

bar appears at the top of the window above the title of your recording which is called Untitled 1 by default (see Figure 7-2). Drag the orange bar to the right until no orange remains and tap the Play button again to listen to your recording.

6. To rename your recording, tap the tape labeled Untitled 1 and enter a new name using the onscreen keyboard.

Working with Pedals and Effects

Effects pedals and stompboxes can be used with the iPad, but with so many virtual amps and effects available in apps like AmpliTube and AmpKit, you might just forget about them. If you are desperate to use a particular piece of hardware, you can wire it in to your line to the iPad using an iRig or similar device. By attaching the pedal between the guitar and your iPad connection, it works as it would with an amplifier. The benefit of using a physical pedal is that you retain foot control, unlike the case for virtual pedals that require manipulation via the iPad's screen.

Alternatively, you could connect a pedal or pedal board to your iPad via IK Multimedia's iRig MIDI and control effects with it through compatible applications. Using this method, you can assign different pedals to effects in your iPad apps so you can use them while you play. This means your effects collection is effectively multiplied while providing the same functionality of pedal control. You can even use this setup in a live environment. You can easily run the output from your iPad or iRig headphone jack to an external amplifier or speaker and achieve the same effect as playing directly to an amplifier.

Recording Acoustic Instruments

You may think acoustic instruments are off limits when it comes to the iPad, with no lead to connect to the device. If so, you're wrong. Not only is it possible to buy a temporary pickup that can be placed inside your acoustic instrument and connected to the iPad, you can also record your instrument via microphone. For acoustic guitars especially, this technique adds great depth and clarity to the sound when done right. Using your chosen microphone, such as IK Multimedia's iRig Mic shown in Figure 7-3, you can record any acoustic instrument with software and monitor the recording through headphones. Not only will this monitoring help your accuracy, it also avoids picking up any sound other than your instrument on the recording and reduces potential feedback.

A mic stand is handy for positioning the mic in the perfect position (offset from a guitar's sound hole is optimal) but you can also hang the microphone or, if you have an able assistant, get someone to hold it for you while you play. If you're tempted to place the microphone on a surface in front of you while you play, beware of potential vibrations caused by sound that might interfere with your recording.

♪ ACOUSTIC RECORDING

This recording was made using the IK Multimedia iRig Mic and a regular acoustic guitar. For the recording, the microphone was positioned just off center from the guitar's sound hole. No effects or editing have been performed on the recording, but you can apply them using a recording app.

FIGURE 7-3

The iRig Mic

Here's how to record acoustic guitar sounds to your iPad:

1. For the best recording solution, attach the microphone to your iPad and then to a microphone stand. If this isn't possible, try hanging the microphone by its lead from any object such as a chair or standing lamp. As you position your microphone, make sure it us level with your guitar when you are in a position to play, be it seated or standing.
2. Check your guitar. Make sure it is in tune and plays cleanly without buzzing. If you do encounter buzz, try replacing the strings and also set up the guitars action for a smoother sound.
3. Next, make sure you're ready. Yes, you. No clothes that ruffle during recording, and no bracelets or other accessories that might tap the body of the guitar while you play.
4. Making surfaces around your recording area a little more reflective to sound is also a good idea. Recording on a hard wood floor helps the sound, as do nearby walls and even doors. Also check that there's no background noise such as building work or traffic that the mic may pick up.

5. Position your mic for recording. At this stage, it can be handy to turn on monitoring in your chosen app and use headphones to listen to how various microphone positions sound when you play. Aiming the microphone at the point where the guitar's neck meets the body is normally a good compromise, as it picks up sound from the fret board as well as from the sound hole without picking up too much of one or the other.

Tip: When recording an acoustic guitar with a microphone, your choice of plectrum is very important. For a strong, punchy acoustic part that will feature prominently in your mix, a thicker pick is ideal. For shiny, glittering accompaniment parts, try using a thinner plectrum. In both cases, try to avoid following through too far with your down strokes and hitting the body of the guitar with your pick, as doing so introduces distracting clicks into your recording.

Recording and Playing Bass

For bass players, much of the information on recording guitars in this chapter applies to your instrument as well. Electric basses can

FIGURE 7-4

Bass Guitar Amp

connect to the iPad using an iRig or equivalent device, and acoustic bass instruments can be recorded using a microphone.

Positioning microphones for larger bass instruments such as a double bass may prove more tricky, and you may need to use a multimicrophone setup, which I describe in the recording drums section in Chapter 10.

In addition to AmpliTube and AmpKit, bassists might look at bass-specific iPad tools. The first is Bass Companion, a free app that not only offers a bass tuner but also has a wide range of chord charts to help you nail your next bass line composition. The app also includes scales for your reference. This is a handy app to have when you're in need of inspiration or need to ensure the correct tuning.

Another great tool for bassists is Pocketlabworks' Bass Guitar Amp (see Figure 7-4), which works in much the same way as AmpliTube and AmpKit but is more bass-focused. For bass players, Bass Guitar Amp is a must-have alternative to a guitar-centric app, thanks to its access to your iPad's music library, time-stretch and pitch-shifting features, and an EQ specially designed for bass players. Bass Guitar Amp works with iRig and AmpKit Link as well as the company's own iRiffPort.

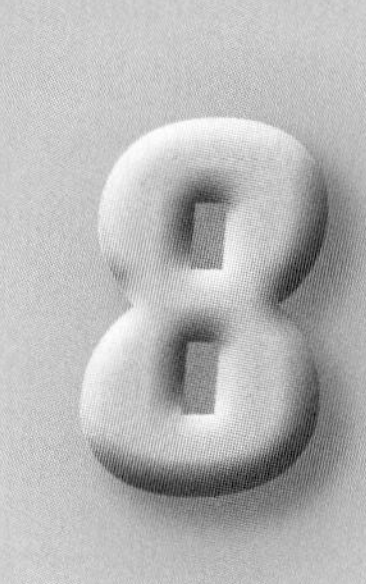

Give Me the Keys

As a musical tool, you would think that the iPad's multitouch screen would be best for pianists and keyboard players but, in truth, tapping a screen is nothing like pressing a real key. What the iPad does offer the ivory tinkler, however, is a wonderful environment for practice and, as with all other instruments, a brilliant hub *through* which to play music with your existing kit. Although sound in my opinion, that theory doesn't hold with everyone. Still, during a performance of "Pulling Mussels from the Shell" on *Late Night with Jimmy Fallon*, Stephen Large of the band Squeeze performed an entire piano solo using the Pianist Pro app on an iPad. It sounded good, too!

Many keyboard players use the iPad as a practice tool but, as proven by this example, it's certainly possible to use as a live instrument as well. Perhaps just not as a substitute for your keyboard.

The iPad can also make a brilliant tool for practice and composition, especially in places where a normal keyboard isn't practical. And for sampling, it is second to none. This chapter focuses on the iPad as a tool for pianists and keyboard players and takes a look at the unique ways it can help you perform, rehearse, and create.

Connecting Keyboards to Your iPad

Connecting a MIDI or USB keyboard through the iPad Camera Connection Kit or IK Multimedia's iRig MIDI (see Chapter 1) is certainly worth it, given the improved control it offers and, in most cases, the additional flexibility to your existing kit that wouldn't be possible without the iPad.

Here's how to connect USB and MIDI keyboards to your iPad:

1. Take a look at your keyboard. If it has a USB socket at its rear, you'll need to use Apple's iPad Camera Connection Kit. If it has MIDI in and out sockets, you'll need to get an iRig MIDI from IK Multimedia (see Figure 8-1).
2. If your keyboard uses a USB connection, connect the iPad Camera Connection Kit to the USB cable and then connect it to your iPad. You can now launch your chosen app and play compatible instruments using your keyboard.
3. If you are using a MIDI keyboard, connect the iRig MIDI to your iPad and then run a MIDI cable from your keyboard's MIDI out port to the iRig. If you want to charge your iPad

FIGURE 8-1

iRig MIDI connections

while you play, connect a Mini-USB cable to the iRig MIDI and to a computer or wall socket.

4. You should now be able to play your keyboard through your iPad. A red LED on the iRig MIDI flashes when each key is played. If you don't see flashes or hear any sound, make sure all the cables are properly connected and your keyboard is connected to a power source.

The option to play and control hundreds of keyboard voices and pads is another advantage. Every application that can be controlled by your keyboard is essentially the same as adding a new bank of sounds or, in some cases, an entirely new instrument.

Performing and practicing with minimal space requirements is yet another advantage.

Overall, the iPad will be more of a supplement to your keyboard playing in a performance or recording context.

You are also free to mix and match when it comes to the iPad and your keyboard. You can play through your iPad using the keyboard as a controller or you can play both at the same time with the iPad offering pads and effects and your keyboard sounds making up the main body. The iPad's compact form makes it an excellent tool to sit on top of your keyboard and, if it has a built-in music stand, should rest neatly on top of it. The iPad can act as an incredibly handy sheet music viewer in this formation as well. Whether you are on stage or in a studio, running the

FIGURE 8-2

Akai's SynthStation49 (Courtesy of Akai Professional)

output from both your keyboard and iPad to speakers or a computer or DAW allows you to use them side by side and harness the power of both.

Connecting a keyboard to your iPad via USB can be a hit-and-miss affair, so it may turn out that you need to downgrade to a lower-power keyboard to use it with your iPad. Compatibility with applications is also a gamble. Check that your app supports the Core MIDI standard — as do GarageBand and Pianist Pro, for example — so that your keyboard can be recognized.

In the best situations, you will find that controls on your keyboard, such as modulation and pitch bend, also work with the instruments you play on your iPad. Apps like GarageBand can recognize these inputs and, for most instruments, allow you to use them to manipulate notes. The keyboard can control other instruments in GarageBand, too, such as the Smart Bass and Guitar instruments, making it easier to record nonkeyboard sections rather than simply tapping the screen or setting GarageBand to play a preset pattern.

If you don't already own a keyboard that you can use with your iPad but are thinking about getting one, I have an absolute gem to recommend. The team at Akai, known for its excellent keyboards, has created a device called the SynthStation49, shown in Figure 8-2. It looks like your average controller keyboard with three octaves of keys,

ARTIST LESSON

Who? Jordan Rudess

Experience: Jordan is the keyboardist for progressive metal band Dream Theater and progressive rock supergroup Liquid Tension Experiment, but his skills and accolades run even further as a solo musician. A serious technophile, Jordan uses Apple's iOS products for music and has created his own apps.

Favorite apps: "I use MorphWiz and SampleWiz the most. Both of these apps were created by me with my partner Kevin Chartier."

Uses iPad for: "I believe the iPad has opened up an amazing world of expressive musical possibilities. When I first touched an iPhone, I knew that things were gonna change forever in the creative world. MorphWiz was my first music app, and we put a lot of time and thought into understanding how to take a device like the iPhone with all its unique capabilities and use them to create a new level of expressive musical control. Instead of taking the approach of using existing technology and shrinking it down, we felt this is something brand-new and capable of pushing the known boundaries of how music is made.

"The iPad fits into my work in the studio and on the road beautifully, although it has not replaced my full-size keyboards or computer for my serious studio work. It constantly opens me up to new ideas and interesting ways to make music. I love the sense of exploration that many developers are able to pursue on these devices. The iPad is a great tool for people to begin to explore the real connection between audio and visuals. Every day I wake up and wonder what the next little miracle will be available for my iPad.

"With MorphWiz, in real time we are able to morph between waveforms both in the audio domain as well as the visual domain. For example, as you slide your finger on a note on the playing surface, you both hear and see the morphing of the waveforms. The really cool addition that has not been possible on any traditional keyboard before; that is, that each finger is treated independently, so you can achieve some very cool, almost pedal-steel-bending articulations!"

Top tip: "Here is one that we are currently developing and people will be doing by the time this book comes out: Start a synthesizer app like SampleWiz and choose a patch. Now close it but leave it running in the background. Start up GeoSynth and have that on the playing surface. You will soon be able to play on the surface of one app while controlling a receiving synth running in the background!"

pitch and modulation wheels, MIDI controller buttons, and even a built-in set of MPC-esque drum pads. But there also is an odd section in the middle. It looks like a sheet music holder but in fact is an iPad dock. Yes, there's a professional keyboard on the market that takes all the connection hassles mentioned in this chapter and does away with them.

The SynthStation49 not only charges your iPad when connected but also allows you to control all the Core MIDI-compatible applications you already own. That's not just keyboard-related apps either, many synth and drum machine apps also respond to the device's controls, including GarageBand.

The SynthStation49 also works seamlessly with Akai's SynthStation app, as you would expect. With your iPad presented at a convenient angle and a full set of velocity-sensitive keys in front of you, the SynthStation is the ultimate workstation for iPad musicians, allowing you more flexibility and the convenience to get on with playing rather than fiddling with onscreen controls. The keyboard also offers stereo outputs, so it's ideal for practice or performing live.

Playing with an Onscreen Keyboard

Although the iPad might not be able to replace a physical keyboard or piano, you might be surprised at just how well you can play on it. There isn't room for complex, multioctave pieces, but you can play simple one-handed parts, as well as solos, fairly accurately.

One of the major difficulties for the iPad keyboardist is holding or mounting the device in a comfortable position. Cradling it in one arm is an option, but not the safest or most convenient method. Placing the iPad on a table while playing also has its pitfalls. The curved edges and smooth back allow it to move around far too much. There are other options, however.

The first is to mount the iPad using a suitable stand or case. Heckler Design's @Rest stand is a decent solution for nonslip iPad mounting. It is heavy, has rubberized feet, grips your iPad, and provides two convenient angles, one of which is comfortable for onscreen keyboard use. It also hides the dock connector cable to prevent accidents and avoid mess. If there's room to place the stand on top of your keyboard, so much the better, as not only can you connect the iPad and keyboard if needed, but you can quickly switch between playing one or the other or use one hand to play each for a truly impressive performance.

FIGURE 8-3

The X-Band

For in-the-hand use, a device like the X-Band from TKO-Solutions, shown in Figure 8-3, is a lightweight winner. Affixed to your iPad with leather corner straps, its neoprene band across the back of the device allows you to slip your hand between it and the iPad as a comfortable way to hold the device with no fear of dropping it or letting it slip from your grasp. With your hand secured firmly between the band and the iPad, you can position the iPad in any way to make it comfortable for your other hand to tap out a tune. For the keyboardist on stage, this is an ideal accessory, especially when you need to rock out a solo.

Saying that you can't really *play* music on an onscreen keyboard isn't completely fair. It is more something you have to learn, especially if you're used to a piano or any other keyed instrument. With GarageBand's onscreen keyboard and the Pianist Pro app, it is possible to access larger keys that take up more of the screen and to show two octaves at once on top of one another. Although it's not the traditional way to play piano or keyboard, this configuration allows you to access more notes and, with a little practice, play more complex parts right from the iPad's screen. Possibly better suited to playing simple chords and triggering pads than more detailed pieces, there is definite benefit to this method. That said, it's also worth exploring a smaller USB keyboard option to attach to your iPad to have more accurate control over your playing.

Synths and Sampling

If you want a synth and sampler designed with the keyboardist in mind, there is probably no better choice than an app created by one. Jordan Rudess of Dream Theater (see more in the "Artist Lesson" sidebar in this chapter) has created an incredible application called SampleWiz that almost defies definition.

It is effectively a sampler but throws in so many more features that it acts like a complete suite of applications: from very basic but pianist-friendly features like being able to set the number of keys displayed, the octave and bass note of that octave, to seriously impressive sampling features such as a granular mode, playable waveforms, and customizable attack, delay, and release settings. SampleWiz is a true powerhouse for sampling fans and keyboard players alike.

The app includes a bank of samples and patches to use right out of the box, and you can record your own samples through SampleWiz at any time. You can then resample these samples by recording a new sample based on your playback of the original sample, which opens up some incredibly creative possibilities.

For creating unique sounds and ambience for your music or for improvisation on stage, SampleWiz is truly a sampling fan's dream.

Many musicians use MooCowMusic's Pianist Pro (see Figure 8-4) for composition, an app that provides a range of instruments, recording, and overdubbing. It can import and export MIDI files, or you can connect to desktop software and use the Pianist Pro onscreen keyboard to control desktop software like Logic.

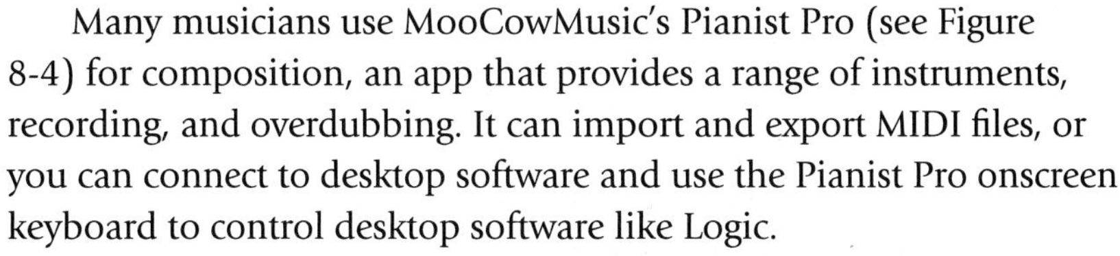

Connecting wirelessly, Pianist Pro lets you use a keyboard with your desktop music software even when you don't have a physical keyboard. It is ideal for traveling with a laptop or working in a different studio setup where a keyboard isn't available. Of course, you need a Wi-Fi network to connect both the computer and iPad for this technique to work.

FIGURE 8-4

Pianist Pro

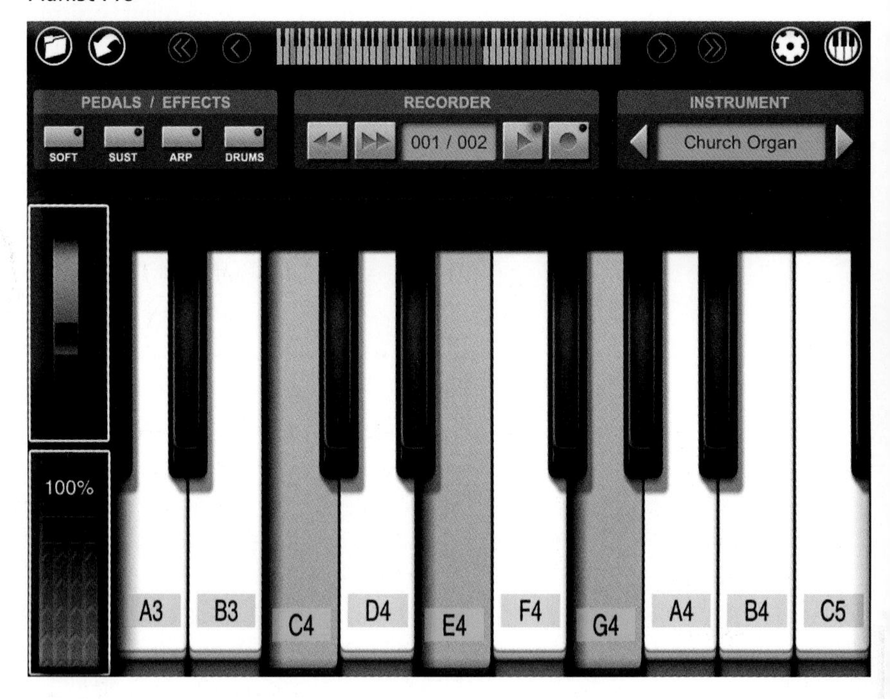

Using the iPad Camera Connection Kit, you can also connect your iPad to some USB MIDI devices and control Pianist Pro from them, adding a wider range of sounds and features to your existing MIDI kit.

Pianist Pro includes its own drum machine, one that is easy to configure using simple step sequences. It also has a full-featured arpeggiator that offers even more flexibility to performances and songwriting. The arpeggiator makes it easier to work in the confines of the iPad's screen, letting you focus on one hand while the app handles the other hand with a wide range of settings from a simple up-and-down arpeggio to random patterns.

Another arpeggiator mode called Pattern Arp lets you set a custom arpeggio pattern for truly creative sequences from only a single keypress. Effects can be applied to your notes, too, so you can build up some really interesting piano parts from your iPad ready to be sent to other apps or exported to your computer.

Here are the steps to record piano parts with Pianist Pro:

1. Launch Pianist Pro and select an instrument sound by tapping the ◀ or ▶ buttons below the Instrument section at the top right of the window.

2. Set any effects or backing you want to use by tapping any of the buttons in the Pedals/Effects section at the top right. These settings include Sustain and an arpeggiator.
3. Slide a finger across the small keyboard display at the very top to select the octave you want to start playing in.
4. Tap the Record button (the far right button in the Recorder section) and wait for the count before starting to play. When you are done, tap the Record button again.
5. Use the Fast Forward and Rewind buttons to the left of the Recorder section to shift your recording forward or backward one bar at a time. Rewind your recording to the first bar and tap the Play button (next to the Record button) to listen to your recording.

GarageBand also excels in the keyboard and piano department, with a wide range of sounds available from organs to grand pianos and synths. It provides arpeggiator features to boot. Sampling is also available in GarageBand, making it a great choice for the iPad-using pianist.

Another piano app worth looking at is Virtuoso Piano (see Figure 8-5). The app is available in paid and free versions and offers great features, including AirPlay support, velocity-sensitive keys, and an option to make each key glow as it is played to provide visual feedback. The free version comes with two keyboard sounds (more are available through in-app purchase) and allows you to adjust the size of the keyboard for more comfortable play. One of the best features offered by Virtuoso Piano is its Duet mode, which splits the keyboard to the opposite sides of the screen so that two people can play at the same time.

To play a duet using Virtuoso Piano:

1. Launch Virtuoso Piano and tap the Duet button at the top right. (The Duet button is next to the settings button and appears as two heads.)
2. The keyboard splits with one copy on each side of the screen. Both players can now adjust the octave they play by sliding a finger across the bars above their keyboard or using the buttons at either side of their bar.
3. Set the keyboard sound by tapping the Options button (the diamond icons) on the left and picking one of the options from the popover that appears.

FIGURE 8-5

Virtuoso Piano's Duet mode

4. Both users can now play on their corresponding sections of keyboard. It's best to position your iPad on a flat surface for playing duets, with the two players standing opposite one another with the iPad between them.

9

Sing for the Moment

It seems, from my research at least, there are more apps for recording vocals in the App Store than any other type of music app. Although pianos and synths may give the singing tools a run for their money, there is a plethora of options for the modern vocalist. From the gimmicky voice-changing tools to professional-level effects processors and recording apps, there's something for everyone — and not just those with pitch-perfect singing voices.

Although simply recording a vocal part and applying effects to that recording might be enough for some, there are more hard-core options in the App Store that reproduce professional studio effects such as vocoding and autotune. If there's one thing that Apple's GarageBand app doesn't excel at, it's vocals, with its Voice Recorder instrument clearly the weakest of the bunch. The effects available aren't brilliant, either, with some bringing about latency when recording live. For that reason, it's worth taking a look at some vocal effects packages as well as making sure your microphone is up to scratch before you embark on a journey into voice recording.

Beyond just recording vocals, there are brilliant apps that allow you to build up complex layers of recordings and loop them so you can create your own backing tracks and even harmonize with yourself. Through careful selection, you will not only find applications that record your voice but those that can enhance it as well.

Although vocal processing was once a dark art known only by experienced sound engineers and music producers, several of the apps listed in this chapter can bring professional improvements to your vocals no matter how bad they might sound in the first place.

Recording Vocals

Unlike instruments that send input to your iPad directly through a lead, the microphone poses a few new challenges — the main one being background noise. Recording vocals through a microphone and into your iPad requires a decent recording space. You are well advised to stay away from busy locations or other noisy areas.

The room also affects the vocal sound you are recording. If you're surrounded by stark, flat walls, the sound you record will be different from a professional vocal booth that has materials to dampen the amount of sound bouncing back off the walls. You don't need to break the bank to create your own dampening; an inexpensive way to reduce the bounceback is to hang heavy curtains or fabric against the walls.

Because the iPad is so portable, an easy yet slightly more peculiar option is to crawl under your duvet with a microphone and record your vocals there.

Similarly, recording in a room with too much space introduces unwanted effects to your vocals, mainly echo and reverb. These might sound good but it is better to apply them after recording, to keep your options open. Several microphones, like the iRig Mic, offer different gain settings for different types of recording. Very-high-gain settings usually result in a very loud recording that also picks up several sounds you don't want, such as the rustling of clothes, cables moving, and, in some cases, noises from the next room. Make sure you set the gain to a level where your vocal is loud but no hiss or noise from the outside world manages to creep in. If need be, hold the microphone closer to your mouth for a louder vocal, allowing you to use a lower gain setting.

FIGURE 9-1

The iKlip

If you're using an iRig Mic for your recording, also take a look at the iKlip from IK Multimedia (shown in Figure 9-1). It lets you attach your iPad to a traditional mic stand for easy access to lyrics and recording software.

GarageBand's Audio Recorder instrument is one route to recording vocals to a project, however there are several other options, some of which are free.

VocaLive is available in free and premium versions from IK Multimedia, and it is designed to work with its iRig Mic microphone. You don't, however, need to own an iRig Mic to download the app or indeed use one with VocaLive. By default, several vocal effects are included, with more available via in-app purchase.

You also have several recording options from recording just a single track or layering as many as four at a time. Like IK Multimedia's AmpliTube, you can also import tracks from your iPad's music library as backing tracks and use the voice-cancel feature so you can add your own vocals over commercial songs. Other features include a metronome to help you keep your vocals in time as well as a suite of tools to help you warm up your voice before recording.

Shown in Figure 9-2, iRig Recorder is another IK Multimedia app I should mention, mainly for its simplicity. If I want to quickly launch an app and record, this is the app I normally use. You can export audio

FIGURE 9-2

iRig Recorder

recordings through several routes, including e-mail and iTunes file transfer.

You do all your editing in other applications, but the main key with iRig Recorder is ease of use: Launch the app, tap the big Record button, and you're off and running. Sometimes inspiration or an unusual sound can catch you by surprise, and this app is the quickest route I've found to capturing these moments.

Like several IK Multimedia's apps, iRig Recorder is designed for iPhone but also runs on the iPad. I recommend having a copy of this app on all your iOS devices, ready to record at a moment's notice.

Here's how to record vocals with iRig Recorder:

1. Connect a microphone to your iPad and then launch the iRig Recorder app. The app is designed for iPhone so, if you want a larger view, press the 2X button at the bottom right of the window.
2. Once the app has launched, tap the large Record button to trigger your recording. The bar above the Record button shows the input volume level, so make sure the bar isn't filled completely or your recording will be distorted.
3. While recording, you can press the large Pause button at the top to stop recording and return to it later. Pressing the Pause button a second time resumes the recording.
4. When you have finished recording, tap the Record button again to have your recording added to the recording list that appears in the center of the window.
5. Tap a recording to play it back or tap the Export button at the bottom of the window to share it via e-mail, iTunes, Wi-Fi, FTP, or SoundCloud.

Vocal Effects and Techniques

One of the more popular categories of vocal apps is pitch correction and adjustment. A selection of apps offers basic chorus effects, vocoding, and pitch adjustment for the iPad that were once solely available through expensive music hardware and professional studios.

The most famous vocal adjustment tool is I Am T-Pain, which has seen extraordinary success and worldwide coverage with its ability to adjust the user's voice using autotune techniques that sound much like the artist the product is named after. The app is designed for iPhone but works fine on the iPad's larger screen, even if it is a little stretched. It's not all fun and games, however. The app allows you to export your work via e-mail or post it to social networks, and you can even add your own music from your iTunes Library as backing. This means that you can finish a track and send it to I Am T-Pain to apply a complete vocal track or add unique vocal elements. You can also work with no backing track and just record your voice, which allows you to export the vocal track and add it to other projects.

Similar to autotuning, vocoding is also a popular effect in the App Store. You certainly have heard vocoding, especially if you have listened to any of ELO's songs. It is effectively a way of altering an input source (normally vocals) using a controller (often a keyboard-driven synth) to adjust the tone and pitch. An app called iVoxel offers the closest reproduction of a vocoder on the iPad, although not to be used as a live effect while you sing.

Using iVoxel, you can record snippets of vocals and then play them as you would on a synth but with the added benefit of making adjustments to the sound. You can also load multiple recordings and play your own voice as if singing through a vocoder. You can also use iVoxel to copy recordings and paste them in to other apps.

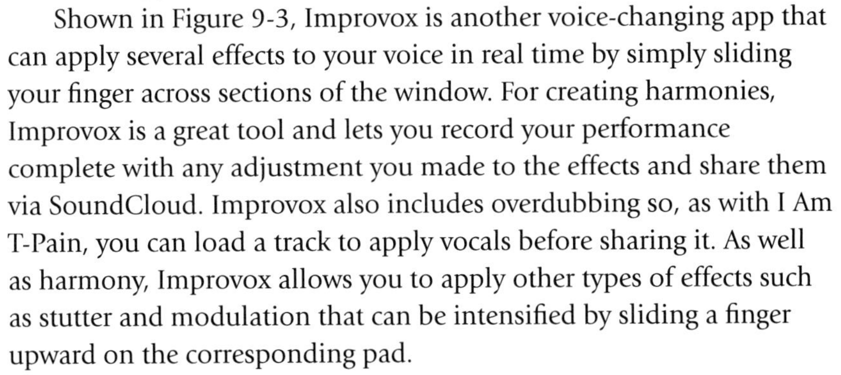

Shown in Figure 9-3, Improvox is another voice-changing app that can apply several effects to your voice in real time by simply sliding your finger across sections of the window. For creating harmonies, Improvox is a great tool and lets you record your performance complete with any adjustment you made to the effects and share them via SoundCloud. Improvox also includes overdubbing so, as with I Am T-Pain, you can load a track to apply vocals before sharing it. As well as harmony, Improvox allows you to apply other types of effects such as stutter and modulation that can be intensified by sliding a finger upward on the corresponding pad.

For real-time vocoding, check out Voix for iPad, which applies vocoding to live vocals by playing keys or chords on its onscreen keyboard (shown in Figure 9-4). For an additional in-app purchase fee, you can use a MIDI keyboard to control the vocoder. It's advisable to use a microphone and headphones for best results although feedback suppression is included. Vocoding can be recorded live, with tracks stored in the application. You can then send these recording via e-mail or copy and paste them into other applications. The app is fairly inexpensive, as well as being a lot of fun, and provides a great way to adjust your vocal parts or create interesting backing vocals for

ARTIST LESSON

Who? Joel Kosche

Experience: Joel is the lead guitarist for Collective Soul, as well as a solo artist with the release of his album *Fight Years* in 2010. A classically trained guitarist, Joel performed with many bands as well as working as a tour tech before being offered the lead guitarist role with Collective Soul. He has also hand-made several of the guitars he plays.

Favorite app: "Right now, I'm really digging on AmpKit. It's an app that's used with a small interface that allows you to play your guitar through a ton of different amp and effect models. You can even do some basic recording, which comes in really handy. It's really great for all around practicing and because it has a basic recording function I can instantly capture any riff ideas that usually pop up."

Uses iPad for: "I use it mainly to practice and to stimulate my creativity when I'm sitting around my hotel room or on the tour bus. I also have the same app on my iPhone so sometimes literally all I need is my little travel guitar and my phone and I'm all set to rock. I have to admit that I'm still partial to firing up my real amps in the studio, especially the one I built myself. Hey, maybe one day they'll model that one too and then I can allow myself to really embrace the future!

"As a guitar player, the iPad allows me to take advantage of some incredible technology without hauling around a bunch of equipment. That's always been the real drag when it comes to the music gear. I used to have my backpack full of stuff like recording interfaces, laptop computers, pedals, amp simulators and cables, etc. Now I just bring an iPad or my iPhone and I'm good to go."

Top tip: "One thing I really enjoy about a lot of these recording/music-related apps is how they work in what is essentially a nondestructive format. For example, on the AmpKit app, one of my favorite things to do is to record an idea for a song and then later 're-amp' the performance. Basically, you capture the performance first and then you're free to listen back to the part through different effects, amps, microphones, etc. that can all be tweaked on the fly and can all be done without affecting or modifying the original recording. This almost always sparks even more ideas, since you're not worrying about playing the part — instead you're just thinking about the music."

FIGURE 9-3

Improvox

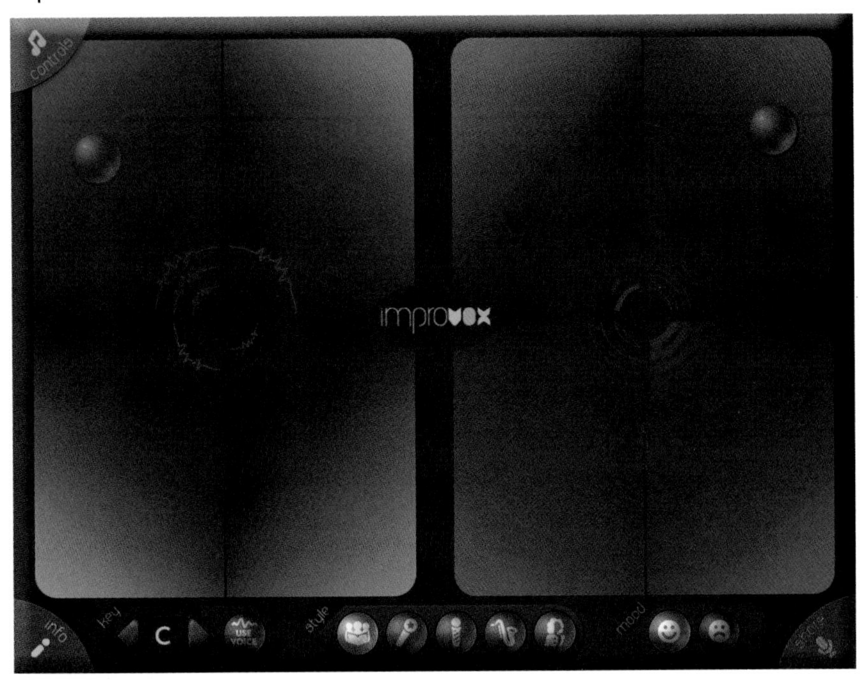

FIGURE 9-4

Voix Vocoder

your projects. A ribbon along the bottom of the window allows you to adjust the pitch of the vocoder's output, although it can be a little tricky to perform when playing chords and holding a microphone, so a stand is recommended.

To record vocoded vocals with Voix, follow these steps:

1. Launch Voix and connect a microphone and headphones to your iPad. A device like the iRig Mic is good, as it lets you monitor your recording without producing feedback. The iPad's headphones with built-in mic also work well.
2. If you are using headphones, tap the Prevent Feedback button to the left of the main LED display to turn off feedback protection for a clearer sound.
3. Tap the Bypass Vocoder button to the left of the Prevent Feedback button and play some notes on the keyboard to check the volume level.
4. Once you have the right volume level set, you can tap the Bypass Vocoder button again and practice your recording. Until you sing or speak into the microphone, no sound is played through Voix, so practice your part while singing and playing the keys.
5. When you're ready to record, tap the Record button at the top right and tap it again when you're finished. You can use the Browse Recordings button to see your recordings. You can then tap a recording to play, rename, copy, or share it.

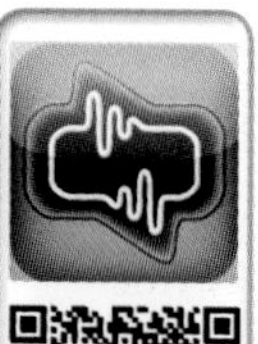

Using Loopers for Unique Vocal Tracks

As well as recording straight vocal tracks, several iPad apps allow you to record snippets of sound as loops and layer them to build a bed of sound. Apps such as Everyday Looper by Mancing Dolecules and TC-Helicon's VoiceJam (shown in Figure 9-5) record through the iPad's built-in microphone or any attached mic in the same way as any recording app, at the tap of a button. The difference, however, is that they allow you to continue to record over the first sound while it loops, allowing you to record harmonies, beats, and rhythms.

Using these simple yet powerful applications, you can build up vocal parts with multiple layers by simply tapping Record, singing, stopping the recording, and repeating the process. Using this method, you can build entire vocal parts with harmonies from scratch; it is a

FIGURE 9-5

VoiceJam

great way to come up with new vocal ideas or interesting rhythms that you might not have developed using traditional music tools.

You don't have to just record your voice, either. Adding in other sounds such as claps or instrument hits brings more detail to the recording that you can then export and use in your projects.

Both apps allow you to export your sound as an audio file but, if you play around long enough, you can even build up a complete track. Everyday Looper offers copy and paste features so you can quickly add vocal loops and layered loops to other applications. British beatboxer Beardyman uses VoiceJam to record entire tracks and even uses the device on stage, so the possibilities for live performance are proven with this style of app.

If this type of audio recording tickles your fancy, you should also check out videos of these apps on YouTube, where some astounding performances have been posted. These videos should be more than enough inspiration to get you humming and wailing into your chosen app.

Rap and Hip Hop

For nonsinging parts like rap lyrics and spoken word, the GarageBand Audio Recorder instrument or other audio recorders for the iPad are ideal tools.

But for more specific rap recordings, there are more targeted apps, including the excellent Freestyle (see Figure 9-6) that is designed for hip hop artists and writers to quickly pen lyrics and record them directly to their device. It includes a rhyming dictionary as well as a selection of built-in beats, and you can buy additional backing tracks through in-app purchase.

You can also add backing tracks from your iPad's music library, which opens the possibility of practicing lyrics over beats you have created yourself. Using the iPad's onscreen keyboard, you can quickly

FIGURE 9-6

Freestyle

jot down your ideas before heading to the Record window to lay down your vocal using the iPad's built-in mic or one you have attached. You can then preview your recordings and use a slider to determine the volume balance between your vocal and the backing track.

Although you can share your recordings via SoundCloud, Facebook, Twitter, and e-mail, you cannot export recordings using iPod songs as backing. However, with several professional-sounding beats included and even more available to download, you shouldn't be short of rhythm options. Note that the export function is a little misleading, as it only allows you to e-mail or share links to your SoundCloud recording, so you need an account. But from your SoundCloud page you can make the track available for download and access the recording that way.

U.K. rap master Rodney P is a big fan of the Freestyle app and even recorded a promotional video that you can view on the app's website. Even if you're not a hip hop vocalist, you might be tempted after seeing the ease of use and convenient features in this rap app.

Vocal Warm-up and Practice

As well as offering a convenient way to record your vocals any time, anywhere, the iPad can serve as a brilliant tool for warming up your voice and even improving your singing.

Liz Caplan Vocal Studios is used by some of the best singers in the business, and its Vocal Tool Kit Pro app for iPad brings this experience to the iPad. With more than 90 minutes of audio and video aimed to enhance the singing skills of beginners and professionals alike, it's a great application to have on hand for practice or just before you go on stage. The app promises to help increase vocal range and power and boost confidence as well as — most important — help you protect your voice from strain with several exercises.

If you're serious about your singing, or you want to improve your vocal abilities, this app will help you learn in the same way the pros do. It is an essential choice for warming up your vocals before recording or performing live. The app is available in various forms specific to the individual, with apps catering to male and female vocals as well as to singing and dancing.

Other apps also offer voice coaching in a more simplistic form on the iPad. Do Re Mi Voice Training, for example, analyzes your vocal and gives you feedback on your pitch which you can then compare to notes on the app's built-in keyboard. Visual feedback on the iPad's screen is a handy way to monitor your accuracy and steadiness on held notes, and it can even help improve your vibrato skills.

A potentially cheaper alternative to both methods is to use apps you already own that include a tuner. If you're after simple feedback or want to practice particular notes, you can launch an app like Cleartune or even GarageBand's Guitar Amp tuner and use a microphone to determine the pitch you are hitting and how close to the note you are. By singing individual notes and watching the tuner's display, you can determine if you're sharp or flat with a reasonable degree of accuracy.

10

Bang the Drum

It's time to explore the backbone of your compositions: the drums. This chapter, although oriented toward traditional drummers, is also important to anyone who wants to make music with the iPad. Whether you can actually play drums, it's important to be able to create custom drum patterns for your songs to avoid using the unoriginal beats provided by music apps that rob you of the flexibility of a real, live drum section. From electronic beats to vintage kits, the iPad offers a wide range of musical possibilities for your drum section, including the ability to connect external devices to your iPad to record live rhythms.

Although GarageBand offers a useful set of instruments for drummers, there are more options in the App Store that can help you design and program truly unique beats that suit your project and let you adapt a wide range of styles. How you create those beats is also flexible. Many apps offer sequencing and programming alongside live recording using MPC-style pads. With these tools, you will never be lost for a beat again.

Annoyingly, drum parts are one of the trickier musical creations to shift between your apps and get them into GarageBand. MIDI files are especially difficult to work with, but you can create an audio version of your MIDI drum beats and move the exported audio between apps. This chapter is all about apps and techniques to help you create and share your drum tracks, so roll up your sleeves and get your sticks (or fingers) ready to lay down some beats.

Recording Live Drums

Like all MIDI devices, electric drum kits and pads can be attached to your iPad using IK Multimedia's iRig MIDI or the Line 6 MIDI Mobilizer, as well as via USB devices that, depending on their power requirements, connect via the iPad Camera Connection Kit. This type of connection method can involve small pads such as the Korg NanoPad and Akai's SynthStation49 or full-blown drum kits like those in the Roland V-Drums series (shown in Figure 10-1). The input from these devices can then be sent to any Core MIDI-compatible application on your iPad, including GarageBand, so you can record directly into your project.

Connecting your iPad's headphone socket to an external amplifier, speaker, or headphones allows you to monitor your performance and even play live through your iPad. The additional bonus of using MIDI

FIGURE 10-1

Roland V-Drums

kits over live recording is that you can edit the recorded MIDI parts in many apps. GarageBand, of course, has to be the stubborn one: It won't let you edit individual drum hits, but you can trim and loop drum parts and copy and paste them to other drum tracks in your project.

Recording a real drum kit requires a little more setup. The kit must be properly miked before you record. A simple USB stereo microphone lets you record decent sound from your kit, and most can connect via the Camera Connection Kit. Of course, for the ultimate drum recording, set up several microphones to record the intricacies of your performance. You need to use additional hardware to accommodate multiple mic inputs as GarageBand, like most apps, doesn't allow multiple, simultaneous input. A USB mixer with multiple channels should do the trick, although you will need to perform any mixing before you record, as the mix can't be adjusted after it is recorded to your iPad.

If you have recorded your drumming using a multimicrophone setup before, simply replacing the device you used to record with the iPad allows you to record drum parts right into any audio recording app or a GarageBand Audio Recorder track. Using this method, you can position several microphones to a multichannel USB mixer, which then sends output directly to a GarageBand track. If your mixer isn't USB-compatible, you can also run its stereo output to a device like the IK Multimedia iRig.

There's no definitive kit list to determine which USB devices, mixers in this case, work with the iPad. The Behringer Xenyx 1204USB mixer has been proven to work with the iPad (it handles as many as 12 inputs). Although you might not be able to record to multiple tracks using this method, you can perform some mixing through the mixer before you record to adjust levels and pan. If your device offers equalization settings, you can make further adjustments, too.

Finally, if you're not up to buying an expensive digital drum kit or a set of pads, you can also use a MIDI or USB keyboard to trigger your drums. Most keyboards read the velocity of each note so the dynamics of your rhythms won't suffer using this input method. GarageBand reads MIDI inputs as do other drum apps that are compatible with the Core MIDI standard, so try your keyboard before giving up on tapping the screen.

Finger Drumming

Tapping the screen is a simple way to input your drum parts. Of course, nobody wants to start hitting their expensive tablet with drumsticks but, using the slightly softer impact of your fingers, you can re-create decent drum patterns directly from your iPad. The first option is obviously GarageBand. Its Drums instrument includes six kits, from

♪ FINGER DRUMMING

This clip features a pattern played by hand using GarageBand's Drum instrument. The first four bars are played with the Live Rock Kit and the second four bars with the Hip Hop Drum Machine. Notice how the kick drum and ride cymbal repeat using the two-finger gesture explained in Chapter 11.

FIGURE 10-2

Shiny Drum

FIGURE 10-3

Drum Meister Grand

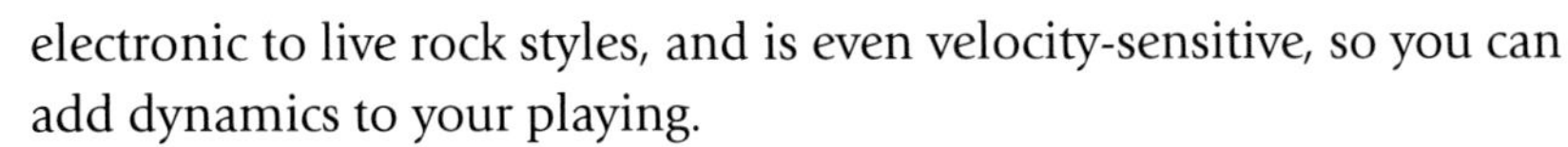

electronic to live rock styles, and is even velocity-sensitive, so you can add dynamics to your playing.

There are also alternatives to the GarageBand drums such as Shiny Drum (see Figure 10-2), Digidrummer, and Drum Meister Grand (see Figure 10-3) that offer more of the same features but, crucially, allow you to position the drums on the iPad screen. This is an important element of drumming with your fingers, as you want the drums you play more frequently close together so that you can tap them with ease. You can position the pads you use less frequently further away.

Here's how to customize kits with Drum Meister Grand:

1. Place your iPad on a flat surface or tilt it slightly using a Smart Cover or other case so it's in a comfortable position for playing drums on.
2. Launch Drum Meister Grand and, on the first window that appears, tap the Info button (the *i* icon) at the top right to display a row of buttons along the bottom of the window. Tap the Arrange button to get a view of the drum kit in which you can move the drums around.
3. Figure out the range of your fingers on the screen by holding them above your iPad. This should give you a good idea of how far each finger can reach to tap each drum.
4. Tap any drum and drag it to a new position on the window that is more convenient to avoid too much overlap between drums. You can also tap the magnifying glass icon that appears when a drum is selected to use a slider that allows you to make the drum larger or smaller.
5. Tap the red button at the top right of the window to introduce two new sections of the window that allow you to add new drums as well as adjust the sound of individual drums. When you are finished, tap the Done button and then Save button (the check mark icon) at the top left to save your kit.

Third-party apps also allow you to adjust the sounds for individual pads, so you can create custom kits and even mix the audio to suit your style. Of course, if you use an app other than GarageBand, make sure the app offers an export feature so you can import the finished product into your GarageBand projects. Most apps allow a mix-down to be shared via e-mail or file sharing and, if you're lucky, you might even find that you can export the MIDI file too.

Ultimately, I recommend using the GarageBand's drum kit. It offers the quickest route to adding your drums and percussion to your music as well as the opportunity to play along with recorded tracks. Although other applications provide more interesting options and a wider variety of sounds, the ease of recording in GarageBand is a major bonus.

When actually playing with your fingers, practice really does make perfect. The most crucial element to drumming on an iPad — to drumming in general, in fact — is consistent timing. Using a metronome and keeping your parts simple are good ways to avoid drifting out of time. Start with a simple kick drum and snare pattern to set the overall timing for your beat without using too many fingers right away. Once you've recorded these basics, you can add more drums on a different track or with your existing drums if your app allows it.

As you get used to playing the drums with your fingers, you can create more complex parts with multiple fingers and, therefore, drums. I also recommend playing along with your favorite songs in your drum app to get accustomed to finger drumming and help you create more interesting patterns.

Drum Programming

For complete control of your drum parts, programming is one of the quickest ways to design a beat while ensuring the timing and accuracy is spot-on when drumming on the iPad's screen. By programming individual hits as you would on any step sequencer, drum parts can be quickly arranged on your iPad without the need to remember which pad triggers which sound.

One of my favorite apps for this kind of work is EasyBeats 2, shown in Figure 10-4. As well as providing pads for live recording, it also offers a sequencer view so you can plot patterns with a simple tap. You can also use both components together. For example, you could record a simple beat using the pads and then move to the pattern editor to add new hits or reposition those you have already recorded.

You can copy and paste patterns, as well as build multiple patterns, that can be triggered at preset intervals for more complex parts. Individual hits can be adjusted using the step modifiers popover to change the velocity and pitch of each hit at a specific time so you can adjust the dynamics of your beat as your song progresses. For added realism, you can even add an element of swing to your pattern, which adjusts the rhythm and makes it sound more like an actual drummer than a machine.

FIGURE 10-4

EasyBeats 2

You can export the finished product as a WAV file to iTunes or share it with the EasyBeats online community. The shared kit and patterns can be browsed in the app, and other users can vote on your music. You can download all kits and patterns to your device so you can add new sounds to the app whenever you have an Internet connection.

BleepBox (shown in Figure 10-5) is a tool for programming beats and includes a number of preset patterns and kits to get you started. Although not as simple to use as EasyBeats, BleepBox does provide a huge number of settings to help you create original beats. If you are familiar with electronic drum machines, you should quickly pick up how it works. You can also share your patterns to SoundCloud via e-mail or Wi-Fi in a variety of formats.

Although expensive, Intua's BeatMaker 2 is worth mentioning as a more complete production app. It includes a great drum machine along with its many other functions. BeatMaker 2 is a true rhythm powerhouse, with a huge selection of kits and effects as well as its Chop Lab that allows editing of loops, pad copy and paste, and overdubbing features that help you add more drum parts to your beats.

FIGURE 10-5

BleepBox

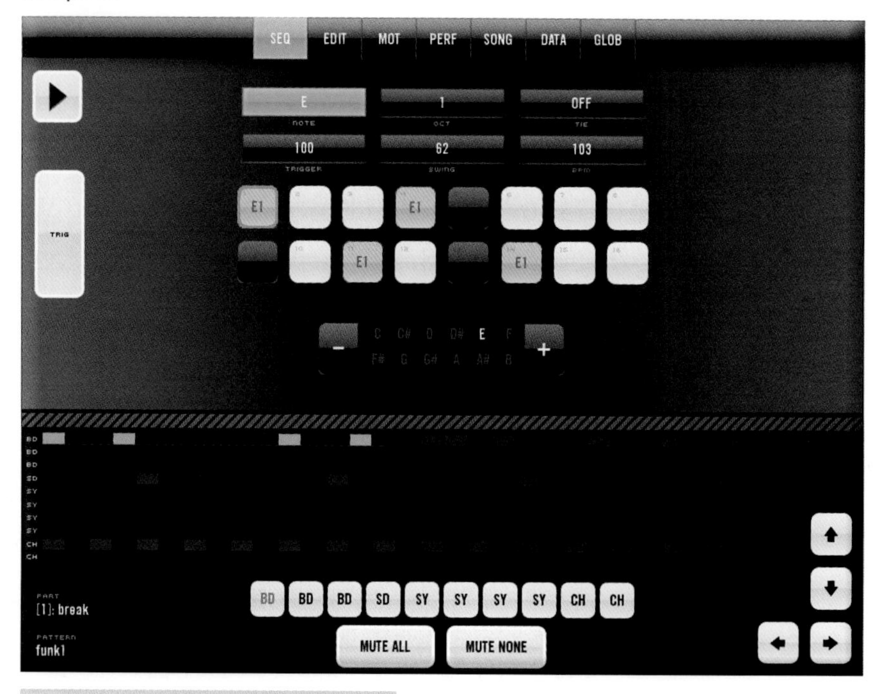

Unique Beat Creation

Drumming with your fingers through a MIDI drum kit or programming beats is all well and good, but what about having some fun while you make your rhythms? Fun is what the iPad is all about, after all.

When it comes to making drum parts there is a bunch of applications that, in just a few taps, can help you make extraordinary patterns without having to think too much. One such app is Beatwave, which offers little more than a window full of dots when first loaded. Tapping one of these dots triggers a specific sound, just like a pattern sequencer, from a kick drum to a musical note. By drawing with your finger across the colorful interface you can swiftly create melodies and beats without thinking about the musical requirements. If you want to dig a little deeper, you can adjust various effect controls for each sound and even add extra patterns to deepen your sound.

There are plenty of apps, a number of them free, that offer beat creation, but Beatwave is worth mentioning purely for how easy it is to play with. There are no built-in export features, so you will need to use

FIGURE 10-6

MadPad

one of the techniques described in this chapter's "Import and Export" section to add the beats you create in Beatwave to your projects.

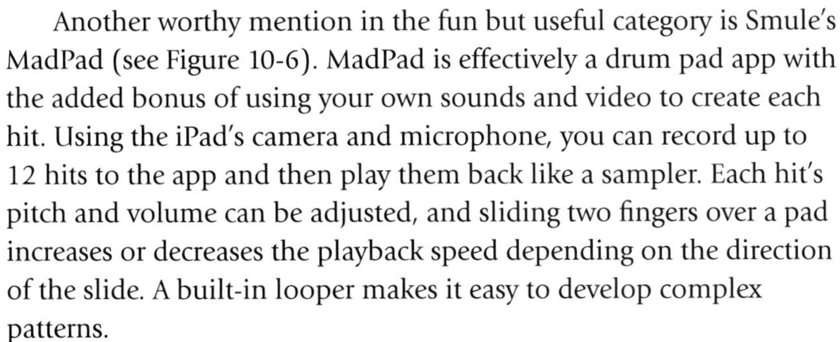
Another worthy mention in the fun but useful category is Smule's MadPad (see Figure 10-6). MadPad is effectively a drum pad app with the added bonus of using your own sounds and video to create each hit. Using the iPad's camera and microphone, you can record up to 12 hits to the app and then play them back like a sampler. Each hit's pitch and volume can be adjusted, and sliding two fingers over a pad increases or decreases the playback speed depending on the direction of the slide. A built-in looper makes it easy to develop complex patterns.

Here's how to create a unique beat with MadPad:

1. Open MadPad and tap the Create Your Own Sets button at the bottom right of the main window.
2. You are then asked to use a slider to set the noise level of your surroundings. When you have set the level, tap the Try This button.
3. On an iPad 2, you — yes, you — appear in a small video window at the top of the window, thanks to its front camera.

Below the video window is a series of pads where you record your individual hits. Prepare whatever sound you want to record and tap any of the pads where it says Tap to Record.

4. Quickly record your sound while Make a Sound is displayed and tap the pad again to stop recording. Your sound and video are played back.
5. Do the same for all the pads on the window and, if you want to change one simply tap the Close box (the X icon) at the top right of a pad and re-record it.
6. When you have all your sounds recorded, tap the Save and Play button at the top right to load your sounds as a drum instrument.

ARTIST LESSON

Who? Kevin Hastings

Experience: Kevin is a classically trained keyboardist educated at the Musicians Institute in Hollywood. Since then he has played with a range of brand-name bands and artists, including tours with Liz Phair and Rihanna. Kevin has also played with Jay-Z, Lady Gaga, and Fall Out Boy, and he has performed at huge events such as the MTV Music Awards and Live Earth. Kevin also has his own band with brother John called Vanity Machine.

Favorite apps: The AC-7 Pro Control Surface and iElectribe

Uses iPad for: "The iPad fits comfortably in my studio as another tool in my ever-growing arsenal of gear. However, on the road, my iPad takes on a much more creative role. I use my iPad for everything from capturing moments of creativity in audio, visual, and written form, as well as for fleshing out ideas I've been thinking about.

"The Korg iElectribe app is a good example of how I can create and capture my inspiration. The app specializes in creating electronic beats. The music Vanity Machine produces all starts with a heavy, usually distorted, drum beat. iElectribe generates deep kicks and trashy snares with plenty of knobs to satisfy any 'tweaker' like myself.

"Once I create a drum beat I am satisfied with, I can easily grab a WAV of my loop via iTunes, drop it into Logic, and I'm ready to chop it up and mess with it further.

"Before I had my iPad, I would miss moments of inspiration while on an

7. You can then record your own beat by tapping the Menu button and then the Record button on the right side of the window.

Your performance can then be recorded and shared with the online community of MadPad users or sent to your iPad's photo library as a video file. Again, export poses a slight problem but you can always extract the audio file using software on your computer or through the iMovie app on your iPad.

MadPad is ultimately a novelty app, but the ease with which you can record quick samples and play them back could be a great use to drummers when playing around with beat ideas. The finished videos

airplane or hotel room. Apps like Dragon Dictation help with capturing lyrics as they come to my brain quickly. I can speak out my lyrics and the app transcribes them so I can edit them further.

"The mic on the iPad is such high quality that I can sample anything around me. While pumping gas, I decided I wanted to sample the sound of the gas pump as it was clanking in a strange rhythm. I grabbed my iPad from inside my car and [sampled the sound.] That sample was placed at the beginning of Vanity Machine's latest single, 'Childlike.'

"The iPad makes life as a musician on the go much simpler. No more lugging a bunch of gear in and out of hotel rooms for one day off from performing.

"In my studio, the iPad offers freedom in its portability. As it's a mobile device, I can easily carry my iPad with me as I move about my studio. I can leave the confines of my computer chair and engineer myself as I play piano across the room. I can control the transport and select which tracks to record, as well as undo and save, all from the iPad. However, these are only the beginning of what's possible."

Top tip: "The best tip I can think of is a bit self-explanatory, but took me a while to figure out. In most beat-making apps like Korg's iElectribe, your loop can be synced to your computer via iTunes. At first, I ran a cable from the headphone out of my iPad into my audio interface and then into Logic to capture my loop. That process, of course, was tedious and would degrade the quality slightly. However, in the Apps pane in iTunes, you can sync the first-generation loop to your computer and then drop it into your DAW. The quality will be higher and the process is much simpler!"

look excellent, so there is certainly the possibility for amateur music video production with this app as well.

Import and Export

So, you have an incredible drum pattern and you want to use it as part of your GarageBand project. What happens next?

As with most third-party apps, it largely depends on the export features available, which will likely be hampered by GarageBand's obtuse nature when it comes to files from outside its walled garden.

At the time of this writing, it is not possible to import MIDI files into GarageBand on the iPad. Although the desktop version accepts the MIDI format quite happily, all attempts to import or copy and paste MIDI files on the iPad end in disappointment. The only route to adding your created drum loops to GarageBand therefore is using one of four methods, some of which require a computer.

1. Export your pattern as an audio file (assuming your app has this option) and add it to GarageBand using either copy and

FIGURE 10-7

Importing Drum Patterns to GarageBand

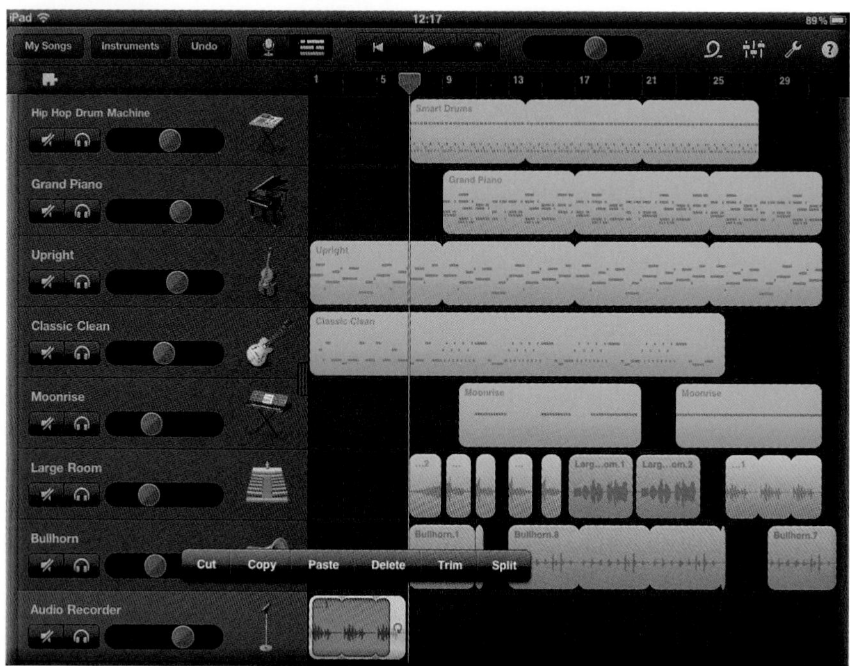

paste (as shown at the bottom of Figure 10-7) or iTunes file transfer.

2. Export the pattern as a MIDI file (again, if your app can) and send it to your computer. Send your finished project to your Mac from your iPad, open it in GarageBand, and then import your MIDI file.
3. You could send the MIDI file to your Mac or PC and then, if your MIDI keyboard accepts incoming MIDI files, store it there. Next, connect your keyboard to your iPad and set the keyboard playing the pattern. The MIDI pattern on your keyboard will then trigger the GarageBand Drums instrument so you can record your pattern into GarageBand.
4. If your app does not have a MIDI or audio export option, you can record its output using a cable from your iPad's headphone socket to an external device or computer or, with some clever manipulation, use an iRig or similar device to send the audio back to a compatible app on your iPad that supports multitasking.

With any luck, Apple will introduce more MIDI features in future versions of GarageBand but, for now, this rather tricky set of techniques is the only way.

PART II

GarageBand Master Class

Where the first part of this book covers third-party apps and accessories, the second part is all about Apple and, more important, GarageBand. Although I mention accessories used with Apple's mobile studio software, in the lion's share of this section I explore the features and possibilities provided in GarageBand.

Whether you have been playing with GarageBand for a while or just installed it, this section is the place to learn how to really make it sing. For the few dollars you spend on GarageBand, the opportunities it affords are almost limitless — and not just for writing complete songs, either. The app features such a wide range of instruments, many worthy of being sold as stand alone apps, that it is the go-to application for music-related jobs, such as recording samples on the fly and practicing your keyboard skills.

The key to GarageBand's success over similar iPad apps is its flexibility to help you make music in a range of genres without needing to use additional apps. Almost everything from instruments to effects can be found in GarageBand, and you can even perform rudimentary mixing before you export your music. Of course, exporting your songs as GarageBand files is far more beneficial to Mac users, as they can use the desktop version of GarageBand, which offers more tracks and loops. But I won't dwell on the Mac aspect for the sake of the PC users.

This section is all about making music on your iPad with GarageBand. What you do with your songs beyond that is up to you.

First, I take a look at the plethora of instruments, both real and software-based, at your disposal. I describe the best ways to use them, send input to them, and record. Beyond that, it's all about the project itself: Setting the tempo, key, and other global adjustments to make your music sound just the way you like.

It's easy to get started with GarageBand and even easy to lay down a few tracks without much guidance, but there are always a few questions that arise as you work. That is what I try to do in this part: Answer those questions and arm you with all the knowledge you need to make brilliant music on your iPad without hitting any restrictions. I fully described GarageBand's features and make sure you look for the tips that appear from time to time.

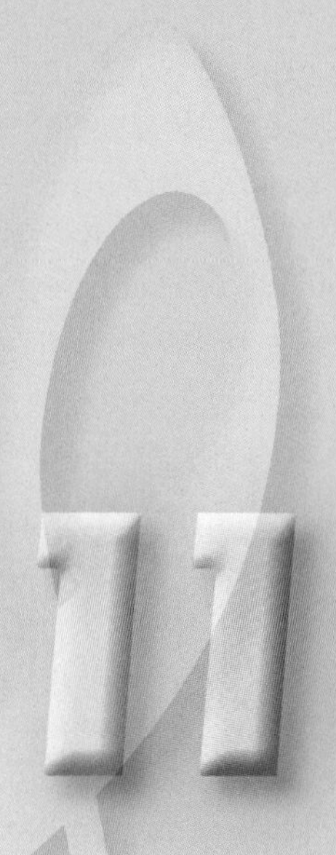

11

Understanding GarageBand

To get started with GarageBand, you first need to launch a new project. By default, GarageBand opens in the My Songs window. If you already have a project loaded, you get to that window by tapping the My Songs button at the top left of the window (see Figure 11-1).

From the My Songs window, tap the New Song button (the + icon) at the bottom left and choose New Song from the menu that appears. When the Instruments view appears (see Figure 11-2), tap the Keyboard image in the center of the window to reach the keyboard instrument. Next, tap the View button in the Control bar (to the left of the Rewind, Play, and Record buttons; the View button is shown in Figure 11-1 as piano keys) to switch from the current instrument to the Tracks view, where you will create your song. The Tracks view looks a little bare at first, but as you add instruments and loops, it will fill.

Regardless of the type of project you are working on, the main GarageBand interface doesn't change so, once you're familiar with all the icons and buttons, you will be comfortable making music regardless of the genre.

Tracks

So, what do you need to know right away? First, that gray space in the middle of the window is where you place your tracks. Any instrument you record or loop you add has its own track running horizontally across the window with the instrument's image on the left. Initially, you should see just the single piano track you added. Once you've recorded a part or dropped in a loop, you see a colored rectangle, called a *region*, added to the track area that includes waveforms or MIDI notes. MIDI regions are green, waveform regions (audio recordings and so on) are purple, and loops are blue. The numbers running across the top of the track denote different bars for that section. Initially, you only have one section with eight bars.

Tip: Swiping your finger from left to right across the image for a particular track shows the track controls for all available instruments. With the track controls displayed, you can set individual volume levels and mute and solo individual tracks without having to use the mixer window.

FIGURE 11-1

The GarageBand interface, in Tracks view

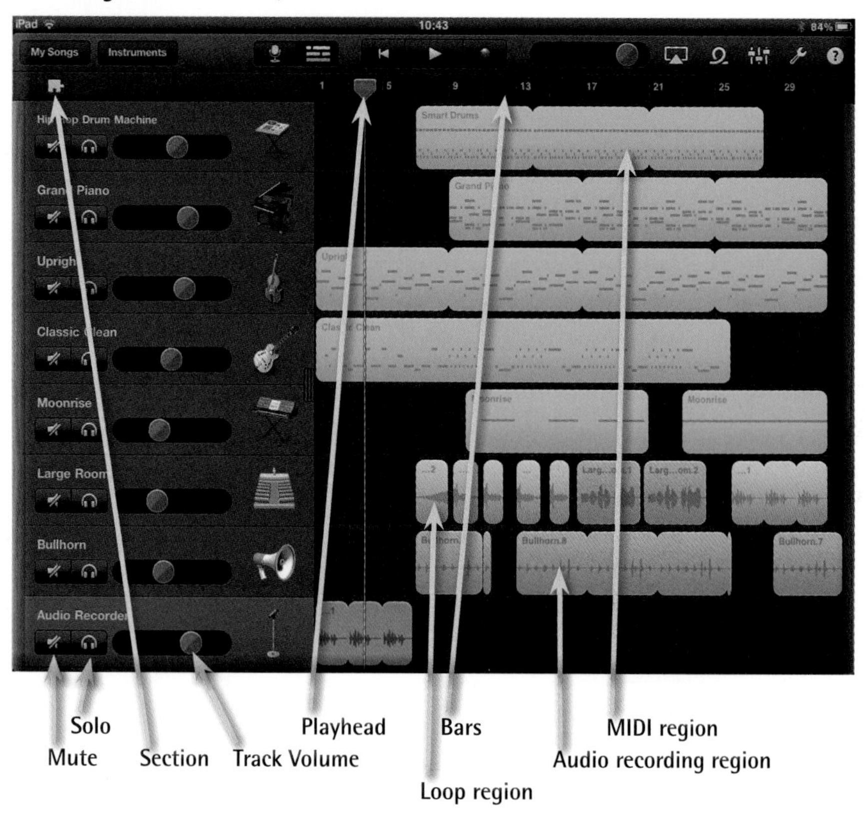

The Control Bar

The Control bar (shown in Figure 11-3) at the top of the window has buttons to help you move among instruments as well as control the playback and settings for your song.

My Songs button

This button takes you from the Tracks view back to the main GarageBand window where you can load new or existing songs, duplicate existing songs, and export them. You can also name your songs from the My Songs window. Every time you move to the My Songs window from the Tracks view, your current song is saved. If you quit GarageBand or put your iPad to sleep, you are returned to your project when you launch GarageBand again.

FIGURE 11-2

The GarageBand interface, in Instruments view

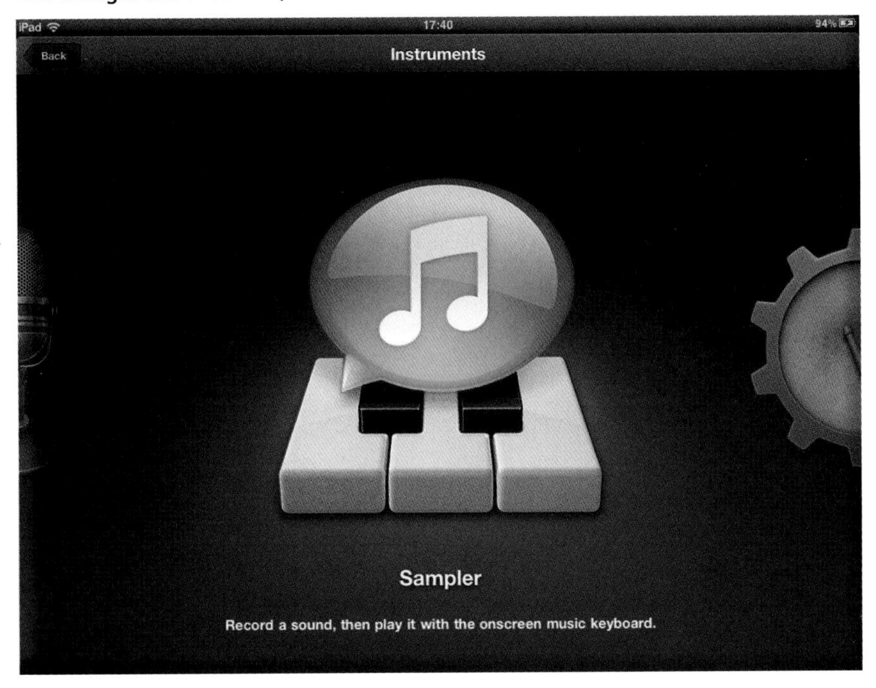

Instruments button

Tapping this button takes you to the Instruments view where you can select a real instrument or a smart instrument to add to your project. Tapping the Instruments button with an instrument selected adds the instrument to your project below the current instrument or at the top of the Tracks view if it's the first instrument you have added. Alternatively, you can change the type of instrument by tapping the Instruments button and picking a new variation of that instrument; for example, changing a grand piano track to an electric keyboard track.

FIGURE 11-3

GarageBand's Control bar

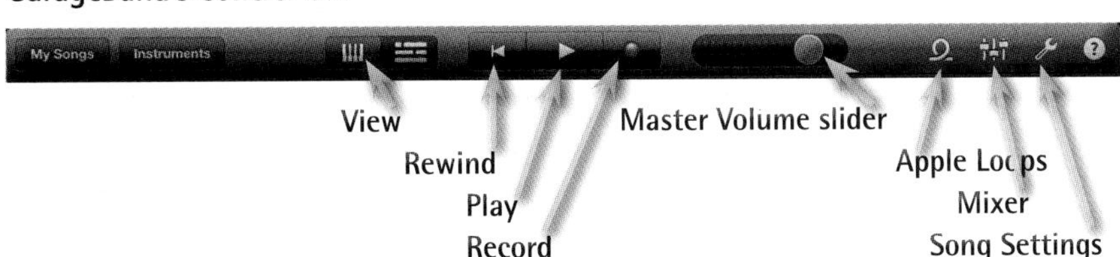

Tip: You can work with only eight instruments at a time when creating a song with GarageBand, so make sure you use your tracks wisely. If you are desperate for more tracks, you can either merge your existing tracks or export the project to GarageBand for Mac, as explained in Chapter 18.

Undo button

As the name implies, use the Undo button to cancel the last action you performed in GarageBand, be it a recording or setting adjustment. This button appears in the Control bar to the right of the Instruments button only after you've recorded an instrument or made changes to tracks or settings in your project. You can tap the Undo button as many times as you want to undo multiple changes if needed. You can also tap and hold the Undo button to bring up a menu with the Undo option to undo the last change you made or the Redo option to reapply the last change you undid. The menu names the action that you are about to undo or redo.

View button

Use this button to move between the Tracks view and the Instruments view for the current instrument. For example, if you have a piano instrument loaded, the View button shows a set of keys that, when tapped, takes you to the onscreen keyboard. The image on the left half of the button changes depending on the current instrument; it shows a drum for a drum track, microphone for an audio recording, and so on. The other half of the button always shows a collection of track regions; tapping this half of the button takes you back to the Tracks view.

Tip: In an Instruments view, you can tap and hold the View button for that instrument to bring up a list of all available tracks so you can quickly move among instruments without heading back to the Tracks view each time.

Transport buttons

This set of three buttons is fairly self-explanatory. The Rewind button moves the playhead to the start of your song or section, the Play button triggers playback, and the Record button starts recording on the current instrument track.

Master Volume slider

The Master Volume slider, to the right of the Record button, allows you to set the overall volume level for your song and also gives you feedback on the volume level. Dragging the circular control to the right increases the volume, while dragging it to the left decreases it. You can also use the iPad's hardware volume buttons to control this level. During playback, green lights show the current level and where the level is peaking. Red lights show that the volume is very high or peaking (hitting maximum volume and distorting).

Apple Loops button

Tapping this button, which looks like a looped piece of string and appears to the right of the Master Volume slider, brings up the Apple Loops popover where you can search for loops to add to your project. Chapter 13 covers the Apple Loops popover.

Mixer button

The Mixer button (the icon of three faders) appears to the right of the Apple Loops button. Tapping it brings up mixing controls for the track you have selected and allows you to edit settings such as Muting and Soloing, Pan, Volume, and effects. Chapter 18 covers the mixer.

Settings button

Tapping the Settings button (the wrench icon) to the right of the Mixer button brings up a settings popover for your entire song, including metronome and key information. From here you can also set the tempo of a track and set up streaming of your audio to external devices.

Info button

This button highlights features in the GarageBand interface and allows you to access the GarageBand help. It basically tells you what I'm telling you now but with much less detail and fewer neat tricks.

Sections button

The Sections button looks like a puzzle piece and appears below the My Songs button in the Control bar. (Figure 11-1 shows both the Sections and New Track buttons.) Tapping the Sections button allows you to add and edit sections in your project. By default, you have one eight-bar track, but you can quickly add more or increase the number of bars in your current track. You can add as many as 320 bars to a GarageBand song, which is effectively ten 32-bar tracks or a mixture of different-length tracks that add up to 320 bars.

New Track button

One of the most important buttons you need is the New Track button, whose icon is the + symbol. The button is at the bottom left of the window, below your tracks. Tapping this icon takes you back to the Instruments view so you can add a new instrument. You'll find yourself using this button each time you need to add a new track or work with a new instrument.

The GarageBand Instruments

So now you know your way around the GarageBand interface, but you're not sure which instrument to use. The first thing you need to know is that there are two varieties of instruments available in GarageBand, three if you include loops. The main two types of instruments are real and smart. A real instrument is one that requires an outside influence to record sound or notes such as the Guitar Amp or Audio Recorder. A smart instrument is one that does some of the work for you, like Smart Bass or Smart Drums. Note that this is not an official differentiation; I split them this way to make things easier, especially given that the desktop version of GarageBand offers real and software instruments.

Real instruments

The real instruments in GarageBand — Keyboard, Drums, Guitar Amp, Audio Recorder, and Sampler instruments — act like virtual equivalents of their real-world counterparts. As you would a physical keyboard, you play the onscreen keyboard on your iPad; like a real drum kit, you tap the drums you want to play using the Drums instrument.

Although the Keyboard and Drums instruments work through touch input, the other real instruments all require audio input. For the Guitar Amp, connecting via the iRig or similar device is a must, although a USB or iPad-compatible microphone like the Apogee Mic are best with the Audio Recorder and Sampler instruments. All real instruments record audio tracks to your project, except for the Drums and Keyboard instruments, which record MIDI notes triggered by your touch input. These MIDI notes can then be transposed or quantized from the mixer, as Chapter 16 explains.

Keyboard instrument

The Keyboard instrument offers 80 sounds from Grand Piano to synthesizers and organs that you can select by tapping the Instrument button in the center of the window (in Figure 11-4, the button shows

FIGURE 11-4

The Keyboard instrument

♪ NOTE DYNAMICS

This audio clip shows the different dynamics available when Velocity is turned on for the Keyboard instrument. Position the Velocity slider's handles at opposite ends of the slider for maximum velocity range. In the audio sample, the first sound is a hard chord, followed by a softer chord, and then a very quiet chord. I produced these different levels of volume by tapping the keys harder or more gently, with GarageBand recognizing the different pressures.

a grand piano). Changing the sound often changes the layout of the instrument.

The Keyboard instrument has several controls to note.

Velocity slider. The Velocity slider appears on the left and looks like a vertical bar with two raised handles at the top and bottom. Moving these handles allows you to set the minimum and maximum sensitivity levels of the keyboard keys. For example, for a very loud piano part with no quiet sections, you might move both handles all the way to the top of the slider for consistently loud notes. Moving the two bars to the top of the slider results in a far louder sound and higher sensitivity, a lower position makes quieter notes. You should experiment with different minimum and maximum sensitivity levels to suit your project.

This slider can be handy for setting the dynamics of your keyboard parts based on your song's requirements. The Velocity slider can be turned on and off from the Keyboard menu, which you access by tapping the Keyboard button at the bottom right of the window.

Octave Selection buttons. These buttons are located above the onscreen keyboard on the left side. Tapping the ▶ and ◀ buttons shifts the keyboard up or down one octave, and the middle button shows how many octaves up or down you have moved the keyboard. Tapping the O button in the center returns the keyboard to its default position. Tapping the ◀ or ▶ buttons multiple times shifts the keyboard up or down multiple octaves.

Sustain button. The Sustain button is located to the right of the Octave Selection buttons and acts like a foot pedal on a normal piano or keyboard. Tapping the Sustain button allows notes to be held

♪ HELD NOTES

This sound shows the difference between playing notes with Sustain turned on and off. The first notes are played without any sustain, whereas the second set has the Sustain button locked in place. Notice how the first set of notes sound very staccato whereas the second set sound like they are held even though the keys are no longer tapped.

longer. To maintain the sustain, slide the button to the right to lock it and slide it back to return to touch control.

Glissando button. This button offers glissando options based on the keyboard sound you are using, as you slide your finger across the keys. By default, each note you swipe across plays, but tapping the button until it displays Scroll shifts the keyboard left or right depending on the direction you swipe. This can be handy if you need to move quickly between octaves without using the Octave Selection buttons. Finally, most of the synth instruments offer a portamento effect that adjusts the pitch of the first note you play as you slide your finger across the keyboard. This effect is applied when you tap the Glissando button until Pitch displays on it.

Scale button. GarageBand keyboards can be set to play notes only from a particular scale such as Pentatonic or Dorian. By tapping the Scale button to the right of the Glissando button, you can choose from a list of 12 options that turn the keyboard's keys into note bars that sound good when played together. If you want to play a scale in a particular key, you can set the root note by changing the project key under Song Settings.

Arpeggiator button. You can turn on the arpeggiator by tapping the Arpeggiator button to the right of the Scale button and sliding the Run switch to On from the popover that appears. Once the arpeggiator is turned on, a new set of controls appears in the popover that allow you to set the order in which the arpeggio's notes are played, the rate at which they play, and the number of octaves the arpeggio spans. At its simplest, with the arpeggiator turned on, a held note plays that note followed by the same note one octave up and beyond, depending on the number of octaves set to play. Turning on Sustain keeps the arpeggio playing until you turn it off or tap another key.

♪ ARPEGGIATED DANCE SYNTHS

Using the arpeggiator, you can turn a single note into a sequence of notes that work perfectly as dance leads using synth instruments. In this audio sample, you can listen to two synth parts, the first playing at a rate of 1/8 and the second at 1/16, with both using the same pattern of four notes as the root. Combine this type of arpeggiated pattern with a house drum beat and you're on your way to making a dance-floor classic.

Tip: Using a synth instrument with the arpeggiator can produce some classic lead dance parts. Turn on the arpeggiator, set the Note Rate to 1/16, and set the Octave Range to 1. You can now play a repeating synth note across a range of keys.

Keyboard popover. You display this popover by tapping the Keyboard button to the right of the Arpeggiator button; it allows you to set how the keyboard is displayed. You can choose a single or double keyboard layout as well as small, large, and medium keys by tapping the corresponding buttons. You can also turn on or off Velocity from the Keyboard popover using its On/Off switch. When turned on, the iPad calculates how hard you are tapping a key and increases or decreases the note velocity accordingly. Setting the Key Controls button to off hides the Glissando button.

Keyboard-specific controls. Certain keyboard sounds offer unique controls or particular styles such as synths. On certain sounds, the Pitch and Modulation wheels display next to the Velocity sliders. The wheels act like those found on real keyboards; you drag up or down to apply their corresponding effects. Both wheels feature an indent that helps you determine the position the wheel is in. The Pitch wheel automatically snaps back to the central position when you lift your finger but the Modulation wheel remains in the position you leave it. When playing notes, moving the Pitch wheel up or down slides the pitch of the note in that direction. The Modulation wheel adjusts the sound, including vibrato and resonance, the intensity of which is determined by the wheel's position.

Other keyboard sounds, mainly synths, offer circular control knobs that look like simple electronic dials to adjust the attack and release of notes as well as other adjustments like decay, sync, and filters. These

♪ PITCH BEND AND MODULATION

Listen to this short keyboard part to hear the way the Pitch and Modulation wheels change the sound of your notes. The first change you hear is the Pitch wheel being moved as a note is played followed by a slow movement of the Modulation wheel on a held note. You can record these changes while you play and GarageBand will recognize the input from external keyboards, too.

knobs appear on the right above the Scale, Arpeggiator, and Keyboard buttons.

Finally, organ sounds offer controls that include a re-creation of the rotating speaker found in real-world organs. This speaker's rotation can be sped up or slowed down using a switch. The rotation of the speaker applies a specific Doppler vibrato effect. Organs also offer drawbars that adjust the waveform of the instrument as well as buttons to control percussion and the chorus effect. There's also a distortion control in the form of a rotating knob.

Drums instrument

The GarageBand Drums instrument is a fairly simple affair, although there are tricks beyond just tapping the virtual pads. There are three drum kits and three drum machines to choose from, each with unique sounds. You select the drum kits by tapping the button in the center of the window; for example, the Classic Studio Kit button shown in Figure 11-5.

Once the kit is loaded, you can then tap the individual drums to trigger hits. Some drums, like the snare ride cymbal, trigger different sounds when you tap different areas. Tapping and holding two fingers on a drum plays a repeating note, and moving your fingers closer together or further apart increases or decreases the rate of the repeat notes. The overall speed of these repeated notes is dictated by the tempo set for your song.

When Merge Recordings is turned on, you can record a single drum and, when the loop returns to the beginning, record another part over the top. You can turn on Merge Recordings by using the Merge

FIGURE 11-5

The Drums instrument

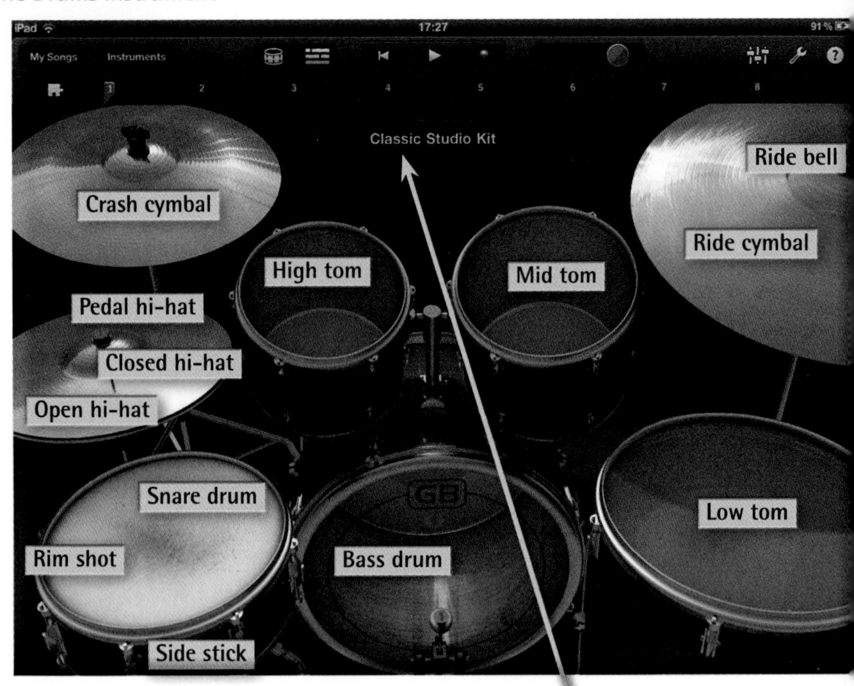

Recordings switch in the mixer popover when a drum instrument is selected.

Electronic drum kits offer pads rather than drums, with an image of the drum type they trigger on each pad. Playing these electronic drum pads is largely the same as playing virtual drum kits, but they don't trigger different sounds when different areas are touched as the traditional kit does. Two fingers still plays a repeated note, and there are control knobs on the electric drum machines. These knobs control the sound's resolution, fidelity, and filtering. Adjusting these knobs can make major changes to the sound of your drum kit and provide interesting creative options for lo-fi effects and processing.

Guitar Amp instrument

The Guitar Amp instrument (shown in Figure 11-6) takes two forms: the amp you see when you first load it and the stompboxes (effects pedals) that connect to it. The amplifier provides the main

FIGURE 11-6

The Guitar Amp instrument

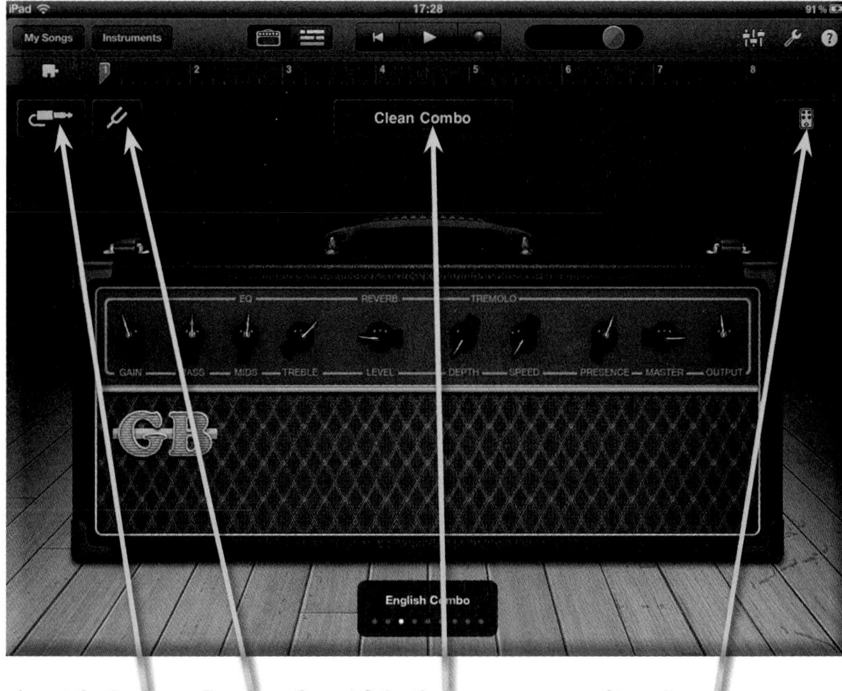

sound for your guitar input, and the stompboxes provide additional effects that can be turned on and off as you want. You can also add chains of multiple stompboxes to create layers of effects. To connect a guitar or other line instrument, you need an iRig or similar device to provide a route from your guitar to your iPad. To make sure all is working as it should, strum the guitar and check the lights behind the volume control to see if they registered the sound.

The Guitar Amp has several controls to note.

Input Options button. Tapping the Input Options button (it looks like a guitar lead) at the top right of the window provides two options when you have your guitar plugged in. The first, Monitoring, sets whether you can hear the input from your guitar as you play through the instrument. The second, Noise Gate, is useful if you have a noisy line from your guitar; it sets the minimum volume level received. Setting the slider to a mid to low level should cut out any background hiss while still recording the main input. Beware of setting the level too high as the more subtle notes you record may be cut off.

Tuner button. The Tuner button is to the right of the Input Options button and looks like a tuning fork. It allows you to quickly check to see if your instrument is in tune. It should go without saying that tuning your instrument is important, so this should be your first port of call when attaching any instrument. When the tuner is selected, a series of gray bars appear across the center of the window.

When you play a string on your guitar, the tuner displays the note it is closest to in the middle of the gray bars. It also highlight the bars to the left or right to show how far away from the perfect tuning the string is. When the note you are playing turns from red to blue on the display with no bars highlighted on either side, you're in tune.

When tuning, watch how the colored lights move to determine whether the note is sharp or flat and turn the tuning pegs on your guitar in the corresponding direction to correct the pitch. If you do the same for all your strings, you should be in good shape. The tuner also picks up chords, so once you have finished tuning, you can check if all is well by watching the feedback from the tuner when you play.

Sound Selection button. Tapping the button in the center of the Guitar Amp instrument (the button shows "Clean Combo" in Figure 11-6) shows a list of available sounds under a variety of headings, from Clean to Processed. Below each category are eight sounds that you can load by tapping them. An amp loads along with any relevant effects and settings, and you can change the various amp control knobs to levels that suit you and then record your part.

Amp and stompbox selection. Once you have loaded a sound, you are free to adjust it to suit your song. Swiping across the center of the window allows you to switch between amplifiers, and tapping the Stompboxes button at the top right shows the loaded effects pedals.

♪ ROCKING THE STOMPBOX

This clip features an electric guitar playing through the Guitar Amp instrument with the Auto-Funk stompbox selected. Notice how the pedal creates a wah-wah effect automatically in time with your playing. The second effect you hear is the Blue Echo stompbox with the Sync button turned on to fit it to the track.

Effects pedals are shown as small boxes that look like real stompboxes laid on a felt background. When you have three or fewer stompboxes loaded, an indent in the felt is shown to the right to denote that you can add another stompbox. Tapping this empty space allows you to pick from any of the ten available stompboxes that appear at the bottom of the window. To add a new one, tap it.

You can reposition stompboxes by dragging them to the left or right, and you can also completely remove a stompbox by dragging it off the window. Stompboxes also have control knobs to adjust their sound and intensity as well as an On/Off button on the front to toggle the stompbox's effect on your guitar sound.

You can tell when a particular stompbox effect is applied as a red light appears on the stompbox when it is switched on. Some stompbox effects also have a sync setting that keeps the effect of the stompbox in time with your music. This is particularly useful when using echo or chorus effects.

Saving custom sounds. If you want to store settings for a particular amp, tap the Sound Selection button again and then tap the Save button at the top right of the popover that appears. You are asked to name your saved amp, which is stored under a new Custom category that you can load again in the future. Any changes you have made to the amp settings, as well as any stompboxes you added, are also stored and applied when you load your custom sound.

Audio Recorder instrument

The Audio Recorder instrument (see Figure 11-7) is as simple as they come: Tap Record, make a noise into the iPad's microphone, and you're done. There are, however, additional features. You don't have to use the iPad's microphone, for example. You can connect headphones with a built-in mic or use a device like the iRig Mic to record sounds. There are also a bunch of effects that you can apply after you have recorded your sound.

Input Options button. Like the Guitar Amp, the Audio Recorder has the Input Options button that looks like a guitar lead at the top right; use it to turn on monitoring and apply the Noise Gate. Monitoring can be handy when recording vocals, primarily to hear your own voice, but also so you can keep in time with your song. Headphones are also the best choice for monitoring as they let you better hear what you are singing as well as avoid other instruments

FIGURE 11-7

The GarageBand Audio Recorder instrument

being picked up by the microphone. If you are in a loud location, the Noise Gate feature can be handy to eliminate unwanted noise from your recording and should be set at a mid to low level to capture your sound without any atmospheric interference.

VU meter. The Volume Unit (VU) meter shows how loud your recording is. If it hovers constantly above 20 VU before you record your sound, you are likely picking up background noise and will need to use the Noise Gate control in the Input Options popover as just described. Also watch out for the needle jumping into the red peak area, which may indicate distortion; again, you might want lower the level of your recording.

Effects. Once you have recorded a sound, you can apply one of eight effects to it. The effects include enhancements such as a more spacious feel using the Small and Large Room reverb settings; others offer more unique styles such as the Bullhorn and Telephone effects. Weirdly, these effects appear only *after* you have recorded a sound. Tapping any of the effects next to the VU meter applies it to your sound, and you can change effects at any time or switch back to the Dry (default) setting when needed.

When you select effects, two sliders appear at the bottom of the Audio Recorder window to adjust various elements of the effect, including equalization, reverb, and compression. Once you have applied an effect, you can record with the effect applied. Recording with effects turned on works well for most effects, but some vocal-changing effects such as Chipmunk and Monster add a little delay to your voice, making it harder to keep in time with your recording when monitoring as you sing.

Sampler instrument

One of GarageBand's more exciting instruments, Sampler (shown in Figure 11-8) offers a quick way to record a sound and play it like a keyboard. Once you've launched Sampler, it is hard to miss the button you need to tap to begin recording — huge, red, and glowing as it is. You can also store samples for future projects. Whether it's a vocal snippet or an interesting background sound, you can then edit and fine-tune the sample using Sampler's editing interface.

Recording and editing samples. Trigger a recording by tapping the Start button. Tap it again to end the recording. You can play back the recorded sample immediately or you can edit it.

The sample is shown as a waveform in the main Sampler window and you can adjust its start and end points by dragging the two handles on either side. Tap the Tune button below the sample to coarsely or finely tune the sample to fit your song using the two sliders. Finally, you can tap the Shape button to drag points across the sample to make a curve. The curve determines the loudness of your sample over time.

The Rev button at the bottom right of the Sampler's waveform plays the sample in reverse and the Loop button loops the sample when you tap and hold a key. At any point, you can set your sample back to its original setting by tapping the Revert button.

♪ SAMPLER USE

This snippet of music uses the GarageBand Sampler to play a sound as an instrument. Notice that the sample speeds up when a higher note is played and slows down for lower notes. There are also chords played from a combination of notes playing the same sound at different pitches.

FIGURE 11-8

The GarageBand Sampler instrument

Saving and reusing samples. If you want to store a sample for later use, you can tap the My Samples button, tap one of your sample recordings from the list that appears, and then tap the Add to Library button (the + icon) above this list. The sample is stored in your library for later use or in another Sampler instrument you add to your project.

Playing samples. Your sample can be played like any other keyboard instrument with each key playing your sample at the corresponding pitch. The same controls as found in the Keyboard instrument can also be used. There are a number of pre-recorded samples in Sampler's library that can be played in the same way. You can load a sample by choosing it from the menu that appears when you tap the My Samples button.

Tip: You can create a scratching effect using the GarageBand Sampler by tapping a note repeatedly and using the Pitch wheel as well as higher and lower notes to make it sound like the sample is being scratched on vinyl.

Smart instruments

For a simpler route to recording instruments or for just coming up with some new ideas, smart instruments make it easier to create professional-sounding instrument parts. Included in GarageBand are Smart Drums, Smart Bass, Smart Keyboard, and Smart Guitar. Aside from the Smart Drums instrument, you play smart instruments by selecting chords or individual notes. You can also play repeating patterns that keep in time with the rest of your song. Although some musicians consider smart instruments as cheating, they are incredibly handy for coming up with new song ideas and melodies and are ideal for when you don't have your real instrument on hand. It is possible to put together an entire song using only smart instruments and, if the digital guilt hits you, you can always record the real instrument parts to replace the smart instruments at a later date.

Smart Drums instrument

The Smart Drums instrument (see Figure 11-9) offers the same kits as found in the Drums instrument and allows you to position individual drums on a grid. You can select a drum kit using the large button on the left of the instrument's display. There are six sets of sounds to choose from: three drum machines and three kits. When a kit or drum machine is loaded, the individual hits are positioned as buttons on the right. Tapping one of these buttons plays a preview of the sound. You can then drag individual drums to create your part.

The main section of the Smart Drums instrument is a grid arranged on two axes. The first range runs from Simple to Complex and the second runs from Loud to Quiet. Dragging drums from the right to the grid adds them to your beat. Placing them at different positions on the grid produces a variety of different drum patterns, based on their volume and complexity. For example, dragging the kick drum to the top-left square of the grid produces a simple and loud drum part. If you decide you want a softer or more complex drum part for a particular sound, you can drag it to a new position on the grid or remove it entirely. If you are not happy with your entire beat, you can tap the Reset button at the lower right of the window to return the instrument to its default settings.

You can place multiple drum sounds on top of one another to share the same volume and complexity in your drum pattern. If you're

FIGURE 11-9

The GarageBand Smart Drums instrument

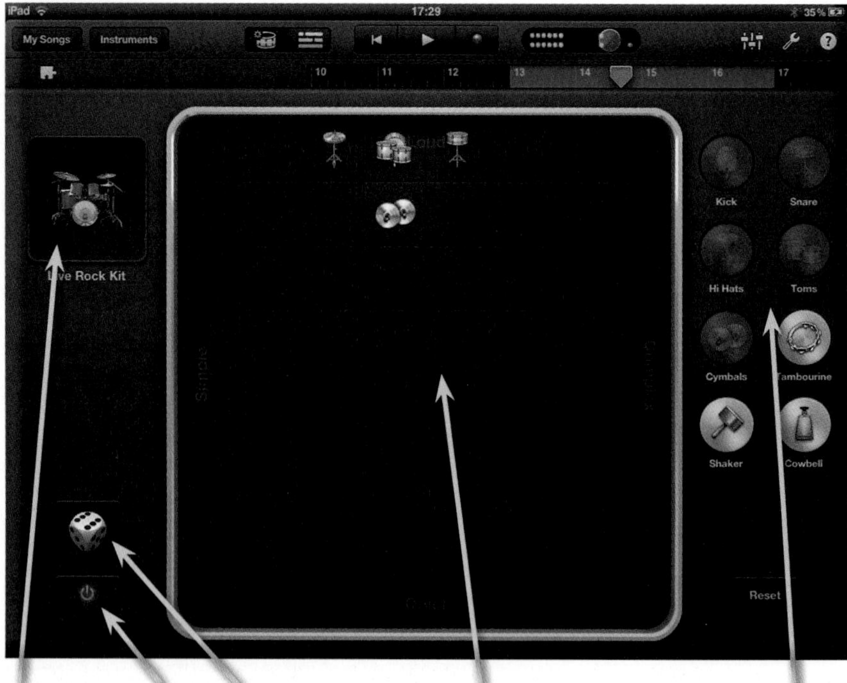

short on inspiration, tapping the Randomize button (the die icon) in the lower left creates a random pattern from a selection of drums. You can tap this button as often as you like to shift things around until you have a beat you're happy with.

Recording and practicing. Recording a drum part with the Smart Drums instrument is as easy as tapping the Record button once you have created a beat. The Smart Drums instrument plays only when the Power button at the bottom left is turned on, which can come in handy if you only want to trigger the drum part during a specific section of your song.

You are not limited to creating your beat all in one go, either. You can start a recording with a single drum or even no drums at all and gradually add them over time. As you record, drag new drums to the grid to slowly build up your drum section until the beat is complete. For example, you can start with a kick drum and then add snares and cymbals a few bars later. This is reflected in your final drum section,

♪ EVOLVING PATTERNS

This recording is of a Smart Drums instrument used as the intro to a song. Notice how the beat starts with just a single tambourine drum playing and develops slowly over 16 bars until it becomes a full drum pattern. I created this sample by adding individual drums to the Smart Drums instrument while the part recorded.

and the added drums play or stop playing at the points you designated during recording.

You can also adjust drum sections after they have been recorded by recording over the entire part or sections with new patterns. The tempo of your Smart Drums track is dictated by the overall song tempo, which you can adjust from the Song Settings popover.

Tip: While your Smart Drums part is recording, try tapping the Randomize button to randomize the beat and make your rhythm more interesting. This can be particularly useful during changes in your song such as a bridge or chorus. The randomize feature doesn't always provide the beat you are after, so you can create a pattern you like by dragging drums onto the grid and record it over the existing pattern if you want.

Smart Bass instrument

The Smart Bass instrument (shown in Figure 11-10) is a convenient way to add a realistic and professional-sounding bass line to your project. With four very different bass sounds to choose from, and the option to play individual notes or patterns in a number of keys, creating a catchy bass hook is easy with this smart instrument. The interface of the instrument is simple to understand, with fewer controls than other smart instruments, starting with the Bass Selection button at the top left from whose menu you can choose a Liverpool, Muted, Picked, or Upright bass.

Once the sound is loaded, you can play individual strings separated into groups denoted by the chord they make up. Tapping the strings records your bass pattern, or you can opt to have the bass play automatically using the Autoplay knob. This knob, at the top right of the window, has five settings and is set to Off by default. Each setting

FIGURE 11-10

The Smart Bass instrument

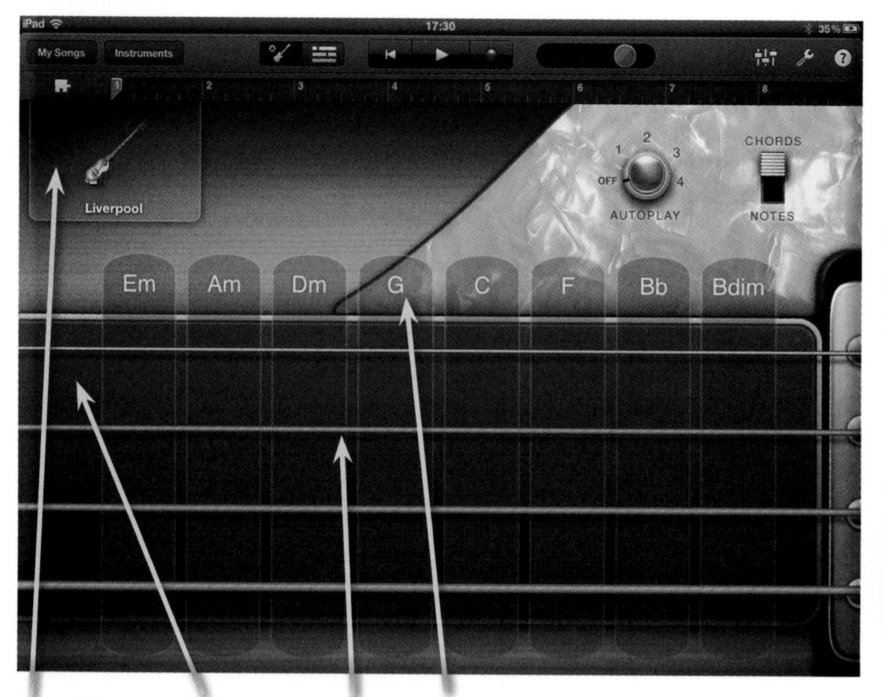

plays a different pattern, triggered when you tap a chord name on the instrument. When you select an Autoplay pattern, the strings disappear from the Smart Bass instrument and you are left with bars that you can tap to begin playing a pattern. Tapping with one, two, or three fingers on a bar produces a different pattern sound meaning that there are in fact 12 pattern styles.

Tip: If you connect a MIDI or USB keyboard to your iPad, you can use it to play notes through the Smart Bass instrument. The Smart Bass can read the velocity input from your keyboard and even responds to the pitch bend and modulation wheels.

To adjust things further, you can head to the Song Settings popover (tap the Settings button, whose icon is a wrench) and choose a different key to provide a different set of chords in the Smart Bass instrument. This affects the pitch of any other smart instruments you may be using. Finally, for complete control of your bass section, you can use the switch at the top right of the Smart Bass window to switch from Chords to Notes. In this view, you are free to tap anywhere

♪ BASS PATTERN

This upright bass part shows how different patterns and chords can be played through the Smart Bass instrument. This part uses three chords and two patterns, triggered by tapping the chord strips with a single finger and two fingers to mix up the patterns.

on the strings to trigger a different note as you would on a real bass instrument. You can even slide and bend notes by swiping your finger left and right or up and down when playing a note.

The Scale button, which appears in this window, allows you to play notes in a particular scale. Rather than using the traditional fretboard, notes are shown as bars when changing the key and help you play notes that fit together nicely.

Tip: To make your bass parts sound more lifelike, try using two fingers when playing in the Notes setting. By holding one finger on a particular string and tapping another finger at a different point on the same string the shift between the two notes sounds more natural.

Smart Keyboard instrument

The Smart Keyboard instrument (see Figure 11-11) is a lot of fun to play and offers creative opportunities for those who aren't trained pianists. Using the chord strips like those found on other smart instruments, you can quickly piece together a melody with a few taps of the window.

Sound Selection button. There are four keyboard sounds available via the Sound Selection button at the left: Grand Piano, Rock Organ, Electric Piano, and Smooth Clav. Each has its own unique traits, with the piano and keyboard instruments offering a Sustain control that works in the same way as in the Keyboard instrument. The organ offers a rotation switch to adjust the sound of the organ's virtual rotating speaker. Both the organ and keyboard instruments offer control knobs to adjust a variety of settings from distortion on the Rock Organ to tremolo and chorus on the Electronic Piano.

Playing chords and notes. By default, the Smart Keyboard instrument is split into chord strips with each strip split into chord variations and bass notes. The gray sections of the strips play the bass

FIGURE 11-11

The GarageBand Smart Keyboard instrument

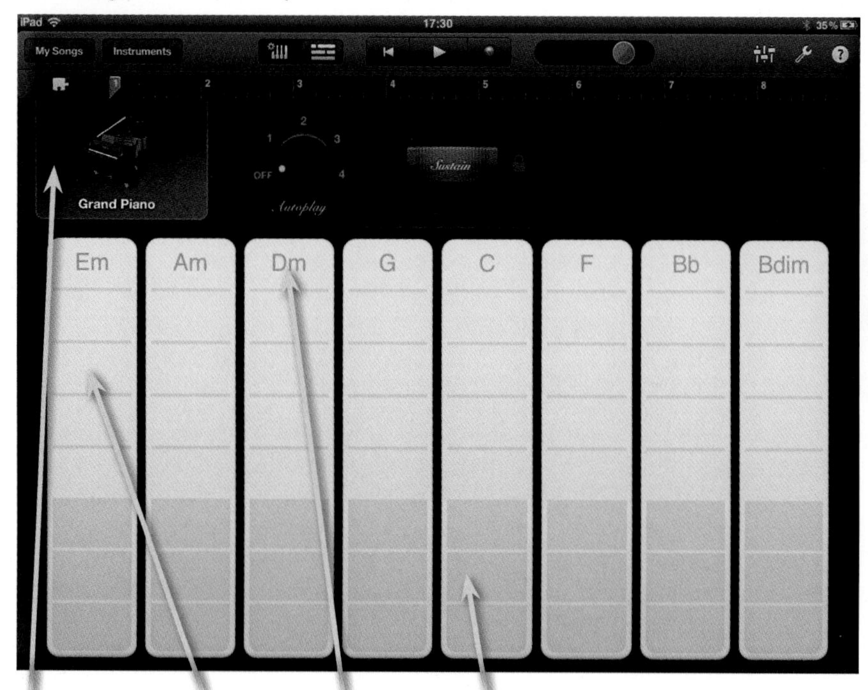

notes although the five white sections on each strip play differently pitched variations on the chord indicated at the top of the strip. By simply tapping these sections, you can quickly put together a simple rhythm made up of bass notes and chords and change chords by moving to another strip.

These strips are also sensitive to velocity, so you can tap them harder or more gently to apply dynamics to your parts. Holding your

♪ FINGER SLIDE

In this clip, the Smart Keyboard is played using the default setting. A combination of bass notes and chords are played between E minor and A minor with a finger slid upward on the A minor chord as a transition back to the E minor chord. There's also a finger slide down on the E minor chord to finish the part.

♪ PATTERN VARIATION

Listen to this clip to hear how patterns and chords can be mixed together using Autoplay to make professional sounding keyboard parts. Using the high part of the rhythm alone to start and then adding the full rhythm as well as variations on other chord parts makes the Smart Keyboard almost indistinguishable from a live performance.

finger on a chord and sliding it up or down plays individual notes rather than chords so you can smoothly link chords together without the staccato jumps that make the playback sound a little too electronic.

Autoplay patterns. Turning the Autoplay knob to position one through four changes the Smart Keyboard window to three sections per chord strip. The top section plays both the high and low parts of a rhythm, and the remaining two play the high and low parts separately. Each Autoplay setting sets a different pattern, and you can further adjust the sound of the rhythm by tapping the central sections of the chord strips with one, two, or three fingers. Depending on the number of fingers you tap the central sections, a different variation of the chord rhythm plays, and you can trigger the bass notes to play at the same time by tapping a single finger on the lower section of the chord strip simultaneously.

Rather than simply shifting between the same pattern across chords, you can create a unique rhythm by using combinations of single-, double-, and triple-finger selections as you play the instrument which makes a far more realistic performance. You are not limited to playing the high part of a rhythm with its corresponding low part. Mixing and matching the high and low parts of a chord rhythm can produce interesting results. By default, your Smart Keyboard offers a set of chords from E minor to B diminished but if you change the key, your project in these chords change to reflect the setting.

Smart Guitar instrument

The Smart Guitar instrument (shown in Figure 11-12) works in much the same way as the Smart Bass, with a selection of chord strips, individual notes, and virtual strings. Each guitar sound (with the exception of the acoustic guitar) includes two effects that can be

FIGURE 11-12

The GarageBand Smart Guitar instrument

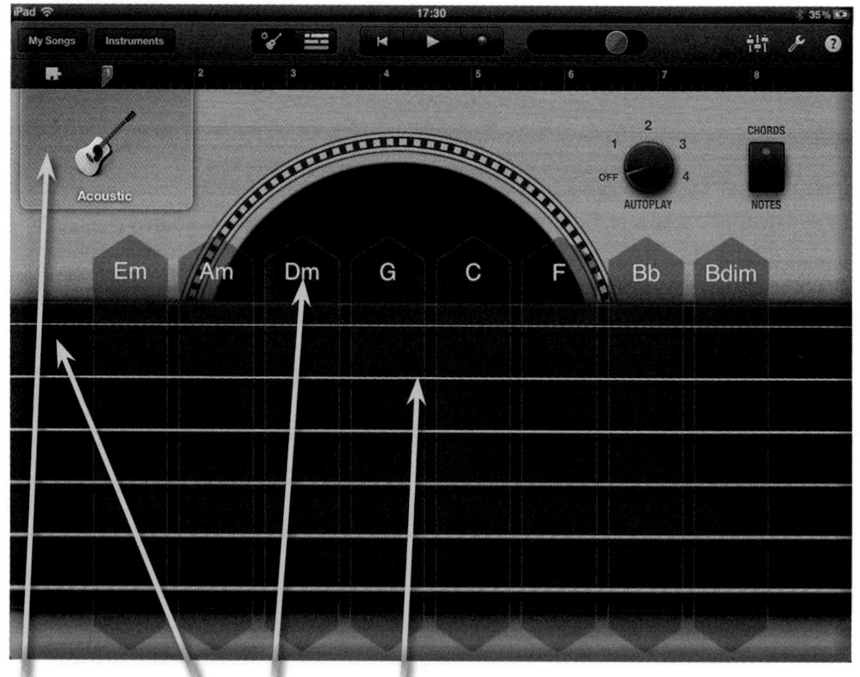

switched on and off with a tap of a button as well as the Autoplay knob at the top of the window. Even if you can't play guitar, this instrument helps you add exciting and realistic sounding licks to your song.

Sounds and effects. There are four available guitar sounds for the Smart Guitar instrument: Acoustic, Classic Clean, Hard Rock, and Roots Rock. You can set them by tapping the large button at the top left of the window. Next to this button are the effects for the guitar sound (unless you loaded the acoustic guitar) that change depending on the

♪ MIXING INPUTS

This clip shows how easy it is to jump between different input methods using GarageBand's Smart Guitar instrument. Starting with a muted chord progression, this part moves to strummed chords with individual picked notes using both the strings on the window and the chord strips to create a guitar part.

FIGURE 11-13

The Smart Guitar's Notes window

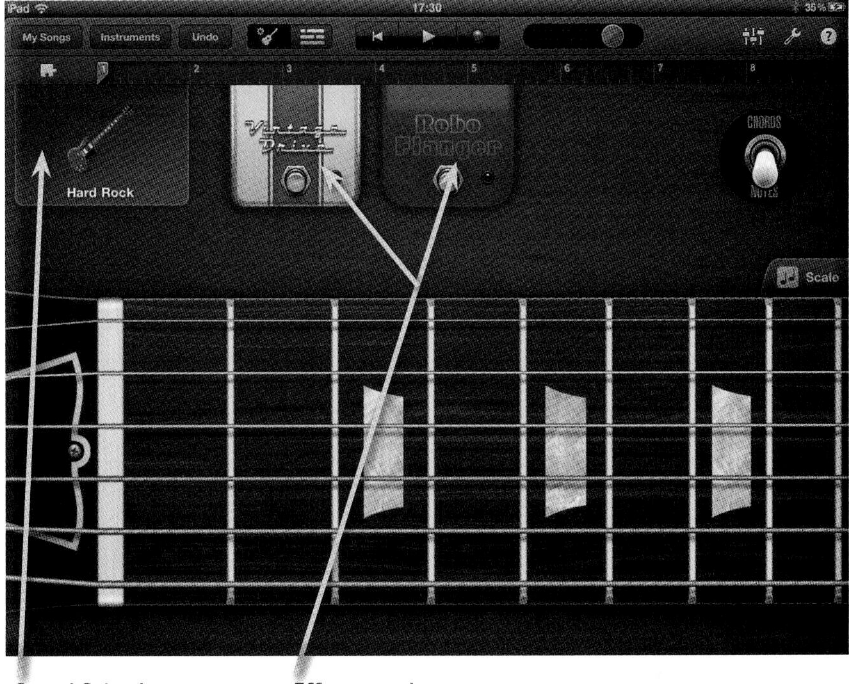

guitar selected. To turn on an effect, tap the button below the effect name so that the virtual LED turns red.

Playing chords and notes. The standard setting for the Smart Guitar shows chord strips with individual notes in the chord played by tapping each string. You can tap the chord name to automatically play the desired chord or sweep your fingers across the strings to create a strumming effect. To play individual strings, you can tap them to produce a picked note. An extra feature of the Smart Guitar is the ability to mute the strings as you would with your palm on a real guitar by holding a finger down at the far left or right of the window on the strips without a chord assigned to them. As long as either of these areas are tapped and held, any note or chord is played with a muted effect.

Autoplay patterns. Setting the Autoplay knob to any setting between one and four turns the Smart Guitar strings into strips and allow you to trigger preset patterns based on the chord you select. Tapping a chord with one, two, or three fingers triggers a variation on the pattern as with the keyboard and Smart Bass instruments.

The Autoplay patterns offer a variety of guitar playing styles from strumming to picked rhythms so there are plenty of options to choose from and suit your project.

Playing individual strings. Tapping the Chords/Notes button on the Smart Guitar instrument displays a traditional guitar neck with strings that you can play with your fingers, as shown in Figure 11-13. The strings play the same notes as a normal guitar and you can drag them up or down to create a pitch bend effect. Tapping the Scale button changes the guitar neck to a series of note bars. The strings work in exactly the same way but play notes only from the scale you have selected. You can also play the individual notes of the Smart Guitar using a MIDI or USB keyboard as well as using the Pitch and Modulation wheels to bend strings and adjust the guitar sounds.

12

Song Settings

As well as controls for individual instruments and tracks, there are also project controls that affect your entire song. These settings are found in the Song Settings popover, accessed by tapping the Tools button (the wrench icon) at the top right of the window. With the Song Settings popover, you can make changes at any point and from wherever you are in GarageBand as well as help you keep your song tight and in the right key.

When you first start your project, it's worth playing around with the settings in the Song Settings popover, shown in Figure 12-1, to help you plan how your song will sound and experiment with new keys and tempos rather than just sticking to the default settings. Here's what each setting does and how it can make a difference to your song.

The Metronome

The first three options in the Song Settings popover control the metronome, which plays a repeating sound to help keep your recordings in time.

FIGURE 12-1

The Song Settings popover

The metronome speed is determined by the project tempo and can be turned on and off using the first switch, Metronome.

The second switch, Count-In, allows you to have the metronome count four beats before recording starts so you can prepare to play.

Using the third option, the Sounds menu, the metronome can play four different sounds, from a simple click to percussion and drum sounds like a woodblock or hihat. The sound you choose depends on your project and the type of recording you are doing. If you already have a drum track in your project, it's best to stick to the click or woodblock so that the sound of the metronome doesn't get lost with all the other drum sounds.

When the metronome is turned on, it plays whenever you play back your project or start a recording. The sound plays on each beat with a slightly different sound played every fourth beat to denote the end of a bar.

Tempo Control

The tempo of your song determines how quickly each beat plays. You can get a better idea of the overall tempo by turning on the metronome and pressing the Play button on the Control bar. You can set the tempo by tapping the up or down stepper controls on either side of the tempo display in the Song Settings popover or tap and hold the stepper controls to move the value more quickly.

Alternatively, you can tap the Tap to Set Tempo button to assign a tempo to your project. This can be useful if you've recorded a part and want to set the tempo to it. Listen to your track and tap the button in time to the beat; the tempo sets itself as you do so. Try to tap along with your recording for as long as you can to make sure the setting is accurate.

Setting the Key

To mix things up in your project, you can change the key by tapping the Key option to bring up the Key popover. The current key is displayed on this menu and is the root note that the rest of the notes in your project relate to. Set whether you want the key to be major or minor using the buttons at the bottom of the Key popover and then choose the key you want from the list of 12. When you're using smart instruments like the Smart Guitar, changing the key also changes the chords available to you when playing the instrument.

AirPlay, Bluetooth, and HDMI

The final switch on the popover — AirPlay – Bluetooth – HDMI — allows you to send audio from your project to an external device. Although it's not a perfect solution, streaming your music in this way is a useful technique to assess how your song sounds on various speakers. It can also be handy in a studio environment to share your creations and collaborate with others.

To turn on the feature, slide the switch to the On position, and you're ready to share your songs. It's worth noting that the wireless audio streaming with AirPlay is not fast enough to allow you to play live, and audio input is switched off when this feature is enabled. This means you can't use the Audio Recorder or Sampler instruments or record instruments through the Guitar Amp. You can play smart instruments while streaming is turned on, but the delay between playing a note or drum hit and hearing it through the speakers makes them practically unusable.

Bluetooth and HDMI connections are somewhat faster, so you may achieve better results when playing live while streaming. Obviously, you'll need an additional kit to make this feature work, but when you do, it's a useful addition to the GarageBand feature set for reference more than anything else.

AirPlay

If you own an Apple TV or a set of speakers that support AirPlay wireless streaming, you can send your GarageBand audio right to Apple TV when you have the AirPlay – Bluetooth – HDMI setting turned on. When it's on, you'll notice the AirPlay sharing button appear on your GarageBand Control bar. Tap it to bring up a menu (see Figure 12-2) of available AirPlay devices on your network. Choose your device and the audio from your project is sent to your speakers with about a three-second delay.

If you don't have any AirPlay devices but are using a wireless network, you can turn your computer into a receiving device using an app called AirFoil Speakers from Rogue Amoeba. The software is available for Macs and Windows computers as well as iOS devices and, when loaded, adds your computer to the list of AirPlay devices. With this software enabled, you can stream your GarageBand project audio to your computer, which you can then connect to standard speakers.

FIGURE 12-2

The AirPlay menu

Here's how to use AirFoil Speakers to stream your music to another iOS device or computer:

1. Launch AirFoil Speakers on the device you want to stream to (another iPad or a computer, for example) and make sure the device is connected to your local network, which should be the same network your iPad is connected to.
2. Launch GarageBand.
3. In the Song Settings popover, set the AirPlay – Bluetooth – HDMI setting to On. The AirPlay icon appears to the left of the Master Volume Control at the top of the GarageBand window.
4. Tap the AirPlay button and, from the list of devices that appear, choose the device you want to stream to (see Figure 12-2). You device should now display AirFoil Speakers and show your iPad as a connected device.
5. Start playback in GarageBand and make sure the volume on the receiving device is turned up. After a short delay, you will hear your GarageBand audio playing via AirPlay on your device, as Figure 12-3 shows.
6. To return to listening to the audio on your iPad, tap the AirPlay button again and choose iPad from the list.

FIGURE 12-3

AirFoil Speakers receiving audio from GarageBand

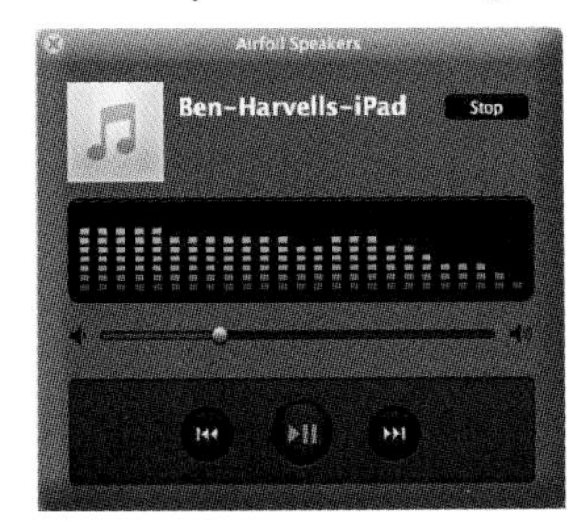

Bluetooth

Bluetooth is faster than AirPlay when it comes to playing instruments live but there's still a little delay. To use a Bluetooth device with GarageBand, first head to your iPad's Settings app's General pane and tap Bluetooth to open the Bluetooth pane. Turn on Bluetooth and turn on your Bluetooth device. Next, select your Bluetooth device from the list of available devices.

The next step depends on your device. You may need to pair it (set up a wireless connection) but most equipment will connect automatically. Head back to GarageBand and your device should be available from the Share menu that appears on the Control bar when you turn on the AirPlay – Bluetooth – HDMI switch. Select it and begin playback to listen to your song through your Bluetooth speakers.

If you don't have Bluetooth speakers, you can also use a computer with built-in Bluetooth: Connect your iPad to the computer using the method described earlier. Then set your iPad as the computer's audio input device from the Mac OS X Sounds system preference or Windows Sound control panel.

HDMI

Apple's Digital AV Adapter is required to send the output from your GarageBand project to an HDMI-enabled device. Most commonly, this is an HD television that you can then connect to a stereo or home theater system to play the audio. Connect the two devices with the AV adapter and then turn on the AirPlay – Bluetooth – HDMI switch in GarageBand to stream to your television.

13

Organizing Instruments

Selecting and organizing your instruments is the next step when making music with GarageBand. Adding instruments is a breeze and, once they're included in your project, you can adjust them quickly from the Tracks view. You should also look into adding loops to your project to provide a background for your instrument parts.

This chapter looks at adding new instruments to your project as well as loops and controlling your tracks once added. I also provide an explanation of the Song Sections window that can help you build up different areas of your song like the verse, chorus, and bridge. For more detailed track adjustments, there's the Mixer Controls for each track described in Chapter 18.

Selecting and Adding Instruments

To add an instrument to your project, tap the Add Instrument button (the + icon) at the bottom of the window to bring up the Instruments view. With your fingers, swipe across the screen until the instrument you want to add is in the center and then tap its icon to add it. You are taken to that instrument's window. To get back to the Tracks view, tap the View button in the Control bar next to the Rewind, Play, and Record buttons. You can continue this process until all the instruments you want are added.

Showing track controls

When you have added the instruments and other tracks to your project, you can extend the Tracks view to show additional controls for each track. By default, tracks on the Tracks view are displayed as a small image of the instrument loaded. By swiping a finger from left to right across this area, the track controls are displayed that allow you to quickly adjust simple track settings and change the order of your tracks (see Figure 13-1).

Three settings appear for each track. The first is a Mute button (it looks like a speaker with a slash through it and is positioned below the track name at the far left). Tapping this button mutes the track so it can't be heard during playback and recording or even when you export your project as an audio file. Muting can be a useful way to remove a particular instrument that is causing problems or can help you focus on other tracks. The Mute button is also used in exporting individual parts (Chapter 18 covers exporting).

FIGURE 13-1

Track controls in the Tracks view

The second button, the Solo button, is to the right of the Mute button and looks like a set of headphones. Tapping this button solos the selected track and is effectively the opposite of the Mute button. By tapping the Solo button, only the selected track plays, and all the others are muted. This feature makes it easy to listen to a specific instrument in your project and make adjustments as needed without distraction from other instruments.

Finally, there's the Volume slider, which looks just like the Master Volume slider but controls only the volume for its track. It appears to the right of the Solo button.

The track volume controls come in handy at the mixing stage and help you manage the levels of each instrument to fit with others.

To reorganize your tracks, press your finger on a track's image until it lifts slightly and then drag the track up or down to move it into a new position. Moving a track can help organize your instruments and group them into sections rather than sticking to the order in which you added them.

Duplicating and deleting

If you want to get rid of a track in your project, simply tap once on the track's image on the left of the window to bring up two floating buttons. Tap the Delete button to remove the track from your project along with any recordings or loops on that track. The second floating button, Duplicate, makes an exact copy of the selected track. Loops and regions you added to the original track are not duplicated, but any settings you applied to the original track are applied to the duplicate. The new track appears directly below the original.

The Apple Loops Popover

You don't have to rely on smart and touch instruments to provide sound for your project, with the Apple Loops popover, shown in Figure 13-2, just a tap away. There are hundreds of instrument samples, audio effects, and beats you can use in your project, and loops are a good way of experimenting with new ideas or to provide inspiration. Loops aren't created from a track, either. You need to drag and drop the track from

FIGURE 13-2

The Apple Loops popover

the popover to an empty space on the time line, where it appears as its own track.

The popover interface

From the Tracks view, tap the Loop button (the loop icon) to the right of the Volume slider to show the Apple Loops popover. You select the loop's specific criteria in the top portion, and the lower section shows the actual loops. By setting certain rules for the loops you are trying to find, you can narrow down the list of loops to only those that are suitable for your project.

Searching loops

Tap Instruments to see the available instrument categories so you can narrow your loop search and tap an instrument that interests you. Next, tap Genre to show the available music styles in the instrument category you selected. Available genres are shown in black while others are dimmed. Tap a genre to return to the main loops window, then tap Descriptors in the Loops popover where you can choose more specific styles such as Clean, Cheerful, Dark, Electric, and Acoustic. This section is useful when you're looking for a specific type of sound and can help you find drum fills to add to your existing patterns.

If there's something more specific you want — a loop name or instrument, for example — you can enter a search term in the top right of the Apple Loops popover and search for loops that way. If at any point you're not satisfied with the search criteria you added, tap the Reset Keywords button to return the search to its default settings.

Previewing loops

After you select the specifications for your loop search, all the loops that fit those criteria are shown at the bottom of the window. You can see how many returns your search had by looking at the number of items displayed at the bottom right of the popover. Each loop has a specific name, often with a number to denote it is part of a set of sounds, and the loops duration in bars shown next to the loop name.

Tap any loop shown to listen to a preview of it. The loop plays back its full length and is set to play back at your project's current tempo so you can hear how it fits in terms of timing. You can also start your project playing and return to the Apple Loops popover to preview your loop. The loop waits until the beginning of a bar to start playing back and then continuously plays until you tap it again. This is a great way to get a feel for how a loop sounds with your other instruments without adding it to the project. You can also adjust the volume level of the loop preview to hear it more clearly over your other tracks or to mix it with the overall sound.

Adding and editing loops

When you have decided on the loop you want to add to your project, simply tap and hold on it until it becomes an icon and then drag it on to the time line. You can drag a loop to an empty area of the Tracks view to create a new track or add it to the track of any existing audio recording or guitar amp track. A yellow line appears at the front of your loop when you drag it to a track to allow you to position it correctly with your other instruments.

Once you have added your loop, you can edit its sound with effects. If your loop created its own track, it becomes an Audio Recorder instrument track. You can head to the Audio Recorder instrument window to add effects as you would any other recording. If, however, you dragged your loop to a Guitar Amp instrument track, you can head to this instrument and adjust anything from the amp used to the effects applied to it. Go back to Chapter 11 to find out how.

The Song Sections Popover

Just below the My Songs button in the Tracks view is a small puzzle-piece icon. Tapping this Song Sections button opens the Song Sections popover, shown in Figure 13-3, where you can adjust the length of the current section and add new ones. By default, GarageBand loads an eight-bar section called Section A. Tapping Section A takes you to the Section Length window where you can choose how many bars the section should include.

If you're planning to record into the section without knowing how many bars you will need, turn the Automatic option to On. The section will now increase once you record or add track regions so you won't get cut off during recording when you reach the eighth bar.

Splitting your track into sections is a good idea as it allows you to focus on individual areas of your song such as the intro, verse, and

FIGURE 13-3

The Song Sections popover

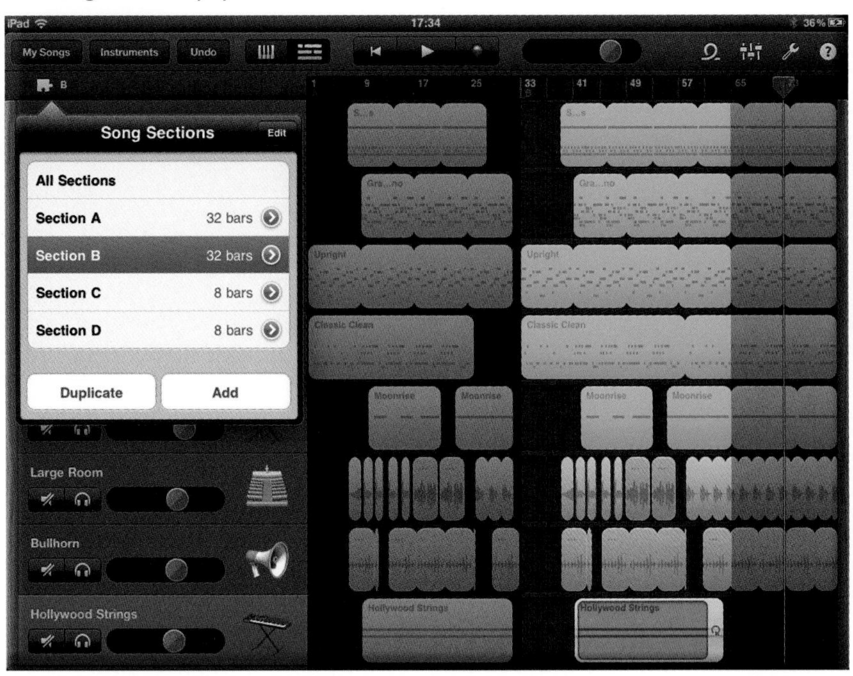

chorus and you can add new sections as you go. Once you are happy with Section A, tap the Song Sections button and tap the Add Section button to introduce a new section or tap Duplicate to create an replica of Section A that you can edit.

When you have multiple sections in your project, they are marked as such with a letter at the beginning of the first bar. The time line is also split into sections so you can only see the selected section. If you want to see all the sections at once, tap the Song Sections button and select All Sections. When creating sections in your project it's worth remembering that there are a limited number of bars that can be added to one project, so make sure one section doesn't hog them all.

If you change your mind about the positioning of a section in your project you don't have to worry about copy and pasting all your regions into a new position. Simply head to the Song Sections popover and tap the Edit button. By using the drag handles at the right of each section titled, you can drag a section into a new position. The change is immediately updated on the time line.

14

Building a Drum Section

Creating a drum part in GarageBand can be as simple as setting the Smart Drums instrument to record a pattern and then loop it throughout your track. However, a drum part that doesn't change for the duration of your song isn't particularly interesting for the listener, regardless of the genre of music you are working with. It's best to use all the tools GarageBand has available to make a beat that is truly unique and one that changes to reflect shifts in your song such as the move from bridge to chorus or as part of an intro or solo section. It's not as difficult to create a more complex drum section as it might sound, and by piecing together a number of drum techniques as well as loops, you can produce excellent patterns that sound realistic and enhance your song.

Start with the Basics

Using either the Smart Drums instrument or the Drums instrument, plot out how the basics of your beat will sound, for example, using a kick drum and snare. Turn on the metronome and set a tempo you are comfortable with before recording a bar or two of this

FIGURE 14-1

Multiple drum patterns

basic beat. If you are using the Drums instrument, you can record this small part and then record over it to add other drums without affecting your original parts. Build more parts on top of your beat until you are happy with the way it sounds and return to the Tracks view to see the pattern you recorded (see Figure 14-1).

Add Intros and Fills

If you shift your drum part along the time line by a bar or two (find out how to move track regions in Chapter 15), you open a space at the start of your song for an intro. This space could be filled with a new part you play using the Drums instrument or the Smart Drums instrument, or even by finding and adding a drum fill from the Apple Loops popover. Whichever method you choose, adding a fill or a drum intro before your main section starts or between two sections of drums will make your song more dynamic and help with its structure.

Here's how to add a fill loop to your drum track:

1. Load the project you want to add a fill to and then add a new Audio Recorder track to your project from the Instruments view.
2. Locate the point in your song where you want to add your loop — for example, at the start or just before a chorus — and open the Apple Loops popover using the Loop button at the top right of the window.
3. From the Apple Loops popover, tap Descriptors and then tap the Fill button to show all the available fills. Preview the fills by tapping them to play them.
4. When you have chosen a loop, drag it from the Apple Loops popover to your new Audio Recorder track at the point you want it to play.

♪ DRUM FILLS

Listen to this clip to hear how a drum fill can be used to denote a change in your drum pattern. Starting with a basic verse rhythm, a drum fill plays on the fifth bar to denote a switch to the chorus. The fill plays again at the end of the chorus as the song switches back to the verse rhythm.

5. Now select one of the drum tracks you already have loaded by tapping it and use the handles at the right side to trim it so that it doesn't play at the same time as your fill (see more on trimming sections in Chapter 15). Do the same with all other drum tracks in your project. Figure 14-2 shows how this should look in the Tracks view.

Use Multiple Tracks

When working with drum parts and multiple drum instruments, it can be easier to use multiple tracks for different sections or even individual drums. Although there are only eight tracks available in a GarageBand project, it can be worthwhile creating your drum patterns first and then bouncing all the individual sounds to one track, as explained in Chapter 18.

By dedicating one track to your kick and snare rhythm, another to your percussion parts, and yet another for any fills or alternate versions of your drum patterns, you will have more flexibility editing your rhythm section rather than if you loaded everything on one track.

FIGURE 14-2

A fill loop added to a drum track

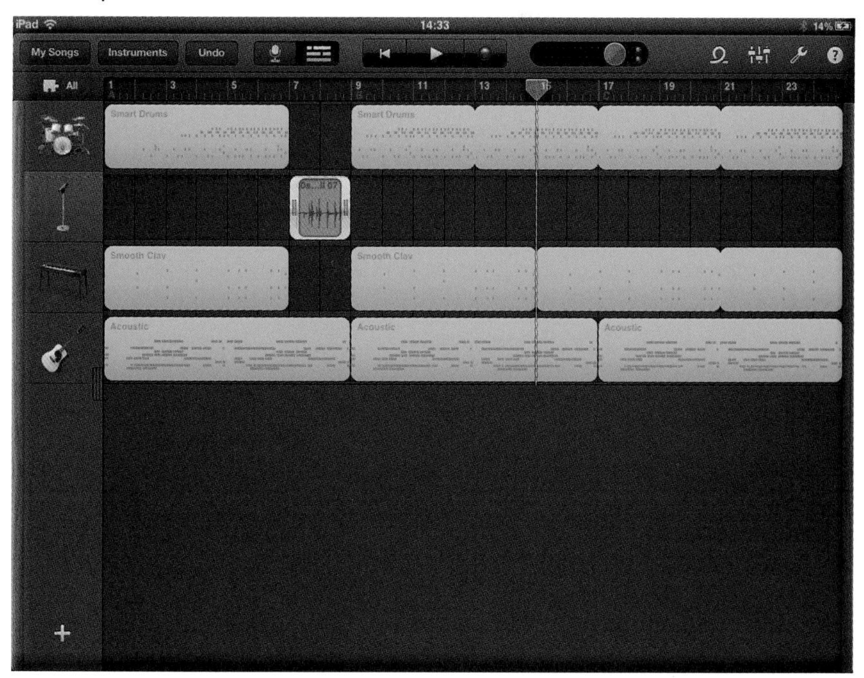

However, if you do bounce all your drum parts down to one track, you need to mix your drum instruments properly before exporting, as you won't be able to adjust the individual drum parts after you've combined them into one track. Make sure you adjust the levels for each instrument so that no instrument is too overpowering or too quiet. Also make sure that any effects, such as reverb or echo, are applied across all drum instruments for a consistent sound. For complete control, consider making individual GarageBand projects for each drum section — for example, verse, bridge, and chorus — and exporting them as audio files. You can then import them when needed to your main project.

Enhance Smart Drums Tracks

Once you have recorded your Smart Drums part, it doesn't have to remain that way. You can still adjust it if needed. You can also go back to the Smart Drums instrument at any time and add new drums or remove them from your original recording. You can even adjust the volume and complexity of a Smart Drums part before recording: Simply load the Smart Drums instrument, tap the Power button at the bottom left of the window, and adjust the drums as you want. Then tap Record to overwrite the drum part on the time line.

For a less destructive enhancement, you can add a second Smart Drums or Drums instrument track to your project and record an additional layer of drums that fits with your original.

15

Editing Regions

Once you've recorded instruments on the time line, you have colorful regions to play with in the Tracks view. These regions don't have to just sit there: You have several editing options to help you tweak individual instrument parts, as well as the sound of your entire project. By using cut and paste, trimming, splitting, and looping, you can shape your song just the way you like and save time as you go.

Working with regions on the time line can sometimes be a fiddly process, so make sure you zoom in and out for a closer look.

Moving Track Regions

The simplest adjustment you can make to regions on your track is to move them around. Tapping and dragging a region to the left or right repositions it on the time line. Notice that the region snaps to the closest beat when you take your finger off the screen. This snapping to the beat is useful to make sure the instrument doesn't play out of time.

Use the bars listed across the top of the time line to help decide where to move your region. Dragging a region up or down moves it

FIGURE 15-1

A mixture of track regions

between tracks. Some tracks allow the region to be dropped onto them and others show a message saying that the region isn't compatible with that instrument.

Generally, green MIDI regions can be moved to other MIDI tracks, but certain instruments (like drums and guitars) are incompatible. Audio regions such as loops, Guitar Amp parts, and Audio Recorder recordings are interchangeable (see Figure 15-1).

Looping Regions

Tapping a region and then tapping the Loop button from the contextual menu that appears repeats the region across the time line until it meets another region or reaches the end of a section. Using the Loop button is a far easier way to repeat a part than using cut and paste, especially for drum sections and bass lines.

Trimming a Region

If you want to adjust the length of a region on the time line, simply tap it and use the bars at either end to drag and make it smaller or larger. Dragging can be handy if you want to remove part of a pattern you don't need or to stop a number of tracks to add emphasis to other instruments.

Before you begin trimming, zoom in close to a region. You will see individual MIDI notes or waveforms (depending on the region you are editing), which will give you a better idea of where you need to trim (see Figure 15-2).

After you have trimmed a region, the notes and sounds you have hidden are not deleted: You can always drag the region to make it larger and reintroduce these sounds if needed.

To make things easier when trimming, I recommend placing the playhead at the point on the time line you want to trim to as a reference point.

Tip: When you want to resize a region with the trimming technique, tap and hold a finger on the end of a region to quickly zoom into the time line. Drag your part to the required length and let go; the view zooms back to normal.

FIGURE 15-2

Zooming into the Tracks view

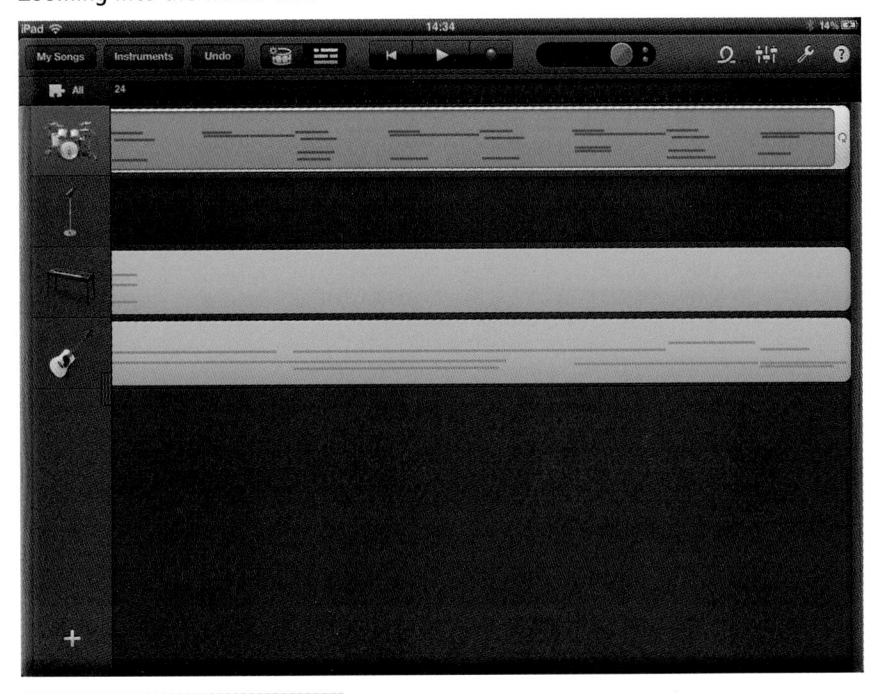

Splitting a Region

To break up a large region into smaller parts or remove sections of a region, use the Split feature. This can be handy if you want to remove a particular section of a track or copy and paste a small section of a region to another track. Here's how it works:

1. Tap the region you want to split, then choose the Split option from the menu that appears.
2. A new marker showing a pair of scissors appears over your region (as shown in Figure 15-3). Drag the marker to the point in the region you want to split.
3. Drag the marker down until the region is split. You can now move the two parts of the region independently and even drag one or both to a new track.

Copying and Pasting Regions

Sometimes you need to add a version of an existing region at another location on the time line or to another track. In this situation,

FIGURE 15-3

Splitting a region

FIGURE 15-4

Pasting a track region

dragging a region won't work because it leaves a gap where the original region was located. This is the time to use copy and paste: Copy a track region and then place an exact replica at another point in your track by pasting it. Here's how to do that:

1. Tap the region you want to copy and then choose the Copy option from the contextual menu that appears (see Figure 15-4).
2. Move the playhead to the position you want the pasted region to appear and tap an empty area of the time line.
3. From the contextual menu that appears, choose Paste. A copy of the original region is placed on the time line.

You can now edit this pasted region and move it like any other section in your song. Pasting is also useful for doubling up instrument parts for more emphasis or for creating harmonies using the Transposition tools explained in Chapter 18.

16

Mixing Your Project

Mixing can make or break a song. Without working on volume levels and instrument positioning, the final result could sound like a messy collection of conflicting sounds. Fortunately, there are mixing options, though basic, available in GarageBand to help you fine-tune your sound.

The most crucial areas you need to focus on when mixing are volume levels and the position of an instrument in the stereo field. The first is simple to address: Don't turn up your instruments so loud it sounds like a jet taking off and, likewise, don't set them so quiet that minimalist music takes on a whole new meaning. Then, of course, you can encounter both problems when one track is too loud and masks the quieter tracks. A bit of balance is what you need.

Addressing the second area — positioning your instruments — can also help with level problems. Believe it or not, when listening to a stereo mix there is not only a left and right perspective but also front and back. Adjusting pan and reverb can help position your instruments so they sit together nicely. By shifting a quieter instrument to one area of the spectrum, for example, it can be heard more clearly because it is further away from the louder tracks. Think of your mix like an orchestra or band: You have your string section in one position, wind instruments in another, and drums and strings elsewhere. If there is a vocalist, he or she is in the front. Likewise, the drummer is also central but placed at the back.

Thinking of the stereo mix as physically positioning your instruments can help you learn where to place them. Ultimately, you should mix until things sound right and, more important, they sound how you want them to sound.

Tip: Make sure you mix using speakers, too; headphones can sometimes give you a false appreciation of your mixing so, even if you do your basic mix in isolation, make sure you listen and adjust through a decent stereo speaker setup afterwards to spot any problems.

Mixing and equalization might sound like complex topics, but I'm not going to be getting too hard-core. This is the iPad after all; even complex sounding tasks are simple.

Working with Levels

Just like the faders you see in professional studios, GarageBand has its own set of volume controls for each track as well as the Master Volume slider at the top of the window. Like the Master Volume

FIGURE 16-1

The mixer controls for the Classic Clean track

FIGURE 16-2

A project set too loudly with distorted audio

slider, the volume slider on each GarageBand track shows a graphical representation of the track's current level to help you determine if an instrument is playing too loudly or too softly.

You can also control a track's volume from its mixer popover (see Figure 16-1; note that the mixer popover's name is that of the current track) for the selected track and, because it is wider than the volume sliders in the Tracks view, it is easier to control when making fine adjustments. Applying the same principle to levels as you do pan helps give prominence to the "main" instruments like vocals and drums but doesn't let them take over the mix and drown out your other instruments. Similarly, you don't want to have loud tracks set too high a level; otherwise, distortion can occur as shown in Figure 16-2.

The Difference between Wet and Dry

In musical terms, a dry track is one that sounds as it did when it was recorded. It is just the instrument with no effects or adjustments. Conversely, a wet track is one that has had effects applied. The general rule is to keep your tracks dry until editing and mixing your song rather than record with effects. And always keep a copy of a dry track in case the wet version doesn't turn out the way you wanted.

With GarageBand for iPad, you can flout these rules somewhat because a dry version of your track is always available. You see, everything you record in GarageBand is recorded dry by the app and stored. You can apply any effects you like to the sound but the dry version is always there for you to go back to apply alternative effects — even if you recorded with an effect applied.

The only time this won't work is if you use any external effects processors such as a guitar pedal that your guitar sound goes through before reaching the iPad. Likewise, any effects applied by external applications, rather than GarageBand: Recording effects in another app and then importing the track to GarageBand means that the effect cannot be removed or reversed when mixing.

Adjusting Pan

Pan is a sound's position in the stereo spectrum. Put more simply, pan determines whether you hear a sound on the left or right speaker and how far across it appears to be on either side. For example, if you play an instrument and shift the pan control from one extreme to another, it will sound as it is moving from left to right.

The pan control for instruments in GarageBand is a slider on the mixer popover for the selected track, accessed by tapping the Mixer button. By default, the Track Pan slider is set to the center position, but you can move it left or right to adjust the position of a particular instrument.

Panning can be helpful when mixing your project as it allows you to segregate your instruments so they don't all sit directly in the middle of the mix in one big blob of sound. Similar instruments — for example, those that have closely related or even identical sounds (say two piano or string parts) — should be the first instruments you separate, as they are more likely to get muddled.

More subtle sounds that could be lost beneath the drums and other loud instruments should also be moved to the side. But make sure that you don't shift too many instruments in one direction or you will end up with a lopsided mix that will sound odd and distract the listener.

As a rule, you should leave your vocals and drums as close to the center of the stereo spectrum as you can to keep them as the driving force of your track.

Reverb

Regardless of whether you know how it works, reverb can add real magic to your recordings and often makes instruments and vocals sound better than the original recording. In layman's terms, reverb (short for reverberation) is the sound remaining after the original sound has ended. Therefore the reverb effect in GarageBand adds the feeling of space to audio and can be a lifesaver when used on flat vocal parts. Although a little bit of reverb can go a long way to improving

♪ ETHEREAL EFFECTS

Listen to how echo and reverb affect the drum and piano parts in this four bar recording. Notice how the repeated notes and drum hits remain in time and the reverb effect adds a spacious feel to the whole recording. This type of effect is good for breakdowns or song intros.

your tracks and adding a more lifelike feel to smart instruments, too much reverb may have the opposite effect, so use it sparingly.

You access the Reverb Level control from the mixer popover for the instrument you have chosen, accessed by tapping the Mixer button. You can apply reverb to any instrument or loop you select.

Echo

This effect applies, as you would expect, an echo (delay) effect of varying intensity to the track you selected. The greater amount of echo you apply to an instrument, the louder and longer the echo lasts.

Echo can be put to good use with a wide range of instruments, from drums to keyboards. Try applying a decent amount of echo to a piano part and play a sequence of individual notes to create an atmospheric intro. Note that not all echo effects in GarageBand stick to the tempo of your song, so you may need to adjust the effect or time your notes so that they remain in time with the rest of your music and the beat itself.

Master Effects

If you would rather have GarageBand handle the effects for your song, there are built-in presets called Master Effects (see Figure 16-3) that you can apply and then control using the Reverb and Echo effects for individual tracks.

At the bottom of the mixer popover, tap Master Effects and then choose either Echo or Reverb from the Master Effects popover. Pick from one of the presets listed (shown in Figure 16-4) and then head back to the main mixer popover by tapping the Back button. Adjusting the Reverb and Echo levels on your tracks applies the Master Effect rather than the default Echo or Reverb settings. The Master Effects feature is a useful way to apply the same effect to all your tracks and create a coherent-sounding mix.

Mixing on a Computer

Although you can do a decent mixing job with the tools in GarageBand on the iPad, computer-based music software provides far more mixing options. If you are a Mac user, you have the benefit of exporting your project and opening it in GarageBand or Logic on your

FIGURE 16-3

The Master Effects popover

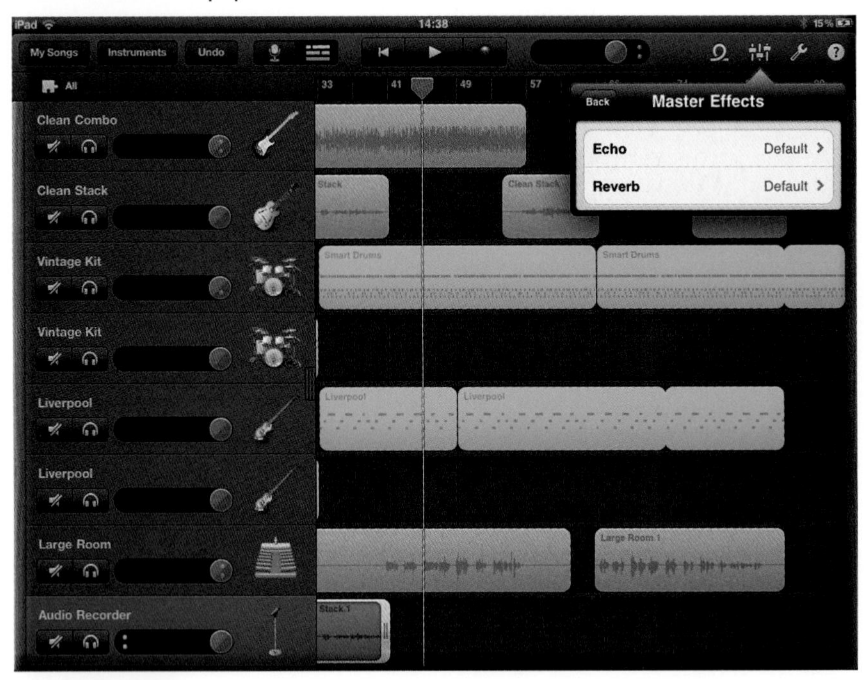

FIGURE 16-4

The Reverb settings in the Master Effects popover

Mac. PC users can also edit on the desktop, but to do so they must export the project's tracks one by one and then import them into their Windows music software.

If you intend to mix your project on either a Mac or a PC, it's best not to apply any mixing to your project before you export it. Keeping your tracks as dry as possible will make it easier to start mixing from scratch on your computer and avoids including effects you can't turn off or reduce once exported.

17

Exporting Your Project

There are a number of ways to extract your music from GarageBand, and how you export depends on the computer you use and the reason you are exporting your song. There are wireless and wired export routes, too, so even if you're not near a computer you can still share your song with the world. GarageBand offers features to help you stay on top of your bulging song library. This chapter looks at the ways you can share your music, send the project to a computer for further editing, and also how to label and track your projects in GarageBand.

Organizing Songs

Remember when you created your first project that you started in GarageBand's My Songs window? This space isn't just for creating new tracks. It's also where you name, import, share, delete, and duplicate your tracks.

The main part of the My Songs window allows you to swipe among all the GarageBand projects stored on your iPad. Tapping the name of the project allows you to rename it using the iPad's onscreen keyboard.

FIGURE 17-1

The My Songs window

Below the name of your project, at the bottom of the window, are four buttons to use with the project you have selected (see Figure 17-1): Share, Import, File, and Delete. Here's what they do:

Share button

Tapping the Share button (its icon is right-facing arrow in a box) provides two menu options (see Figure 17-2). The first is Send to iTunes; choose it to send the selected project to your computer via iTunes file sharing. When sending the file to iTunes, you get two export options: as an audio mix-down of the song or as a GarageBand project file.

The second option is Email Song and, you guessed it, this option adds your GarageBand project to a new e-mail. The song is mixed down as an audio file when you choose this option, and your iPad opens the Mail app with a new e-mail loaded that includes your song as an attachment. For a quick way to share your song with a friend or simply to yourself, this is your best bet.

FIGURE 17-2

GarageBand's Share menu

Import button

If you've sent GarageBand projects to your computer or someone has sent you a GarageBand for iPad project, you can import the project into GarageBand using the Import button (its icon is a down-pointing arrow in a tray).

You first have to load the files in iTunes on your computer by selecting your iPad in the iTunes Devices list in the Sidebar, then going to the Apps pane's File Sharing section, where you select GarageBand.

Click the Add button to select the files you want to import. Once the files have been added to the GarageBand file list in iTunes, GarageBand on the iPad can import them when you tap the Import button and choose the Copy from iTunes option.

File button

Tapping the File button (its icon is a + symbol inside a rectangle) opens a menu with two options. The first option allows you create a new song (that's about all you need to know) and the second allows you to duplicate an existing song. The duplicate feature is handy if you want to experiment with changes to a song but are worried about messing up the original. By duplicating the project and launching the copy, you can fiddle to your heart's content without fear or damaging your existing work.

Tip: Get in the habit of using the Duplicate menu option. There is no Save As feature in GarageBand, so you can't start working on a project and then decide you want to save your changes as a separate copy — you have to make that copy before you make any changes using the Duplication menu option.

Delete button

The Delete button (the trash can icon) is my least favorite button in GarageBand. Every song is a work in progress, so there is no reason to throw out an idea that you may want pick up and work on again. So don't use it — unless, of course, the song is truly terrible and you are running out of space on your iPad. Then, and only then, should you use the Delete button.

FIGURE 17-3

Renaming a project

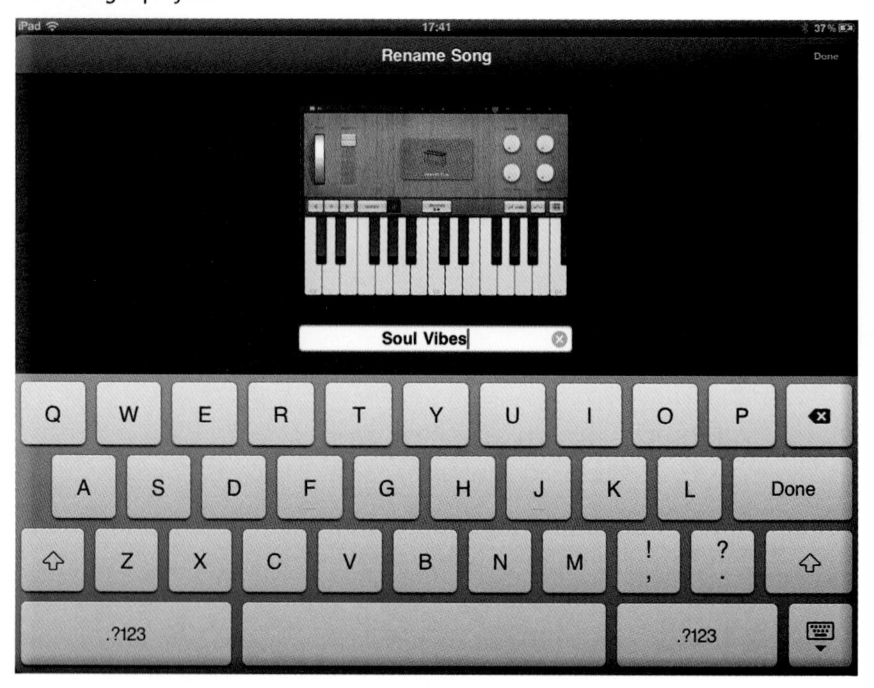

Renaming a project

If you want to apply a different title to your project other than GarageBand's default `My Song 01` convention, there's no button for that. Instead, simply tap the title of the project when in the My Songs window (see Figure 17-3). You can now enter a new name using the onscreen keyboard, which appears when you tap the project title.

Another Way Out

There is one other way to export your song from GarageBand, but it is not ideal. You can play your project on your iPad and record it by running a lead from your iPad's headphone jack to the line-in jack of a recording device or computer. The quality is likely to suffer using this method and, if you want to keep individual tracks, you need to record each track on its own. But it works in a pinch.

18

Advanced Techniques

Beyond the basics of making music with GarageBand, there are a handful of techniques that I hope will help when you reach a dead end in your project. If you find yourself thinking, "Oh, you can't do that in GarageBand," turn to this chapter before giving up. Most of the techniques in this chapter are actual features of GarageBand, but some require an additional app purchase or getting extra kit to make them work.

Although GarageBand is a great app, it has its limitations and this chapter is my attempt to break through those barriers and help you do more, even when traditional methods suggest you can't.

Importing Audio Files from E-mails

GarageBand has copy and paste features but there's no way to import a file sent to your iPad via e-mail. Of course, you could send that file back to your computer and use iTunes file sharing to send the sample to your iPad, but what about when your computer isn't available?

To get an audio file from your e-mail to GarageBand, you need an audio application capable of copy and paste. I tend to use Hokusai Audio Editor, which is free but requires an in-app purchase to access the copy and paste features. Here's how it works:

1. With Hokusai Audio Editor installed, tap and hold on an audio file in the Mail app to open the Open In menu and open it in Hokusai (see Figure 18-1).
2. Once the file is loaded, tap and hold on the waveform and drag across to select the entire sound.
3. Tap it again and choose More from the contextual menu that appears. Choose AudioCopy from the Effects menu to send the audio file to the iPad's Clipboard.
4. Head to GarageBand, add a new Audio Recorder instrument to the project you want to paste into, and tap the time line for the Audio Recorder track until a menu appears. Tap Paste to import the audio file from your e-mail.

Hokusai Audio Editor offers several other tricks as well as copy and paste, including splitting stereo tracks, so it's well worth the money and is a lifesaver when iTunes file sharing isn't an option.

FIGURE 18-1

Importing a song from the Mail app

Bouncing and Merging Tracks

There are many reasons why you might want to bounce (export) individual or groups of tracks from your GarageBand project. The first could be because you are running out of available tracks. By exporting a selection of tracks, say four drum tracks as a single audio file, and then reimporting them into your project as a single audio file, you free up three tracks in your project.

You might also want to share individual tracks with other GarageBand users directly from your iPad so they can add the tracks to their project, in which case bouncing tracks to the Mail app is an option. Here's how:

1. Select which tracks you want to export from your project. To do this, make sure you are in the Tracks view and tap the Mixer button at the top right of the window.
2. From the mixer popover, set Show Track Controls to On. Now, mute all the tracks you don't want exported by tapping the Mute button for each track.
3. Tap the My Songs button.

4. Tap the Share button (its icon is an arrow emerging from a rectangle) and choose to send your project to iTunes or via e-mail from its menu. The tracks are exported with only the unmuted tracks left.

You can re-import the exported tracks using the importing technique explained in this chapter.

Bouncing Tracks Manually

If you have an iRig (shown in Figure 18-2) or similar input device, there is a faster way to bounce multiple tracks into one track:

1. Connect your iRig or other device as normal but instead of connecting a guitar or other instrument, run a compatible cable from the line-in jack to the iPad's headphone jack. You could also use an adapter to convert your existing guitar lead.
2. In Tracks view, mute all the tracks you don't want to bounce using the Mute button on each track.
3. Now load a new Audio Recorder track and return to the Tracks view by tapping the View button.
4. Make sure your new Audio Recorder track is selected by tapping it.
5. Tap Record to play your unmuted tracks through the iRig, where they will be sent back to GarageBand and recorded on your new Audio Recorder track.

You need to make sure the levels are set correctly before recording to avoid any distortion, but this technique is a far faster way to combine tracks in GarageBand.

FIGURE 18-2

The iRig

Transposition

MIDI instruments, such as the Smart Piano and Keyboard, have additional controls in the mixer popover, one of which is Transposition (shown in Figure 18-3). Transposition is shifting a part up or down by a set amount, and in GarageBand you can move a part up or down by three octaves. This is a useful technique for creating harmonized parts.

Here's how to use this feature:

1. Start by duplicating an existing instrument track (any track with green regions on the time line) and copy and paste the region from the original track to the new track so that it is positioned at exactly the same point on the time line.
2. Select the duplicated track and choose Transposition from the mixer popover, accessed by tapping the Mixer button.
3. Move the part up or down as many octaves as you want and return to the Tracks view.

Your two tracks should now play in harmony, and you can change the instrument sound on the duplicate track for an even more diverse effect.

FIGURE 18-3

Setting GarageBand's Transposition control

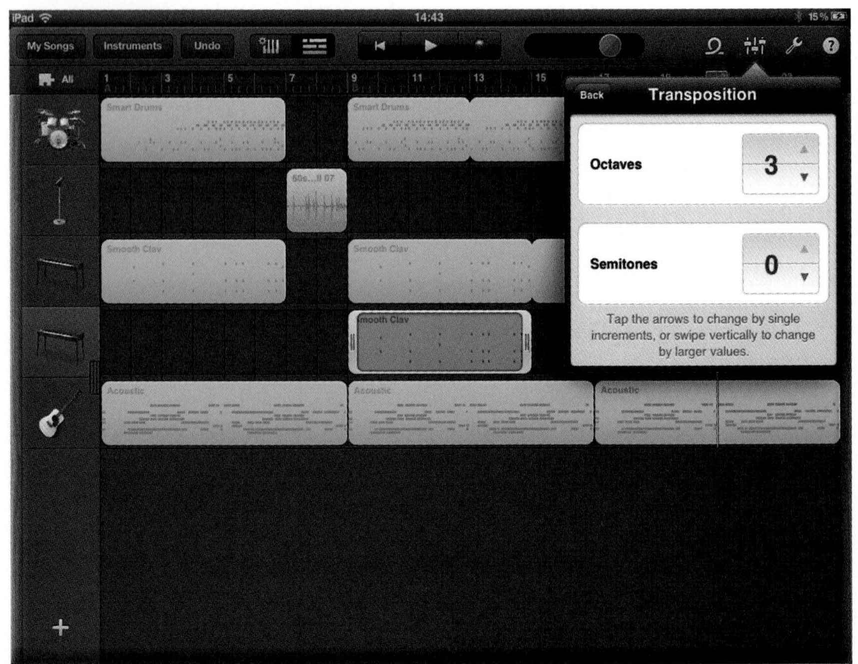

♪ TRANSPOSITION HARMONY

For the first four bars of this recording, a simple piano part plays on its own. Over the next four bars, two duplicate parts are added with the same pattern, with one transposed up an octave and the other down and octave. Notice how the three parts playing together fill the sound out and give the recording more depth.

Quantization

The Quantization setting in the mixer popover can be used with a range of MIDI instruments, including the Smart Piano and Drums instrument, and allows you to adjust the timing of recordings. Quantization can also create new and interesting rhythms from your existing tracks that may provide inspiration.

To apply quantization, select the track you want to adjust, tap the Mixer button, and then select Quantization from the mixer popover. Now choose the desired quantization settings. There is a wide range of quantization options available from 1/1 notes that set notes to play at the beginning of each bar to 1/4 notes, triplets, and more. There are even quantization options that include Swing, which makes your parts sound more realistic as their timing shifts by tiny amounts to simulate a real performance.

Not only can quantization help fix your dodgy timing when playing instruments but it can also help create new sounds from smart instrument patterns. Try experimenting with different quantization settings to mix things up in your project.

♪ QUANTIZED KEYS

You mainly want to quantize your drum parts to keep them in time, but listen to this clip to understand what quantization can do for keyboard notes as well. The first four bars of this part feature a simple electric piano part without quantization, whereas the second part has 1/4 note quantization applied.

FIGURE 18-4

Changing Smart Keyboard sounds

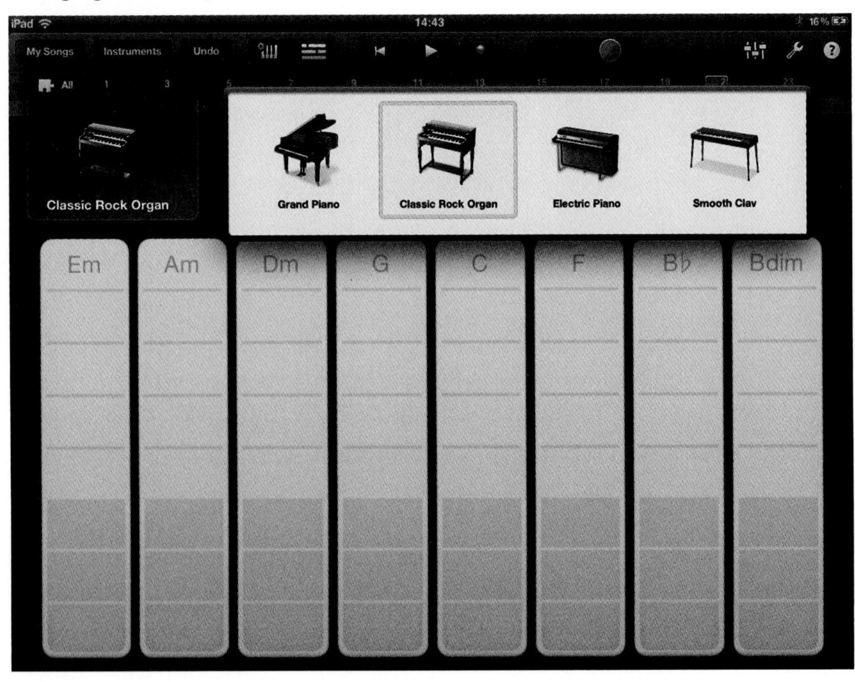

Create New Smart Instrument Patterns

Each smart instrument sound in GarageBand has its own set of patterns, but it is possible to mix and match patterns between different sounds; for example, a Rock Organ pattern that you think would sound better played on a Grand Piano.

To apply the pattern to a different instrument sound, simply record the part using the original instrument sound and then change the instrument's sound after recording (see Figure 18-4). The part uses the

♪ SWITCHED SMART PARTS

In this clip, you can hear the Smart Guitar instrument's acoustic guitar sound playing a picked pattern. This pattern isn't available for the Classic Clean sound but can be played through it by switching instruments after recording. Listen to the change for the final four bars.

new sound when you play your song or record. This technique works for all smart instruments, including Smart Drums and Smart Guitar.

PART

Your First Song

The first two parts of this book provide information and techniques to help you decide the best route to making music on your iPad. This part draws on what you have already learned to help you create your own song. From writing lyrics and picking chords to recording and sharing, I show you how to make a complete song using GarageBand, with each chapter a lesson that focuses on a single aspect of creating a song.

Even if you're a complete beginner to music or, at the very least, to digital music, this part's chapters will allow you to come away from this book with a piece of music that you created yourself.

I know I won't be able to please everyone here, especially if the song I'm about to show you how to create doesn't fit your preferred genre, but bear with me. Although I do look at specific chords and styles in this project, the basic techniques apply to most songs and genres, so you can tailor the project to your own requirements. I also highlight sections in the song where you might want to go a different way from what is described, using a real guitar over the Smart Guitar instrument, for example.

Not only does this part bring together the tips and techniques found in the earlier sections, but it will give you a feel for the entire process of writing, recording, and mixing a song on your iPad — I hope set you up for many more projects in the future.

To keep things simple, the track I have created for you to follow is a basic pop/rock piece with the traditional arrangement of bass, drums, guitar, vocals, and keyboards, with a few neat tricks thrown in along the way. Of course, once you've mastered this song, you can go on to use the techniques you've learned to make any genre of music you want and using whatever instruments you may own.

For now, let's take a look at the basics and start making a song together.

19

The Planning Stage

This first lesson is fun. Assign yourself a couple of hours — or at least a half hour — to simply listen to music. You could dig through your record collection, play songs from your iPad's music library (see Figure 19-1) or use one of the many music apps like Pandora, Spotify, or Rdio.

Find Inspiration

By listening to songs you love and artists you admire, you'll not only be spurred on to make your own song but you'll also be able to pick out just what you love about the music you listen to. Is it the way the guitar parts sound? Is it a unique vocal performance? Is it the mixing and overall production that brings you the most enjoyment?

Make a note of all the things you like about the music you listen to and also pay attention to how the music is put together. Discover whether a particular song follows a traditional verse, bridge, or chorus structure, or if it deviates to include a mixture of sections, breakdowns, and instrumental parts. It might sound like an obvious thing to do, or you may already have a clear idea of the song you want to write, but immersing yourself in music will definitely put your head in the right place before you begin working on a song.

Of course, the downside to this process is that you may inadvertently create a copy of a song you really love. This in itself isn't a bad thing. Re-creating an existing song can be just as valuable as writing your own in terms of learning and will set you up to create more original songs in the future.

Now that you have a feel for the music you're about to make, let's move on and start planning how it will sound.

Get Writing

Now let's go to the hands-on stage part of the planning process, where you can begin writing your lyrics and plotting chords and melodies for your song. The order for planning songs tends to differ from musician to musician: Some prefer to write the music first and add lyrics later, and others prefer the reverse. There's no hard-and-fast rule. For me, it's a combination of both: I tend to work on the chords and build vocal melodies to go with them as I work. From there, the lyrics begin falling into place.

FIGURE 19-1

Listening to music on the iPad

Using an app like Simple Song Writer (covered in Chapter 2) is a great way to plan chord progressions, and it's as easy as tapping a button to play a chord. If you intend to play a real instrument as part of your song, you can have Simple Songwriter display the chords you have chosen while you practice (see Figure 19-2).

You can plan chords with GarageBand by launching one of the smart instruments and experimenting with different sets of chords and listening to how they sound alongside each another.

In this chapter's project, you'll put together intro, verse, bridge, and chorus parts, so think about variations on your main chords and melodies to use in these sections, too. At the end of this process, you should have a basic chord progression for the intro and verses, as well as a different chord progression for your chorus and bridge parts. These could all be the same chords if you want, but your song runs the risk of becoming a little monotonous if the same series plays throughout.

You should also have your lyrics set in the same way (if, of course, you want your song to have lyrics), covering three to four verses, plus the bridge and chorus. Your bridge and chorus lyrics can be the

FIGURE 19-2

Plotting chords with Simple Song Writer

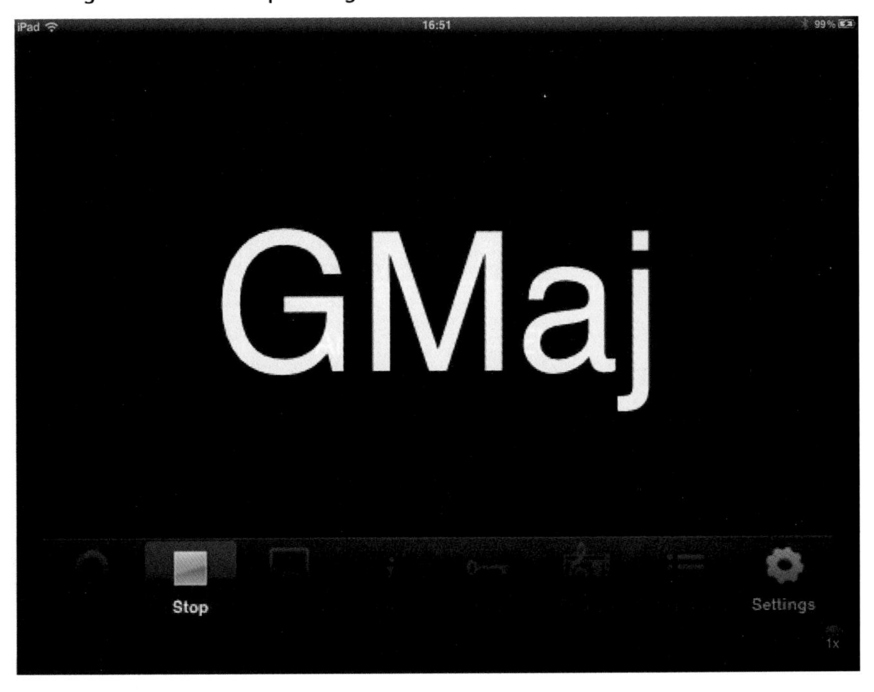

same if you want, or you could vary them as the song progresses. It's completely up to you.

You may want to handwrite your lyrics as you plan out your chords, but it's always best to have a digital copy as well. Not only does a digital copy provide you with a backup should you lose your handwritten version, but it also means you can print multiple copies and make changes more easily as you develop your song.

Tune Up

The project in this chapter uses GarageBand's smart instruments throughout, but I give you a nod at any point where you could use a real instrument instead. If you do intend to use a guitar or keyboard, or just record your own vocals, now's the time to make sure they're ready to record.

Some of the tuning tools such as Cleartune Chromatic Tuner mentioned in Chapter 3 help get your instruments in tune at this stage. It's also worth retuning to Cleartune after every other take to make sure you don't slip out of tune during recording.

FIGURE 19-3

Tuning in GarageBand

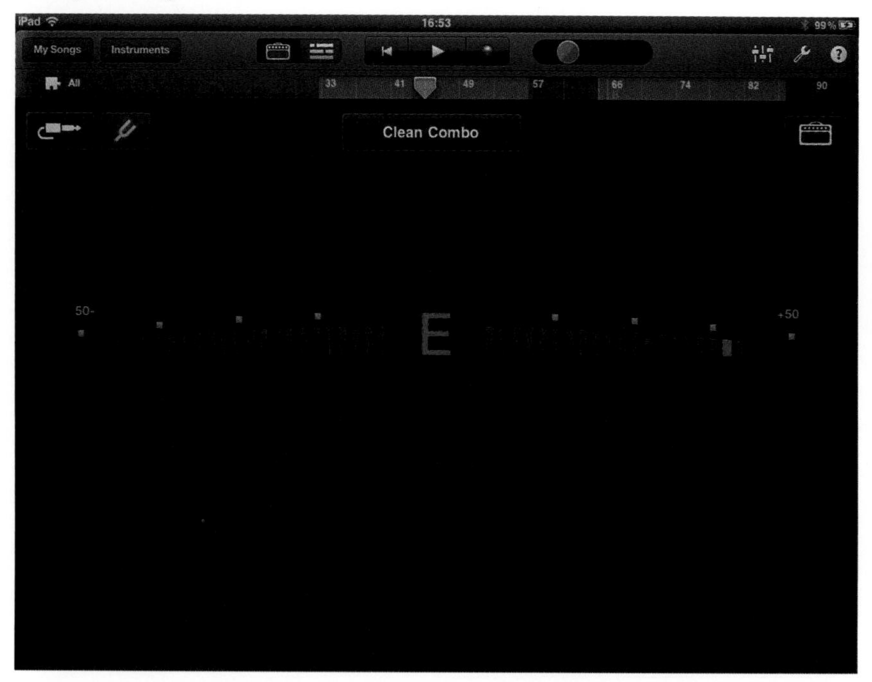

GarageBand's tuner can also help, especially for stringed instruments and you can access it from the Guitar Amp instrument (see Figure 19-3).

You should also begin to warm up your voice by singing a few scales, gently singing along to a favorite song, or anything you like to do to get your voice ready. There's nothing more disheartening than recording a vocal take without warming up your voice first and finding flat notes and off-key melodies when you listen back to it. You're also not doing your vocal chords any good by trying to belt out a tune without preparing. I also recommend avoiding caffeinated drinks and food before you begin recording vocals, as I find they tend to constrict the vocal chords more than normal and result in lesser vocal range and flexibility.

20

Set Up Your Project

Now it's time to bring GarageBand into the equation, if you haven't used it already. You need to determine individual sections in the Tracks view, as well as set the key and tempo of your song. All these settings can be changed at a later time, but it's worth deciding on them now so you have a solid base from which to work.

Bear in mind, however, that adjusting the tempo at a later stage may cause problems if you have recorded live instruments or vocal tracks. Unlike its desktop sibling, GarageBand for iPad can't adjust the tempo of recorded tracks and therefore a shift in the song's speed will mean everything around the MIDI tracks change while the live vocal or instrument recordings stay the same. This could mean your chorus vocals start in the middle of the bridge section or begin long after the chorus section has already begun. That's why I've left the vocals as the last section to record, so you can make changes to the tempo before you've committed to vocal recordings.

The same consideration applies to recorded guitar parts and bass parts, too, so if you opt to use a real instrument over a smart instrument, keep in mind that adjusting the tempo won't be a realistic option once you've laid down these parts.

Make Minor Adjustments

When it comes to recording your instruments, make sure everything is in time and that you are prepared before a recording begins. To ensure that you are in time with the instruments, you need to turn the metronome on as well as set it to count you in. You can apply both settings from the Song Settings popover, accessed by tapping the Song Setting button (the wrench icon) at the top right of the window. Simply move the switches for both the Metronome and Count-In settings to On (as shown in Figure 20-1) and, if you want, tap the Sound button to pick the type of sound of the metronome.

Define Song Sections

To make things easier when recording your individual tracks, it's best to plan out your song's sections first, even before you start adding instruments and loops. For the project in this chapter, I've used a simple format shown in Figure 20-2: an eight-bar intro, an eight-bar

FIGURE 20-1

Metronome settings

FIGURE 20-2

A GarageBand project divided into song sections

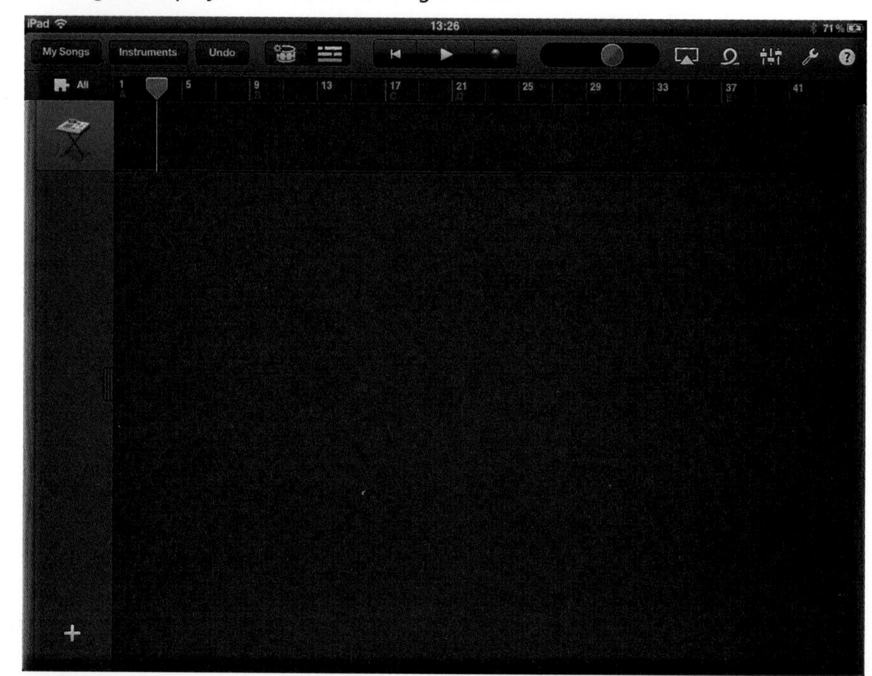

verse, a four-bar bridge, a 16-bar chorus, two more eight-bar verses, another four-bar bridge, and two more 16-bar choruses.

By setting a section for each part of your song, you can quickly jump to the part you want using the Song Sections popover as well as make sure you record only in these sections. Breaking the song into sections also gives you the option to quickly increase or decrease the number of bars in a particular section as well as move the bars to different positions in your project.

Breaking the song into sections can come in handy should you decide to add another verse or chorus to your song at the last minute, as moving a section shifts all the instrument parts in the section to the new position.

To speed the process, add just one section for each part of the song to begin with. That's one intro, one verse, one bridge, and one chorus. To avoid having to record them again for each section, use the Song Sections' duplicate feature to add the remaining sections once you have recorded some instruments.

To create and arrange song sections, do as follows:

1. Launch GarageBand and create a new song project from the My Songs window. You are asked to pick an instrument so, as you'll be working with drums in Chapter 21, select the Smart Drums instrument by swiping across the screen until the Smart Drums image is in the center and then tapping on it.
2. When the Smart Drums window appears, tap the View button to the left of the transport controls to move to Tracks view. Tap the Song Sections button below the My Songs button. By default, an eight-bar section has already been added. You will be using this as your intro.
3. Tap the Add Song button (the + icon) in the Song Sections popover to add a new section, Section B. This will be your verse section. Again, this has a default eight-bar setting, so it doesn't need to be adjusted. Tap the Add Song button again to create Section C, your bridge part.
4. For the bridge, you want to use only four bars, so tap the arrow on the Song Sections popover next to Section C and tap the down-arrow stepper controls on the next popover to change the number of bars to four. Next tap the Song Sections button at the top left of the popover.
5. Tap the Add Song button again to create Section D and then tap the arrow next to Section D on the popover. Change the

number of bars to 16 for your chorus part using the up-arrow stepper control on the Length of Section D popover that appears.

Set the Key and Select Chords

During your planning, you will have a selection of chords to use in your project. You now need to set the key for your GarageBand project to make sure all these chords are available when playing smart instruments. The easiest way is to make a list of the chords you want to use and then launch a smart instrument. The Smart Guitar and Smart Keyboard are best for this process.

By default, a GarageBand project is set in the key of C major with the default chords E minor, A minor, D minor, G, C, F, B sharp, and B diminished available. Changing the key, however, provides a different set of chords and helps you pick out the chords you want to include in your song. Changing the key affects all smart instruments in your project, and each uses the same set of chords.

In some situations, you may have to compromise, as some of chords you have chosen might not be available. In this case, you either need to adjust your chord selection or find the nearest chord to the one you wanted to use as a replacement. For the song here, I have kept the default C major key.

Tip: To use a physical keyboard or guitar in your project instead of smart instruments, your chord selection isn't quite as important, as you can play any chord on your chosen instrument. You do, however, need to make sure that any smart instruments you use in your project can play the same chords, or they won't be able to match the chords of your real instrument.

To set your project's key:

1. Load the Smart Guitar, Smart Bass, or Smart Keyboard instrument by tapping the Instruments button at the top left of the window.
2. If none or only some of the chords you intend to use are listed on the instrument's chord strips, you need to adjust the key to find a better option. Tap the Settings button (the wrench icon) at the top right of the window.
3. From the Settings popover, tap the Key section and change the root note using the buttons at the top of the Key popover, and change to a major or minor key using the buttons below (see

FIGURE 20-3

Setting a song's key

Figure 20-3). The chords on your smart instrument update accordingly.

4. When you find a key that includes all the chords you want to use, tap anywhere on the smart instrument's window to close the Key popover and keep the key you require set. This affects all other smart instrument you have loaded, too.

Set the Tempo

From the planning stage, you no doubt have an idea of the speed you want for your song. Although rock songs normally sit in the 100 beats-per-minute (bpm) range, ballads are around 90 bpm — or even lower. Dance songs can be anywhere upwards of 120 bpm. If you don't know the precise tempo you are looking for, try humming your song (or playing it on your instrument) and play at a comfortable speed. If you can establish how quickly four beats would be counted between chord changes (try actually counting to four between chords), you can tap your tempo into GarageBand and the app will figure out the tempo for you (see Figure 20-4).

FIGURE 20-4

Tapping to set a tempo

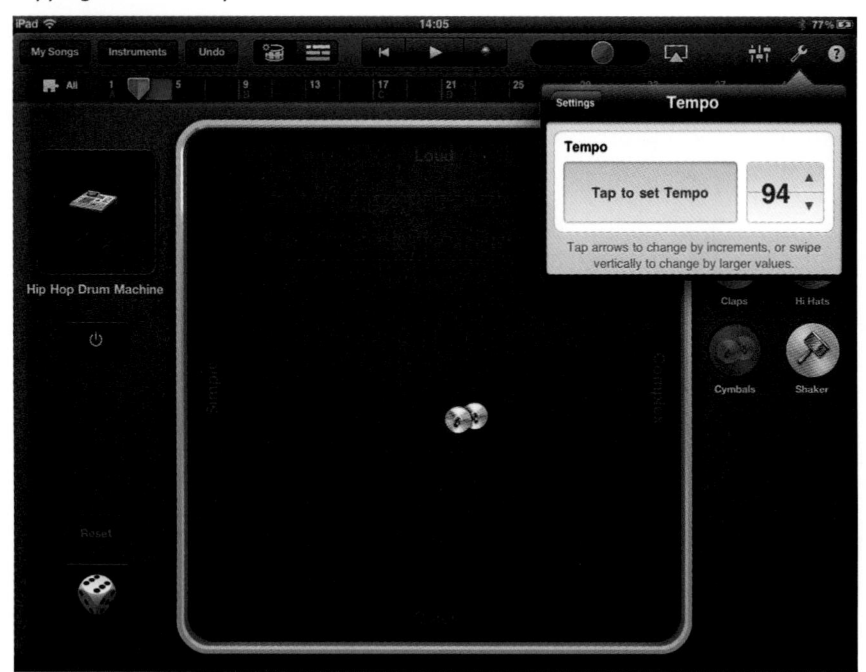

In this lesson, I'm working with a standard 110 bpm, so if you don't want to fiddle with the tempo just yet, leave it as it is.

To find your song's tempo:

1. Tap the Settings button at the top right of the window and then tap on the Tempo option to show the Tempo settings.
2. Tap on the Tap to Set Tempo button in patterns of four beats at a speed you feel is comfortable. This should be the same speed that four beats pass between chord changes when you practice or hum your song.
3. As you tap your beat, the tempo rate increases or decreases accordingly. Continue to tap your beat until the figure levels off between one or two beats per minute. This will be the tempo of your track.
4. If you need to make adjustments to the tempo, use the up and down stepper controls in the Tempo popover to shift the tempo up or down by one beat at a time.

21

The Beat

Now that the basics of your song have been put together, you're ready to start adding instruments to the song, starting with the drum section. I use the Smart Drums instrument in this chapter's lesson but you're free to record a drum part using the Audio Recorder instrument if you prefer. (For more information on how to record a live drum part, head back to Chapter 10.)

In this lesson, I describe each part of the drum track, how to record an intro beat, vary the drum pattern between verse and chorus sections, and how to add a drum fill loop for added realism.

The Intro

As the song begins, the drum part should be introduced slowly rather than hitting the listener right away. Some songs benefit from getting right into the rhythm from the offset, but this lesson's method of gradually building the drums in the intro gives room for other instruments to setup the song.

1. Start by loading a Smart Drums instrument if you haven't already, and select the sound you want to use. I use the Live Rock Kit in this chapter, if you want to follow the project exactly.
2. Tap the Song Sections button below the My Songs button and choose Section A. The time line above the Smart Drums instrument window now shows only the eight bars in Section A.
3. You want the drum intro to build slowly, so add a single hi-hat to the grid about half way down and slightly to the left so that it is fairly quiet and plays a simple beat. You can adjust the position of the hi-hat on the grid if you want a different style.
4. Tap the Record button and let the hi-hat you have added play until the playhead reaches the end of the fourth bar.
5. Next, drag a snare drum to the top of the grid a little to the left, followed by a kick drum and cymbals a bar or two later (see Figure 21-1).
6. The result is a slowly building drum intro over four bars. If you don't like the way your intro develops, you can tap the Undo button next to the View button and record the part again.

FIGURE 21-1

Drum intro positioning

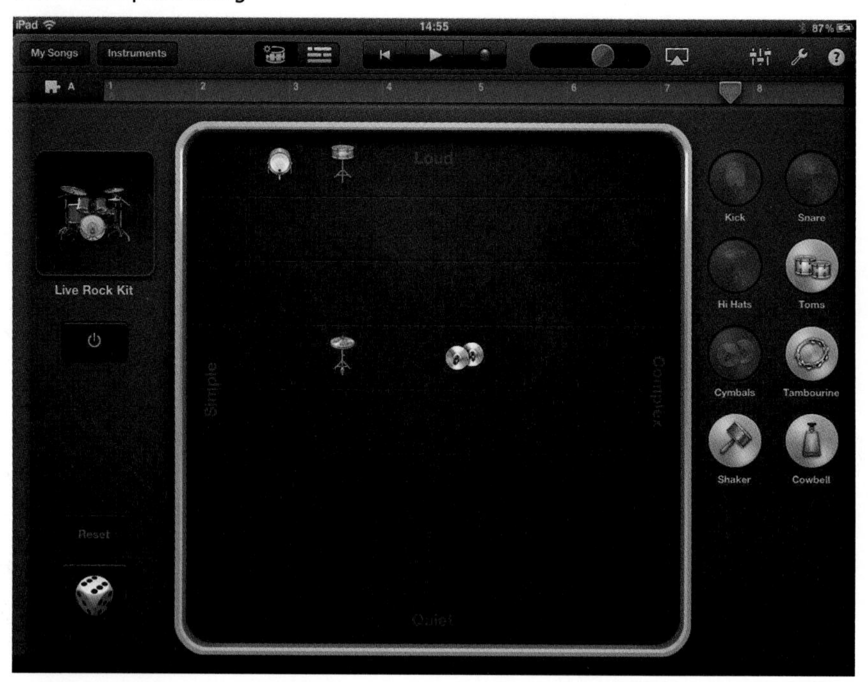

The Verse

Now it's time to add the main drum section of your song, the verse pattern. Ideally, this will sound the same as the last couple bars of your intro section so that the two flow together neatly without too much of a change when the verse starts.

The easiest way to make a seamless transition is to copy the position of your drum instruments at the end of the intro part and apply them to your verse drum part. The verse drum section then plays the same pattern over eight bars until it reaches the bridge.

1. Tap the Song Sections button below the My Songs button and tap on Section B. This loads only your verse section. Tap the Power button on the bottom left of the Smart Drums window.
2. Now drag all the drums used in your intro drum section to the grid in the same positions as before. If you need to refer back to your original drum part so you can remember where the drums were positioned, use the Song Sections button to load Section A before moving back to Section B.

FIGURE 21-2

The verse drum part in Tracks view

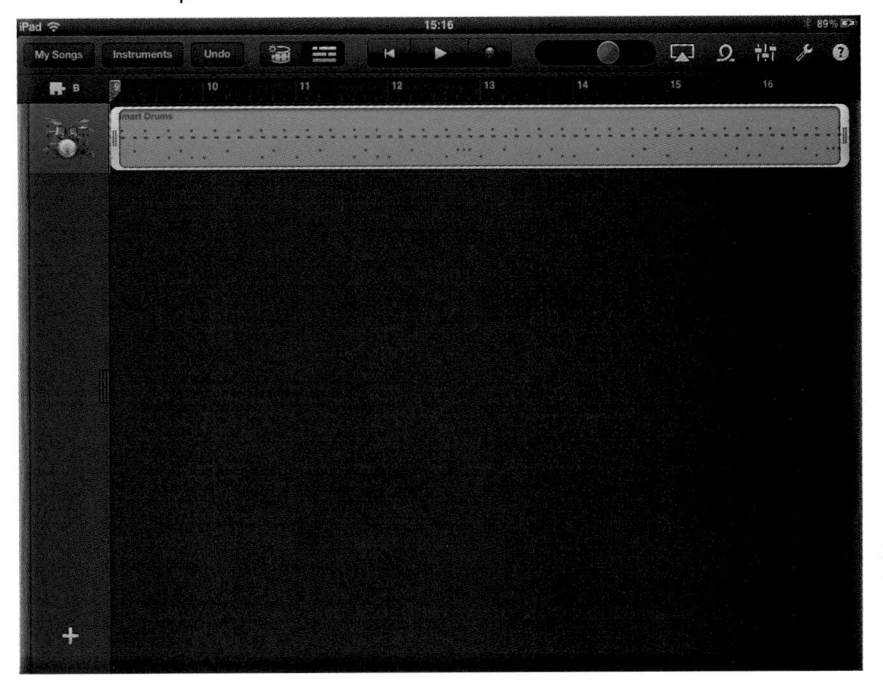

3. Tap the Record button and let your drum pattern play for 16 bars. This records all the drums you have added to the grid to create your verse drum pattern (see Figure 21-2).

The Bridge

With the intro and opening verse drum parts recorded, it's time to move to the bridge section. Here, you're going to use a drum fill loop as well as the Smart Drums instrument to spice things up a little as the song heads into the chorus. The bridge shouldn't sound drastically different to the verse drum part, if at all, but the addition of a loop to lead into the chorus pattern adds a more professional feel to your song.

1. Tap the Song Sections button and select Section C, your bridge section. Now tap the Power button at the bottom left of the Smart Drums window. Drag the drums you used in the verse part to the grid in the same positions as before.
2. If you want to tweak your drum part for the bridge, try removing some drums or adding some more subtle sounds such as a shaker or tambourine part.

3. Now tap the Record button and let your pattern record across the four bars of Section C.
4. Tap the View button to move to the Tracks view and then tap the Loops button next to the Mixer button. On the popover that appears, tap Instrument and select All Drums from the Instruments list before tapping the Apple Loops button to return to the Apple Loops popover.
5. Tap Descriptors and then tap the Fill button from the Descriptors popover. Tap the Apple Loops button again and sample the selected loops from the list at the bottom of the popover by tapping to preview them.
6. When you find a fill you want to use (I used Crowd Groove Fill 07 in my song), tap and drag the loop's name from the popover to the Tracks view below your Smart Drums track.
7. Position the loop on the last bar of Section C below your Smart Drums track where a new track will be created. Now tap the Smart Drums region on the time line to select it and use the handle on the right of the region to reduce the size of the

FIGURE 21-3

The bridge drum fill loop and bridge Smart Drum region

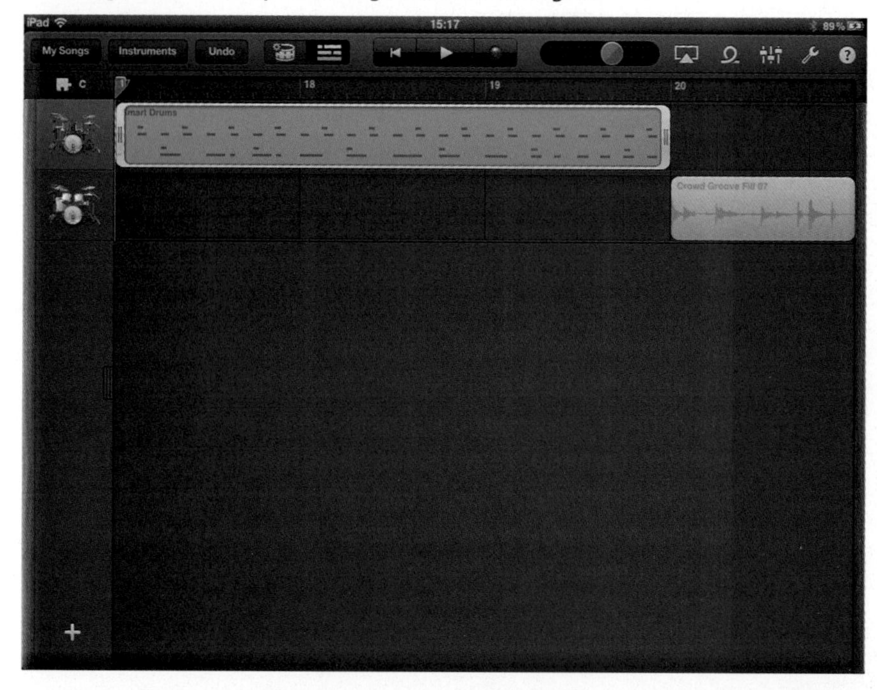

region by one bar. The Tracks view should now look like Figure 21-3.

Tip: The loop added to the bridge section is a waste of a track given that it only plays a couple of times in the song. If you want to free up that track by combining all your drum tracks into one, head back to Chapter 18 and check out the section on bouncing (exporting) tracks from GarageBand.

The Chorus

Now to the chorus, the last of your drum sections for now. This part should be slightly different from your existing verse and bridge drum parts to highlight for the listener the change from verse to chorus. Using a different beat also enlivens the chorus and makes it stand out from the rest of the song, as it should. Of course, you don't want the chorus to be too radically different or you could risk losing the overall feel of your song and confusing the listener, but mixing things up a bit certainly helps.

Here's how to adjust and record your chorus drum pattern:

1. Tap the Song Sections button and select Section D, your chorus section. If you're not already in it, move to the Smart Drums instrument window by tapping the View button.
2. At this stage, it's worth experimenting with your drum part for a different feel during the chorus. To try random patterns, tap the Randomize button (the die icon) at the bottom left of the screen. You can always add new drum sounds to these patterns as you go.
3. For a little more emphasis on your chorus drum part, move some of the main drum sounds — the kick and snare drum, for example — to the top of the grid so they are at their loudest.
4. When you're happy with your chorus pattern, tap Record to apply this pattern to the 6 bars of your chorus section.

Final Checks

Now you have recorded all your drum sections, it's worth checking to make sure all looks as it should. Your project should now include two tracks: the Smart Drums instrument and an Audio Recorder track with your drum fill loop on. Smart Drums regions should appear in Sections A through D. Tap the Song Sections button and then tap All

FIGURE 21-4

Intro, verse, bridge, and chorus Smart Drums regions in Sections A through D

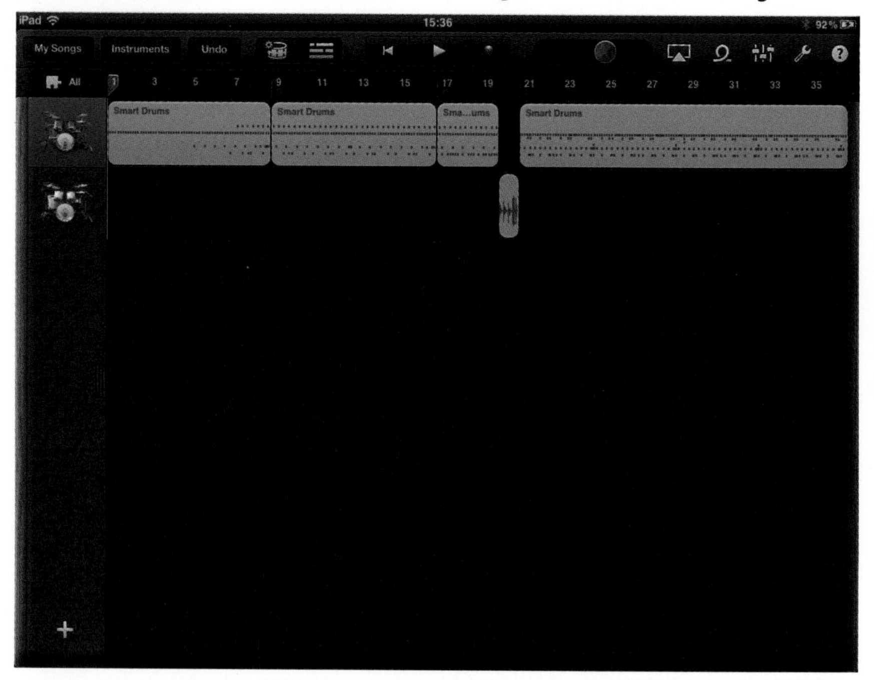

Sections to see all your recordings and sections when in Tracks view. It should look like the setup in Figure 21-4.

Tip: If you want to record your own drum parts using a MIDI drum kit or keyboard, you can follow the same steps for the intro, verse, bridge, and chorus in this chapter but record them yourself rather than using the Smart Drums instrument.

22

The Bass Line

With the drumbeat in place, next comes the most important part of your song's rhythm section. The bass provides the musical background to your song and, for an easier ride, I use the Smart Bass instrument in this lesson to create these sections. You are, as always, free to use the Guitar Amp instrument to record bass parts if you want. I also use the same chords for the bass sections as I do in the other smart instrument sections in later chapters, so if you have chords planned out already for the verse, bridge, and chorus sections go ahead and use them as you record your bass parts.

The Intro

It will be easiest to use the same chords in your bass intro part as you do in the verse sections, as doing so sets up the chord progression before you reach the main body of the song. You are, however, free to use any bass notes or chords you want. In this section, I show you how to record your bass intro part using the Smart Bass instrument and an Autoplay pattern.

1. Start by loading a Smart Bass instrument into your project by tapping the Add Instrument button (the + icon) at the bottom left of the window. The instrument is below your drum tracks in the Tracks view.
2. In the Smart Bass window that appears, pick a bass sound by tapping the large button at the top right of the window (I used the Liverpool sound in my song) and then tap the Song Sections button and choose Section A, your intro section.
3. From here, you can use either chords or notes via the Chords/Notes switch. Using Chords is the easiest option as it allows you to use Autoplay patterns. Set the Autoplay pattern by sliding a finger across the Autoplay knob at the top of the window. In my song, I set the Autoplay knob to position two.
4. Select the chords you want to use for the intro and tap the chord strip for your opening chord.
5. Tap the Record button and play your chords in sequence across the eight-bar intro by tapping the desired chord strips in time with the beat. I used two chords in my intro, A minor and G, alternately every two bars. See Figure 22-1 for a rough idea of how it should look.

FIGURE 22-1

The Smart Bass and Smart Drums intro regions

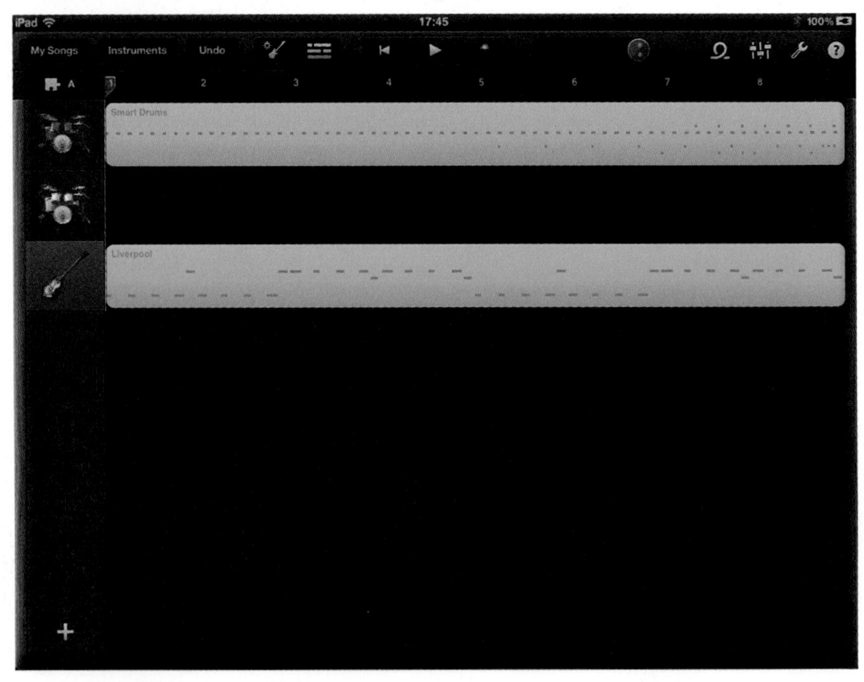

The Verse

For a smooth transition between intro and verse, it's best to continue with the same set of bass chords you used in the intro part. You may have other ideas for this section but if you want to take the easy route for now, I suggest using the same pattern and chords as I have with my song. Should you decide to use the same chords, recording the verse part is essentially the same process as recording the intro section. But if you want to use different chords, you should play them during this recording stage.

1. Tap the Song Sections button and then tap on Section B, your verse section. Tap the View button to move to the Smart Bass instrument if it isn't displayed.
2. Tap the Record button and tap the chord strips in time to add your bass patterns across the eight-bar verse. If you want to copy my song, I used the Liverpool Smart Bass sound with the Autoplay knob at position two (see Figure 22-2). The chords are the same alternating A minor and G as in the intro.

FIGURE 22-2

Recording the Smart Bass verse part

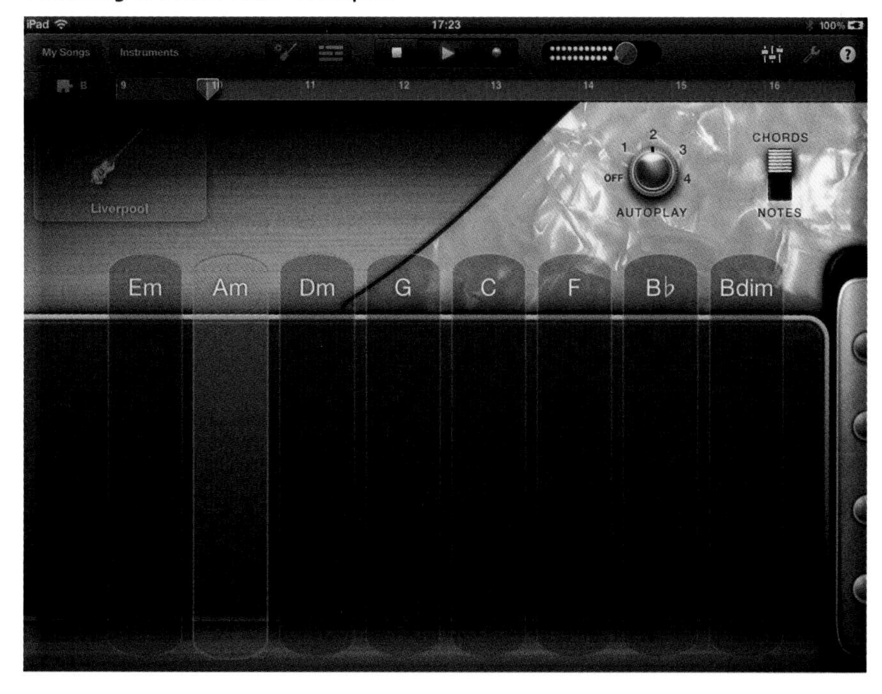

3. Tap the Record button again to stop the recording and tap the Play button to listen to your recording.

The Bridge

As with the drum section, the bass bridge section needs to provide a lead into the chorus, and a slight change of chords will do just that. Using the same pattern, but with different chords, suggests to the listener that a change is coming and also fits with the other instruments playing alternate bridge chords that you'll add in the next few chapters.

1. Tap the Song Sections button and then choose Section C, your bridge section, to restrict the time line to just that section.
2. If it's not shown already, switch the view to the Smart Bass instrument with the View button and then tap the Record button.
3. Record your bridge bass chords using the chords strips across the four bars of the bridge. In my song, I play F for two bars, E minor for one bar, and G for the final bar.

The Chorus

The chorus, like the drum section, should also involve a change in pattern to make it stand out from the rest of the song. Fortunately, this is easy to do using the Smart Bass instrument's Autoplay knob. The chords for the chorus should also be different and match those that you chose when you planned your song earlier.

In this section, you record a new bass section with a different pattern and different chords to provide the backing to our chorus. When you are done recording your chorus section, tap the Song Sections button and then tap All Sections before moving to the Tracks view using the View button. Your time line should look something like that in Figure 22-3.

1. Tap the Song Sections button and then choose Section D. This is your chorus section. Use the View button to move to the Smart Bass instrument if you're not already using it.
2. Change the Autoplay setting to a new pattern by dragging a finger across the Autoplay knob at the top of the window. In my song, I set the Autoplay knob to pattern one.

FIGURE 22-3

The Smart Drums and Smart Bass sections from intro to chorus

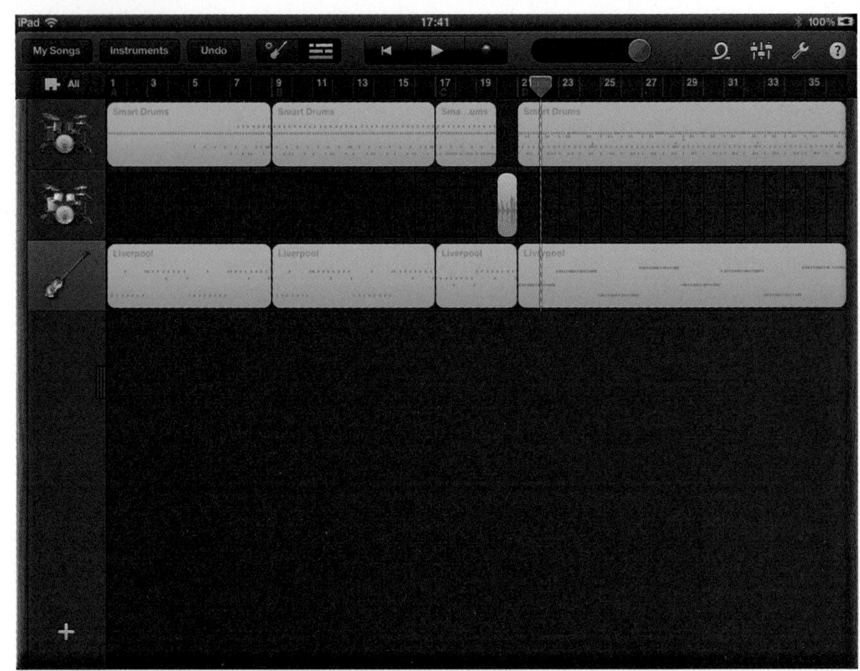

♪ DRUM AND BASS SECTIONS

Listen to this clip to hear how my project sounds after the drum and bass sections have been recorded. If you're following my chords and instruments, listen for any differences and head back to the relevant chapters to fix any issues you may have.

3. Tap the Record button and use the chord strips to play your chorus chords over the 16 bars of the chorus section. I use C, G, A minor, and F in my song, repeating the progression twice, as shown in Figure 22-3.

How Does It Sound?

With the drum and bass sections complete for now, you should have the beginnings of a song put together on your iPad. If you're following the chords, instruments, and settings I'm using, you can listen to the audio sample in the sidebar to hear how your song should be sounding right now. If not, now would be a good time to check your song anyway. Tap the Song Sections button and then choose All Sections before playing back your entire song to check how it's sounding so far.

23

The Rhythm

Now it's time to add another driving force to your song: a rhythm guitar, keyboard, or both. For this lesson, I opted to add a rhythm guitar section to my song as well as a rock organ to provide a bit more color to the chord progressions. As with the bass and drum instruments, you'll add these parts section by section and use the chords you chose in the planning stage to start putting some meat on the bones of the song.

The Intro

It's best not to introduce your main instruments too early in your song, which is why I've left out the rhythm guitar section from the intro. Feel free to add a guitar part to your intro if you want. Instead, I've added a very subtle rock organ part the plays along with the bass line and introduces the chord progression before I reach the rhythm guitar during the first verse. Here's how to add the organ part to your intro:

1. Add a new Smart Keyboard instrument to your project by tapping the Instruments button and swiping until you reach the Smart Keyboard. Tap it to load it.
2. Choose a sound using the large button to the left of the window (I used Classic Rock Organ) and adjust any settings you believe would work with your project. I set the organ's rotation to fast, for example.
3. Tap the Song Sections button and choose Section A to load your intro section.
4. Tap Record. Play chords using the chords strips across the eight bars of the intro. Again, I used A minor and G alternately every two bars, playing the section third from the bottom of each chord strip to play bass notes. The end result should look like that in Figure 23-1.

The Verse

Now it's time to introduce a guitar part as well as the organ that was already played as part of the intro. The guitar part should use the same chords you chose at the planning stage, the same chords that your bass part has been playing for each section. The organ also returns and effectively plays the same part throughout the verse as it did during the intro.

FIGURE 23-1

The organ intro part

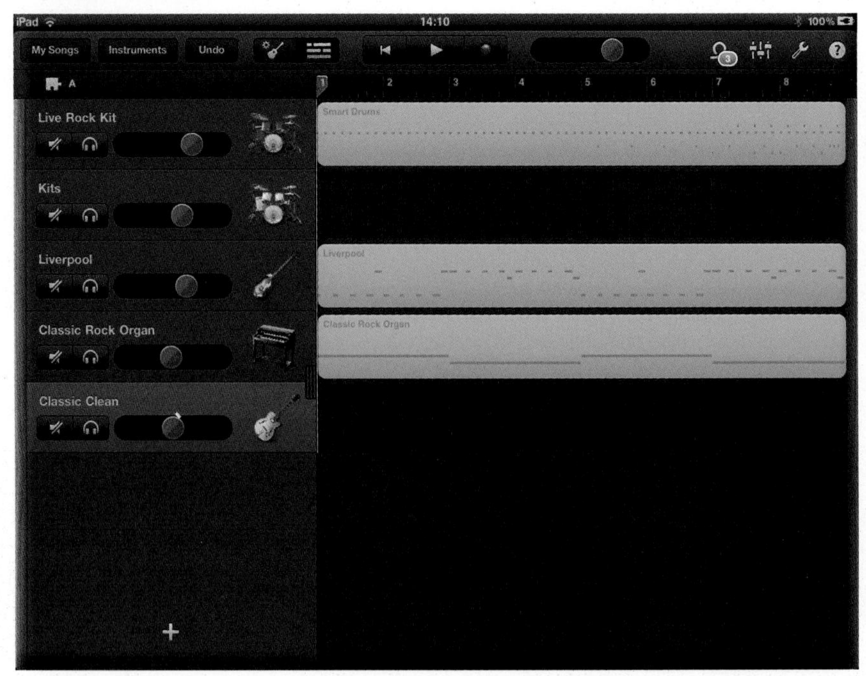

Here's how to add the organ and guitar part. The process is the same for both instruments, so you just to repeat the following steps for each instrument:

1. Either select the Smart Keyboard instrument to add the organ part or add a new Smart Guitar instrument to your project from the Instruments menu.
2. If you are using the Smart Guitar, load a sound using the large button to the left of the window and set an Autoplay pattern. I used the Classic Clean sound with the Autoplay knob at position four. If you are recording the organ, keep the settings the same as for the intro.
3. Tap the Song Sections button and choose Section B, your verse part.
4. Tap the Record button and play your chords across the eight bars of the verse (see Figure 23-2). For both the Smart Guitar and Smart Keyboard organ part, I again used the alternating A minor and G pattern.

FIGURE 23-2

The organ and guitar verse parts

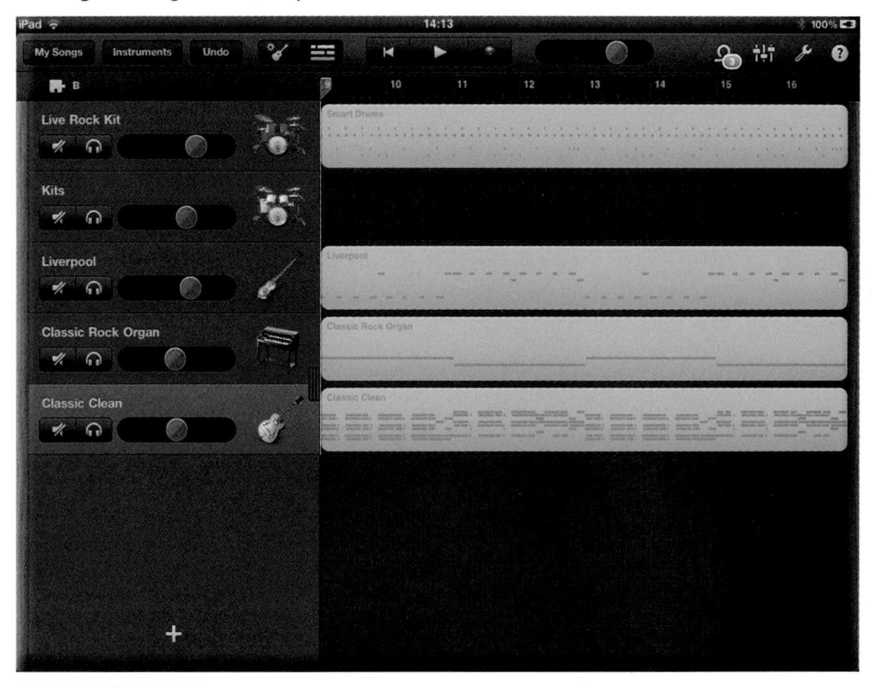

The Bridge

Now for a quick change of chords for both the organ and guitar parts as the song reaches the bridge. The chords should follow the same progression you used with your bass part for the bridge; both the organ and guitar parts will drive the song through to the chorus where the chords change again.

As before, recording the Smart Keyboard organ part and the Smart Guitar part are identical processes aside from choosing the instrument you want to record in the first step. But I have shifted the organ chords up by one section on the chord strip (the fourth section from the bottom) to add a little more weight to the bridge. Let's record a bridge part:

1. Tap and hold the View button and select either the Smart Guitar instrument or the Smart Keyboard instrument depending on which instrument you want to record first.
2. Tap the Song Sections button and then choose Section C to load your bridge part.

FIGURE 23-3

The organ and guitar bridge parts

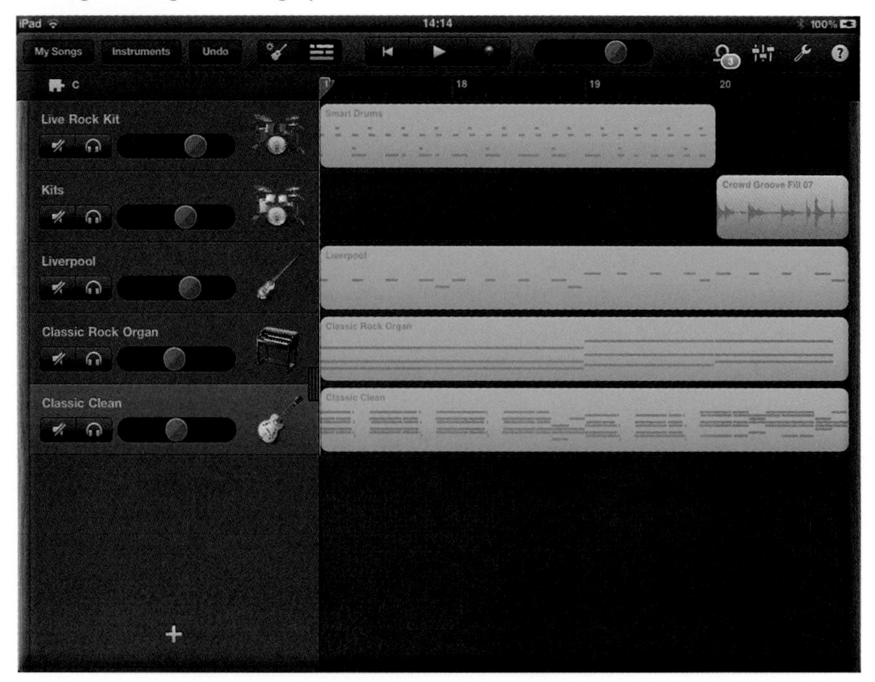

3. Make a note of the chords you use for the bridge (the same chords your bass part uses) and tap the Record button.
4. Play the chords you have chosen across the four bars of the bridge to add them to the time line. For both the organ and guitar parts, I used the same F, E minor, G progression used for the bass bridge part.
5. When you are done recording, repeat steps 1 through 4 with your other rhythm instrument. The final recordings should look like Figure 23-3

The Chorus

Like the bass and drum parts, things need to change for the guitar and organ parts during the chorus. You should already have picked out the chords you want to use; they're the same chords you used for the bass part in the chorus section.

I also adjusted the chord sounds for the organ part during my chorus and used the full chords (tapping the top of the chord strip) rather than the bass notes for a more punchy and dynamic rhythm

FIGURE 23-4

Recording the chorus guitar part

across the chorus. Here's how to record both the organ and guitar chorus parts:

1. Load either your Smart Guitar or Smart Keyboard part by tapping and holding the View button and selecting it from the list of available instruments that appears.
2. Tap the Song Sections button and tap on Section D to load your chorus section. Make a note of the chords you are about to play and tap the record button.
3. Play your chorus chords across the 16 bars of the chorus (see Figure 23-4). If you're following my song, you'll be using the progression C, G, A minor, F, and will repeat the progression after eight bars.
4. When you're done recording, repeat the process with your other smart instrument, either the organ or guitar part, depending on which you recorded first.

Tip: As with the other instruments, recording a real instrument such as a guitar or keyboard is fine at this stage, too. You can use the Keyboard instrument or the Guitar Amp instrument to add any of these

FIGURE 23-5

Guitar and organ across all sections

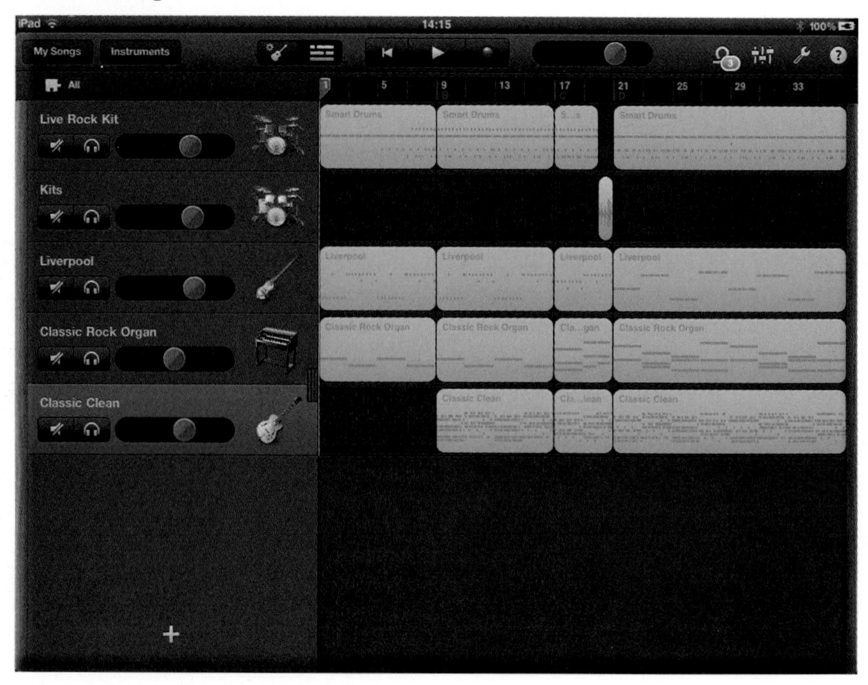

rhythm parts to your sections using the chords you want as long as they match the bass chords you've already added.

How Does It Sound?

Now that the organ and guitar parts have been added, your song should be taking shape. Listen to the audio clip in the sidebar to hear how my project sounded after I added these rhythm instruments across

♪ DRUM, BASS, ORGAN, AND GUITAR

Here's how my song sounded once the rhythm guitar and organ were added across all the sections. Notice the changes in the organ chords, starting with a subtle background note and progress to full chords in the bridge and chorus sections.

each section and check that your song is shaping up in the same way. It should look the same as Figure 23-5 when you are in the Tracks view.

24

The Lead

Here comes the fun part of the lesson: recording your lead instrument. A stage in the recording where you can let your creativity flow, improvise, and put together a dynamic section that runs throughout your song. You're free to choose the instrument you use as your lead; it could be a piano, keyboard, organ, or even a synth, or you could go down the same route I did and opt for the traditional lead guitar.

Recording this section is a little less structured than those before it, and you can choose whether to record your lead in sections, which might help the structure and editing, or record in one long take throughout your entire song. If you do intend to record your whole lead part in one go, it might be best to hold off recording it until you have extended your sections and mixed your project so that you won't have to re-record the lead section should you make any changes to the order of your sections or chords in your song.

Also, if you don't believe you have the required chops to record a lead section, you can always use one the Autoplay patterns on a smart instrument to add a simple lead part. Guitar parts with picked notes would be ideal in that case.

Recording the Lead

Here's how to record the lead part in sections:

1. Add a new instrument to your project by tapping on New Instrument button (the + icon) at the bottom left of the window. This could be a keyboard, Guitar Amp instrument, or Smart Guitar instrument. Here, I use the Smart Guitar instrument and the Hard Rock sound.
2. Tap the Song Sections button and then tap the section where you want your lead instrument part to start. I've included the lead guitar part from the intro of my song.
3. Tap the Record button and record a lead part over the number of bars in your chosen section. It might be worth playing the section back and practicing a few times before recording.
4. Continue to load song sections and record lead parts until you are happy. I recorded the intro section as one take and then recorded across all sections by setting Song Sections to show All Sections. I then split the region at the start and end of each section (see Figure 24-1).

FIGURE 24-1

The lead guitar part split across sections

Tip: Now is the perfect time to break out a real instrument and record a lead section for your project. A guitar, through the Guitar Amp instrument, or a keyboard part would work well here, and you can record in sections as above or as a single take.

How Does It Sound?

It would be pretty tricky for me to explain the exact notes I used for my lead part but you can listen to my recording using the QR code in the sidebar and follow them if you want. I used the Smart Guitar instrument with the Hard Rock sound applied and a USB keyboard

♪ LEAD GUITAR

This clip includes the lead guitar part added to the intro, verse, bridge, and chorus sections. Using a USB keyboard, I used the pitch bend wheel for the string bend effect but you can do it by dragging a string up or down using the Smart Guitar's notes window if you don't have a keyboard you can use.

using the iPad Camera Connection Kit to record that part, but you could create just as good a section by using the Notes window on the Smart Guitar instrument if you prefer.

25

Mix and Edit

With almost all the main sections in your song in place, it's time to make some adjustments to the project before adding in the vocals as the final job (as described in Chapter 26). If you do not want to add vocals, these are your final steps before sharing your song.

The first work that needs to be done is on the song structure. So far, if you've been following my song, you have an intro, verse, bridge, and chorus with recordings for each instrument on each track. A commercial song normally includes more than one verse and one chorus, so you need to add in new sections for the extra material. A clever trick is to use the Song Sections duplicate feature to add new verses and choruses rather than record the parts again.

The second task is to mix your song and most of the information you need in Chapter 16. In this chapter, I describe some of the mixing I used in my song for this lesson. As I've mentioned previously, GarageBand for iPad isn't the ultimate mixing platform. Ideally you'll export your project to GarageBand for Mac to apply effects and mixing but, that said, by using the Pan and Level controls in GarageBand for iPad as well as the Reverb and Echo effects, you can achieve decent results.

Finally (no pun intended), you need to find a way to end your song rather than have it stop dead. I recommend the Fade Out feature but, if you want, you can add one final section and record an "outro" to bring your song to a gentle stop.

Add New Verses and Choruses

Rather than record entirely new verse and chorus sections, it's far easier to duplicate the existing sections in your song by using the Song Sections popover. For this lesson, you'll repeat the verse and chorus sections. If you're worried that your song may become repetitive when using the same sections, you can always re-record any instrument parts in a given section to keep things interesting.

1. Tap the Song Sections button and then choose Section B, your verse section.
2. Tap the Duplicate button at the bottom of the popover. A duplicate of your original verse is now placed at the end of your song, just after the first chorus.
3. Do the same with your bridge part by tapping section C on the Song Sections popover and then tapping the Duplicate button.

You need to add two more chorus sections, one to follow your new verse and bridge and the other to provide a finale for the song. Choose

FIGURE 25-1

Duplicating the verse, bridge and chorus sections

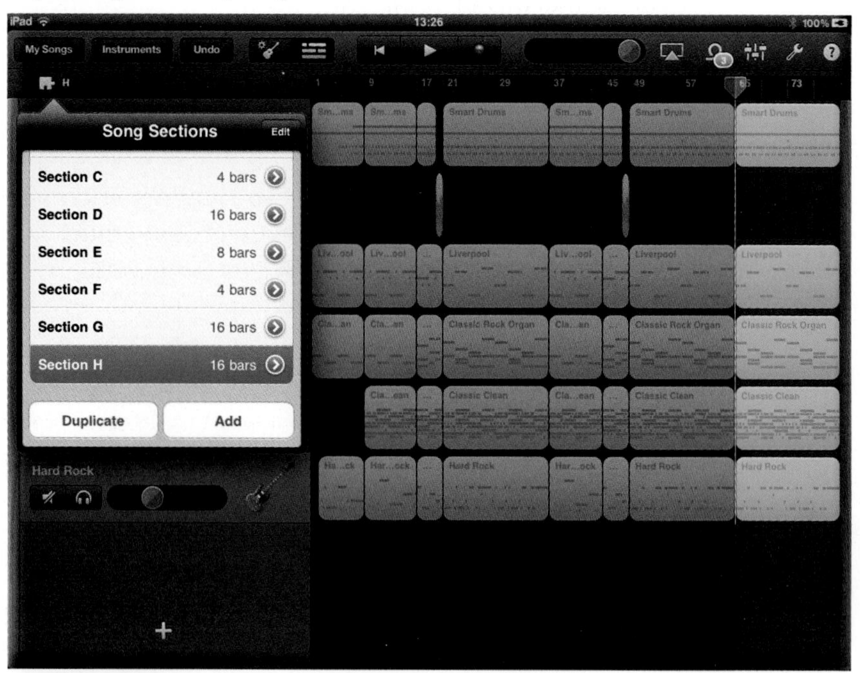

FIGURE 25-2

The Fade Out switch in the Song Settings popover

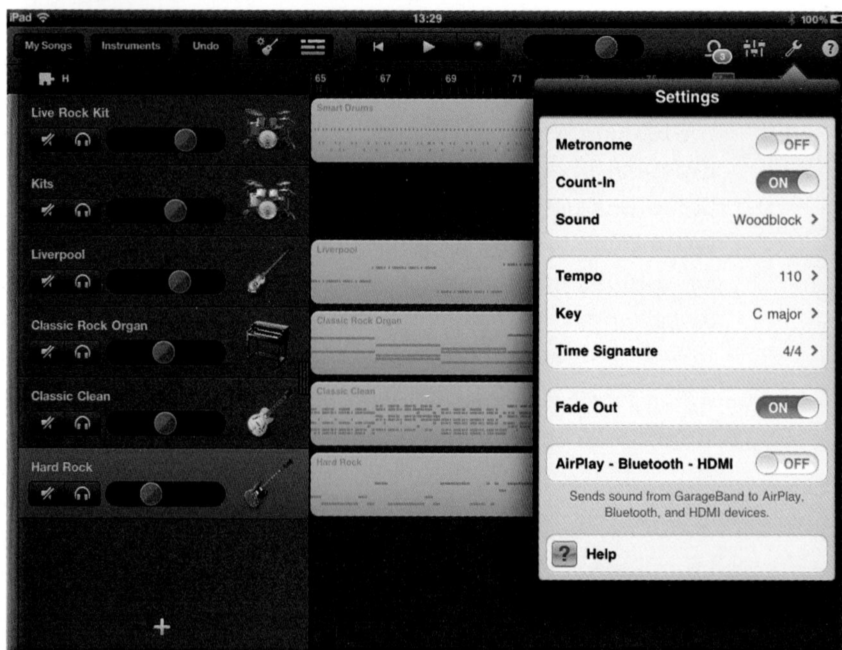

Section D in the Song Sections popover and then tap the Duplicate button twice to add two more chorus sections (see Figure 25-1).

Here's how to add a fade-out:

1. To add a fade-out to the final few bars of your song, tap on the Song Settings button.
2. From the Song Settings popover, set the Fade Out switch to On (see Figure 25-2).
3. Head back to the Tracks view and play the last few bars of your song to make sure the fade doesn't cut too much off. If it does, consider adding a few more bars to your song.

Mixing Your Song

Mixing is largely up to you, because you're the one who knows how you want your song to sound and which instruments are given prominence in the mix —and, most important, because you're the one listening to it! Using the advice in Chapter 16, you should be able to enhance your song and avoid clashes between instruments by using the Pan and Reverb controls from the mixer popover for each track.

When I mixed the song I've been creating over the last few chapters, I applied a degree of reverb to the drum section as well as the lead guitar part and added a very small amount of echo and reverb to the lead vocals (covered in Chapter 26). I also used the pan controls to separate the Smart Guitar instrument's rhythm and the organ rhythm as well as to slightly shift the lead and bass guitars to one side.

I left the vocals dead center, along with the drums. The key to mixing this track is to make sure that the similar-sounding instruments don't muddle together when you play the song back. The two guitars, for example, share tones that might cross over if you don't adjust their pan level to keep them apart.

Experiment with your mixing using the level controls for each track as well as the pan, echo, and reverb settings and you'll soon create a much clearer mix. You should also try listening to your song through different devices such as headphones, small speakers, and larger hi-fi speakers to make sure your mix sounds good on all devices. If, however, you're planning to export your song to GarageBand on the Mac for mixing, leave all the mixing controls alone and do it all on the computer.

26

The Vocals

I've left this part of the lesson until last, as it'll likely be the part of your song you work on the most and won't want to adjust once you've perfected it. Conversely, you might not want to bother with vocals at all: Not all of us can hit the right notes when it comes to producing a vocal track (you'll find that out when you listen to my wailing on the finished project!), which is why I've included a small section on prepping your song for another vocalist. But if you do have some vocal talents, step right this way, as it's time to lay down your mellifluous tones.

Preparing to Sing

The advice on recording vocals in Chapter 9 should be the first place you look when it comes to laying down your voice tracks. It will also help you figure out the equipment you need to perfect your vocal parts.

When you've gathered all your gear together and are in a comfortable and sonically desirable location, it's best to do a few vocal exercises to prepare yourself. Then, of course, you need to make sure your lyrics are in easy reach so you can refer to them as you record.

When recording vocals, the best practice is to use headphones to monitor your singing and avoid recording the rest of the song along with your voice. If you don't feel comfortable singing wearing headphones, try singing with only one of earpads against an ear so you can hear the song and your recorded vocals. Your other ear can accurately monitor your voice in real time and, hopefully, keep your voice from drifting out of tune. For an even more focused vocal recording, try muting some of the louder tracks in your project while you record, making sure to turn the metronome on so you can stay in time.

Recording Vocals

How you record your vocal tracks is up to you. The process works in much the same way as the lead instrument part covered in Chapter 24: You can record section by section or, if you believe your lyrics and singing will flow better, record the vocal track in one take.

1. Add an Audio Recorder track to your project by tapping the Instruments button and swiping until you see the Audio Recorder option. Tap it to add it to the song.

FIGURE 26-1

Audio Recorder input options

FIGURE 26-2

Adding a harmony as part of the chorus

PREPPING YOUR SONG FOR A VOCALIST

If you can't sing but want a vocal part for your song, it can be tricky to explain to a singer how you want the vocals sung. Often, vocalists have their own ideas about how to sing a particular song and, of course, of what feels comfortable to them.

To give them some direction, you can create a "mock" vocal track. Ideally, you'll use the Keyboard instrument and find a nonintrusive sound like the Electric Piano. Using an external or onscreen keyboard, play the notes you would like the vocalist to sing, or at least roughly try to replicate them. You can then record the vocals following the tips in Chapter 9 and in this chapter, and either mute or delete your mock vocal track afterward.

2. Plug in your headphones (and microphone, if you are using one) and then tap the Input Options button at the top left of the Audio Recorder window.
3. Sing into your microphone to gauge the input levels and adjust the Input Level slider to make your voice louder or softer (see Figure 26-1).
4. If you want to hear yourself singing while you record (which I recommend), turn on the Monitor setting on the Input Settings popover and sing into the microphone again to check that you can hear yourself through the headphones.
5. When you're ready to record, choose a section or All Sections from the Song Sections popover and tap the Record button when you're ready to sing.

Adding a Harmony

Harmonies always make a vocal track sound better (at least in my opinion), so I've added one to the song as part of the chorus (see Figure 26-2). It's easier than you think to add harmony to your vocal track, but it does require concentration to hit the right notes. Here's how:

1. In Tracks view, tap the microphone image on your Audio Recorder track and then tap the
2. Duplicate button that appears. Your vocal track is duplicated.

♪ THE FINISHED SONG

Here's the finished song for you to listen to. Your track should sound roughly the same if you've followed the same chords and instrument sounds that I used. This version includes the duplicated verse, bridge, and chorus sections as well as a fade out at the end.

3. Move the playhead to a point just before your chorus part, then double-tap the duplicated Audio Recorder instrument to move to the instrument window. (It might be better to start with a fresh track so the rest of your lead vocal is not doubled, which could complicate your mix.)
4. Tap the Record button and sing along with your chorus, but sing a harmony part an octave or two higher (a harmony part) than your original vocal. You may need to practice this a few times.
5. Tap the Mixer button and in the mixer popover slightly reduce the volume of your harmony track, move the pan a few millimeters off center, and add a decent amount of reverb and echo.

How Does It Sound?

Okay, you've made it to the end of the song. How is it sounding? Are you impressed that such a small piece of electronics can produce a sound that big? Using the QR code in the sidebar, you can listen to my finished song, which — if you've followed the same chords and instruments as me — should sound fairly similar to yours. If not, listen to the differences and try to learn where you (or I) went wrong.

It's not a Grammy-worthy production by any means, but for a first attempt and using only the smart instruments, I think you'll agree that it doesn't sound bad. Just think what you could achieve with a few more attempts and some real instruments thrown in there. This is just the beginning!

Index

A

B

C

D

I

J

K

L

M

N

O

P